OGLALA SIOUX INDIANS
PINE RIDGE RESERVATION
BIRTH & DEATH ROLLS
1924-1932
BOOK II
Including Illustrations

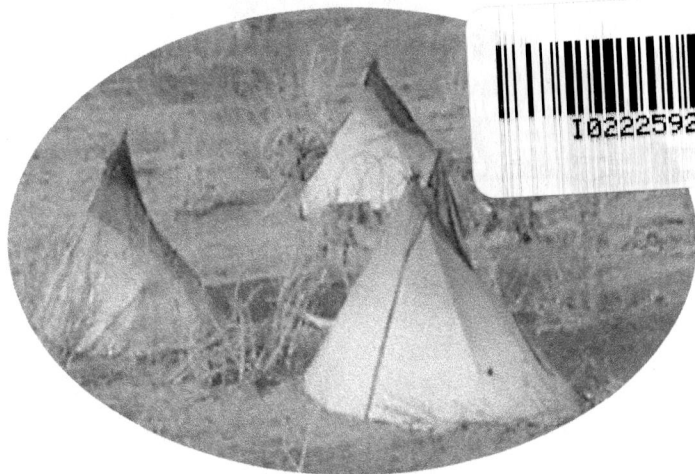

TRANSCRIBED BY
JEFF BOWEN

NATIVE STUDY
Gallipolis, Ohio
USA

Native Study LLC
Gallipolis, OH
www.nativestudy.com

Library of Congress Control Number: 2020923011

ISBN: 978-1-64968-118-8

Book cover: "The Great Hostile Camp" 1891, Photographer:
John C. H. Grabill; Bird's-eye view of a Lakota camp (several
tipis and wagons in large field)--probably on or near Pine
Ridge Reservation.
All photos including the one for the book cover are
complements of the Library of Congress.

Made in the United States of America.

Other Books and Series by Jeff Bowen

1901-1907 Native American Census Seneca, Eastern Shawnee, Miami, Modoc, Ottawa, Peoria, Quapaw, and Wyandotte Indians (Under Seneca School, Indian Territory)

1932 Census of The Standing Rock Sioux Reservation with Births And Deaths 1924-1932

Census of The Blackfeet, Montana, 1897- 1901 Expanded Edition

Eastern Cherokee by Blood, 1906-1910, Volumes I thru XIII

Choctaw of Mississippi Indian Census 1929-1932 with Births and Deaths 1924-1931 Volume I
Choctaw of Mississippi Indian Census 1933, 1934 & 1937, Supplemental Rolls to 1934 & 1935 with Births and Deaths 1932-1938, and Marriages 1936-1938 Volume II

Eastern Cherokee Census Cherokee, North Carolina 1930-1939
Census 1930-1931 with Births And Deaths 1924-1931 Taken By Agent L. W. Page Volume I
Eastern Cherokee Census Cherokee, North Carolina 1930-1939
Census 1932-1933 with Births And Deaths 1930-1932 Taken By Agent R. L. Spalsbury Volume II
Eastern Cherokee Census Cherokee, North Carolina 1930-1939
Census 1934-1937 with Births and Deaths 1925-1938 and Marriages 1936 & 1938 Taken by Agents R. L. Spalsbury And Harold W. Foght Volume III

Seminole of Florida Indian Census, 1930-1940 with Birth and Death Records, 1930-1938

Texas Cherokees 1820-1839 A Document For Litigation 1921

Starr Roll 1894 (Cherokee Payment Rolls) Districts: Canadian, Cooweescoowee, and Delaware Volume One
Starr Roll 1894 (Cherokee Payment Rolls) Districts: Flint, Going Snake, and Illinois Volume Two
Starr Roll 1894 (Cherokee Payment Rolls) Districts: Saline, Sequoyah, and Tahlequah; Including Orphan Roll Volume Three

Cherokee Intruder Cases Dockets of Hearings 1901-1909 Volumes I & II

Indian Wills, 1911-1921 Records of the Bureau of Indian Affairs
Books One thru Seven
Native American Wills & Probate Records 1911-1921

Turtle Mountain Reservation Chippewa Indians 1932 Census with Births & Deaths, 1924-1932

Other Books and Series by Jeff Bowen

Chickasaw By Blood Enrollment Cards 1898-1914 Volume I thru V

Cherokee Descendants East An Index to the Guion Miller Applications Volume I
Cherokee Descendants West An Index to the Guion Miller Applications Volume II
(A-M)
Cherokee Descendants West An Index to the Guion Miller Applications Volume III
(N-Z)

Applications for Enrollment of Seminole Newborn Freedmen, Act of 1905

Eastern Cherokee Census, Cherokee, North Carolina, 1915-1922, Taken by Agent
James E. Henderson   *Volume I (1915-1916)*
                           Volume II (1917-1918)
                           Volume III (1919-1920)
                           Volume IV (1921-1922)

Complete Delaware Roll of 1898

Eastern Cherokee Census, Cherokee, North Carolina, 1923-1929, Taken by Agent
James E. Henderson   *Volume I (1923-1924)*
                           Volume II (1925-1926)
                           Volume III (1927-1929)

Applications for Enrollment of Seminole Newborn Act of 1905 Volumes I & II

North Carolina Eastern Cherokee Indian Census 1898-1899, 1904, 1906, 1909-
1912, 1914 Revised and Expanded Edition

1932 Hopi and Navajo Native American Census with Birth & Death Rolls (1925-
1931) Volume 1 - Hopi
1932 Hopi and Navajo Native American Census with Birth & Death Rolls (1930-
1932) Volume 2 - Navajo

Western Navajo Reservation Navajo, Hopi and Paiute 1933 Census with Birth &
Death Rolls 1925-1933

Cherokee Citizenship Commission Dockets 1880-1884 and 1887-1889
Volumes I thru V

Applications for Enrollment of Chickasaw Newborn Act of 1905
Volumes I thru VII

Cherokee Intermarried White 1906 Volume I thru X

Applications for Enrollment of Creek Newborn Act of 1905
Volumes I thru XIV

Other Books and Series by Jeff Bowen

Applications for Enrollment of Choctaw Newborn Act of 1905 Volumes I thru XX

Choctaw By Blood Enrollment Cards 1898-1914 Volumes I thru XX

Oglala Sioux Indians Pine Ridge Reservation 1932 Census Book I

Visit our website at **www.nativestudy.com** to learn more about these
and other books and series by Jeff Bowen

This book is dedicated to
Kent Anderson,
Forever the Faithful Friend
to the Pine Ridge Sioux.

"One does not sell the land people walk on."

Crazy Horse

TABLE OF CONTENTS

LIST OF ILLUSTRATIONS

MISCELLANEOUS PHOTOGRAPHS

PINE RIDGE RESERVATION OR AGENCY
PINE RIDGE SOUTH DAKOTA

The following illustration names are either within the 1932 Oglala Pine Ridge Census Book I and/or the Pine Ridge Birth and Death Rolls 1924-1932 Book II or are a party with a family name or relation of the same; or the photograph itself was taken at or near Pine Ridge.

Photographer: Gertrude Käsebier, 1852-1934 (ca 1900)

Joe Black Fox, a Sioux Indian from
Buffalo Bill's Wild West Show.

Photographer: Gertrude Käsebier, 1852-1934 (ca 1900)

Joe Black Fox, a Sioux Indian from
Buffalo Bill's Wild West Show, cigarette in his right hand.

Photographer: Heyn Photo (ca 1899)

Bone Necklace, Council Chief

[Within the 1932 census there is a Bone Necklace #2 age 64.
Also in the 1900 census (page 17) there is a Bone Necklace #2
at 32 years of age, Census #745 with the Sioux name of *Hohu
Napin*, likely the same individual or a close family member.]

Photographer: Unknown (ca 1899-1900)

Bone Neck Lace

Photographer: S.D. Butcher & Son, Kearney, Neb. (1891)

Two Strike['s] band [Brule Lakota] Pine Ridge 1891. A group of Sioux men full-length, standing, facing front, in a half-circle behind a group of five Sioux sitting on the ground, three wrapped in blankets and with their backs to the viewer.

Photographer: Gertrude Käsebier, 1852-1934 (ca 1900)

Charging Thunder, a Sioux Indian from
Buffalo Bill's Wild West Show

Photographer: Gertrude Käsebier, 1852-1934 (ca 1900)

Charging Thunder, a Sioux Indian from
Buffalo Bill's Wild West Show

Photographer: John C. H. Grabill (1891)

Rocky Bear, Oglala chief, standing to the left of a Euro-American man on horseback; three tipis in the background--probably on or near Pine Ridge Reservation.

Photographer: Herbert E. French, National Photo Company
1929

Chief Spotted Crow of the Sioux tribe of Pine Ridge, S.D. and his five months old granddaughter, Lena Lou White House, who was named by Vice President Curtis a few days ago.

Photographer: Heyn & Matzen (ca 1900)

Eagle Shirt, Sioux Indian, full-length portrait, facing slightly right, standing in front of studio backdrop.

Photographer: Heyn Photo (ca 1899)

Eddie Plenty Holes, a Sioux Indian, half-length portrait, facing front, holding tomahawk.

Photographer: Heyn   (ca 1899)

James Lone Elk

Photographer: Heyn (ca 1900)

James Spotted Elk, Sioux Indian boy wearing feathered headdress and beaded vest.

Photographer: Heyn Photo (ca 1899)

John Comes Again

Photographer: Heyn Photo (ca 1899)

Joseph Bird Head, Lakota or Sioux, seated on blanket holding
handcrafter club.

Photographer: Heyn & Matzen (ca 1900)

Joseph Two [Two].

[In the 1897 Sioux and Cheyenne Census, Pine Ridge, on page
60, Census #2426, there is a Joseph Two Two at age 37.]

Photographer: Heyn & Matzen (ca 1900)

Julia Lone Elk.

[In the 1897 Sioux and Cheyenne Census, Pine Ridge, on page 58, Census #2330, age 27, shows Julia as the wife of James Lone Elk.

Photographer: Gertrude Käsebier, 1852-1934 (ca 1900)

Kills Close To The Lodge, a Sioux Indian from Buffalo Bill's
Wild West Show, wearing breastplate and headdress.

Photographer: Heyn Photo (ca 1899)

Last Horse, Sioux, wearing paint above waist, holding spear
and shield.

Photographer: Heyn Photo (ca 1899)

Left Hand Bear, Chief

Photographer: Heyn Photo (ca 1899-1900)

Little Horse.

Photographer: Unknown (ca 1899-1900)

Little Wound, wife and son.

Photographer: Unknown (ca 1900)

Luke Big Turnips.

Photographer: Heyn Photo   (ca 1899)

Philomen Turning Hawk.

Photographer: John C. H. Grabill (1891)

Indian chiefs who counciled[sic] with Gen. Miles and settled the Indian War
- 1. Standing Bull, 2. Bear Who Looks Back Running [Stands and Looks
Back], 3. Has the Big White Horse, 4. White Tail, 5. Liver [Living] Bear, 6.
Little Thunder, 7. Bull Dog, 8 High Hawk, 9. Lame, 10. Eagle Pipe.

Photographer: W. R. Cross' Studio   (ca 1907)

Indian woman and small child seated. Pine Ridge Agency Indians.

Photographer: S.D. Butcher & Son, Kearney, Neb. (ca 1908)

Pine Ridge Sioux Indian woman standing between two frames on which meat is dried near tents on the far left.

Photographer: S.D. Butcher & Son, Kearney, Neb.   (ca 1908)

Back view of the Squaw dance Pine Ridge S.D. Rear view of a group of Sioux
women, standing, some wearing headdresses. Also shows a wagon, a tent,
and a young Sioux girl.

Photographer: Heyn Photo   (ca 1899)

Poor Elk.

Photographer: Heyn Photo   (ca 1899)

Running Horse, wearing feather headdress and bone
breast plate.

Photographer: Gertrude Käsebier, 1852-1934 (ca 1900)

Sammy Lone Bear, a Sioux Indian from Buffalo Bill's
Wild West Show, wearing breastplate.

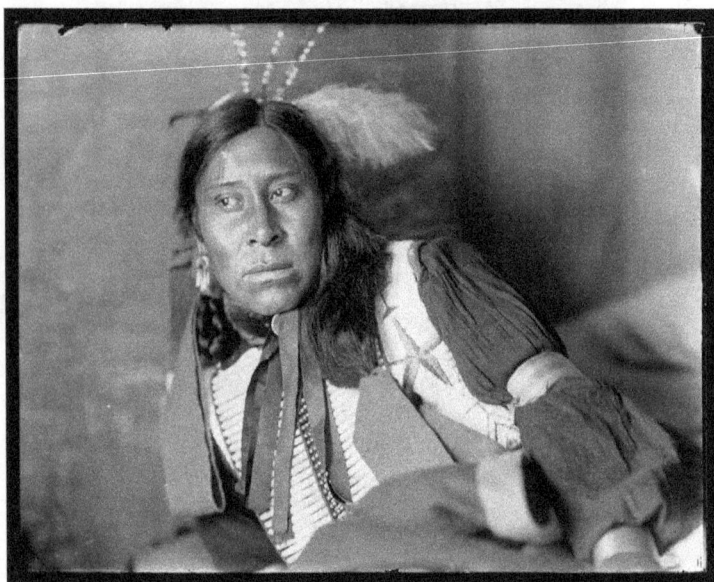

Photographer: Gertrude Käsebier, 1852-1934 (ca 1900)

Sammy Lone Bear, a Sioux Indian from Buffalo Bill's
Wild West Show, wearing breastplate.

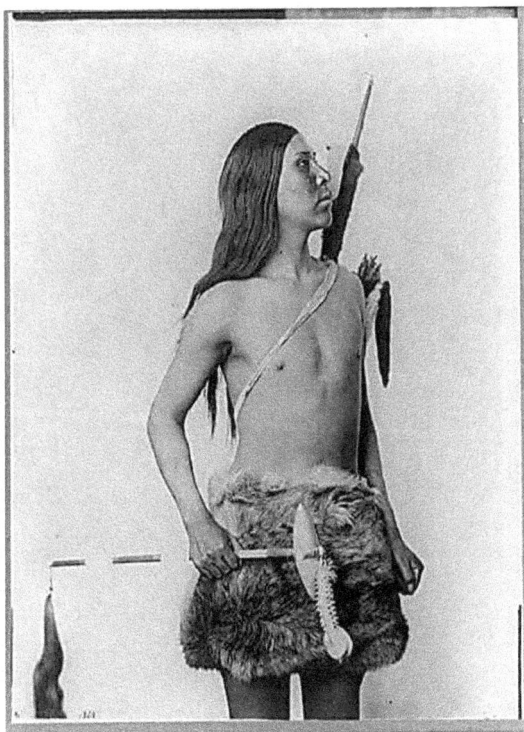

Photographer: Heyn & Matzen (ca 1900)

Samuel Lone Bear, holding tomahawk.

Photographer: Heyn & Matzen (ca 1900)

Chief Samuel Lone Bear

Photographer: Heyn Photo (ca 1899)

Shout At

Photographer: Heyn   (ca 1899-1900)

Standing Bear.

Photographer: John C. H. Grabill (1891)

A young Oglala girl sitting in front of a tipi, with a puppy beside her, probably on or near Pine Ridge Reservation.

INTRODUCTION

The best way to start this introduction is to quote author Joe Starita who wrote *The Dull Knifes of Pine Ridge* in 1995. He mentions a gentleman who is on page 106 of this census along with his wife Rosa by the name of Guy Dull Knife, Sr. "'My name is Guy Dull Knife Sr. I am Oglala Sioux.' His people, the Oglala, were once the largest and most powerful of the seven subtribes of Teton Sioux, prairie dwellers who lived farther west than the other tribes of the Great Sioux Nation. In their own language, Teton tribal members traditionally referred to themselves as *Lakota*, 'alliance of friends.'"[1]

"Pushed out by the Ojibwa from their ancestral woodlands home near the headwaters of the Mississippi in northern Minnesota, the displaced Lakota began migrating west and reached the heart of the Great Plains about 1760. By the early years of the nineteenth century, they had become superior horsemen, skilled hunters and fierce warriors, commanding a huge section of the northern plains that at one time stretched from the Missouri River of South Dakota to Montana's Big Horn Mountains."[2]

At one time, the Oglala were the most vast and able-bodied among the seven Teton bands or subtribes, the Brule, Oglala, Sans Arc, Hunkpapa, Miniconjou, Blackfeet or Blackfoot and Two Kettles. For generations they were strongly associated with the Northern Cheyenne through marriage as well as customs, similar dress and rituals. They wintered together within the same mountains and had the same enemies in common. Even with their great numbers and tribal confederations they couldn't hold back the destruction of their mostly peaceful existence. Their life sustaining abundance of food and many uses of the buffalo during the late 1700's to the mid 1800's was about to be destroyed by those coming from the east bringing with them what was thought to be civilization. The buffalo from early times were estimated at 50 million but by the 1870's they were decimated by fur traders and next by hired railroads' private armies of extermination. Then came the government policies of destroying Sioux individualism by finishing off the food supply by having the Army slaughter helpless animals that provided economic stability to the Sioux people. The buffalo wasn't just food for a plains tribe but they provided skins for tipis, clothing, moccasins, bedding, saddle covers, and sinew for bow strings, even a buffalo tongue could be used as a hair brush. The use of the buffalo for the Sioux and other tribes was literally unlimited. The buffalo was a way of life for the people and they watched it disappear before their very eyes just so they could be controlled and have their lands stolen.

---

[1] The Dull Knives of Pine Ridge; Pg. 4 Para. 4-5
[2] The Dull Knives of Pine Ridge; Pg. 4-5 Para. 7

Over the years the Sioux have had to contend with many struggles, one such event was the massacre of Wounded Knee during December of 1890 and, "On the morning of December 29, the U.S. Cavalry troops went into the camp to disarm the Lakota. One version of events claims that during the process of disarming the Lakota, a deaf tribesman named Black Coyote was reluctant to give up his rifle, claiming he had paid a lot for it. Simultaneously, an old man was performing a ritual called the Ghost Dance. Black Coyote's rifle went off at that point, and the U.S. Army began shooting at the Native Americans. The Lakota warriors fought back, but many had already been stripped of their guns and disarmed.

By the time the massacre was over, more than 250 men, women, and children of the Lakota had been killed and 51 were wounded (4 men and 47 women and children, some of whom died later); some estimates placed the number of dead as high as 300."[3]

In bringing up Wounded Knee it's understood that Chief Bigfoot at the time had gotten pneumonia and was extremely ill, therefore not able to keep his promises of turning in the Hunkpapas the next day after he had taken them in when they were in need a Colonel Sumner took it as resistance to follow instructions. But the pressure was great from General Miles who had wired Sumner to gain control of the situation and arrest Bigfoot. Sumner later reported that Bigfoot's people looked so pitiable that he didn't consider them hostile. But he sent a rancher he thought they could depend on to relate to Bigfoot to at least travel to Fort Bennett. This rancher obviously translated the wrong message which seems like it was on purpose and told him to go to the Pine Ridge immediately, 50 miles away, if you want to save your lives. When Sumner had gone to Bigfoot's village looking for him and him not showing up at Bennett, Miles sent a message stating that Bigfoot was clearly being defiant and hostile. Sumner was ordered to arrest and disarm Bigfoot's band immediately. So Miles was in fear that Bigfoot was making for the Stronghold on Pine Ridge and was afraid he would arouse the Ghost Dancer's into a frenzy.

In finishing the story of Wounded Knee and its circumstances it was felt that one last quote from Joe Starita's book was needed to balance out the history of what worth there was to Wounded Knee. "The Reverend Charles Cook hastily removed all the pews and then he covered the floor of the Holy Cross Episcopal Church with a bedding of straw and quilts. The Christmas season was upon Pine Ridge. Garlands and wreaths decked the walls and a homemade sign—Peace On Earth, Goodwill To Men—still hung above the altar of his church. Shortly after 9:30 p.m., the first wagons arrived carrying survivors from the Miniconjou village. When Dr. Charles Eastman, a Santee Sioux in charge of treating the wounded, and the Reverend Cook and his church staff first saw the men, women and children carried in from the wagons, they cried out in anguish. 'All of this,' said Eastman later, 'was a severe

---

[3] Wounded Knee Massacre; Wikipedia

ordeal for one who had so lately put all his faith in the Christian love and lofty ideals of the white man.'

Steals a Running Horse, age five, was among thirty-eight survivors laid out in rows on the church floor that night. Bullets had torn apart the small boy's throat, and when doctors tried to feed him, the food and water came out the side of his neck. Blue Whirlwind had been wounded fourteen times. Her two small sons were shot up, but still alive. Her husband, Spotted Thunder, was dead. Louise Weasel Bear had been one of the first to flee the village for the ravine. 'We tried to run but they shot us like we were a buffalo. I know there are some good white people, but the soldiers must be mean to shoot children and women. Indian soldiers would not do that to white children.' Bertha Kills Close to Lodge, seventeen, ran with her relatives through the ravine, stopping when she heard a burst of gunfire behind her. 'I went over there and it was my sister and her mother was pregnant at that time. I found she was killed. I was wounded but was able to go to where they were. My sister was near death and I stayed with her. When she died I straightened her out, laid her out the best way I could.' Alice Dog Arm saw a soldier on a bay horse riding toward her family. 'I ran and hid in a ditch with my mother and two brothers. My father came and took my older brother to care for him. Soon he came back and said that they had killed my brother. Then my mother cried and as she wanted us all to be together and die together so my father took us to a safer hiding place and then he left us and soon a man named Air Pipe came and told us that my father was killed.' Afraid of Enemy, thirty-six, said she saw an officer on a sorrel horse swing around the left end of the camp. 'I heard him give some command and right after the command it sounded like a lightening crash. That is about all I know. When I became conscious I was lying down. As I rose and started to go I began to get unconscious again. For that reason I do not know a great deal of what took place after this. I have my old cloak and it has nine bullet holes in it.' After the initial cannon salvo, Rough Feather and her family fled toward the ravine under heavy fire. 'My father, my mother, my grandmother, my older brother and my younger brother were all killed. My son who was two years old was shot in the mouth that later caused his death.'

On New Year's Day, 1891, a burial detail rode out of the agency headquarters in Pine Ridge with an army escort. Under contract at two dollars per body, the civilian detail of thirty men spent two days combing the snow-covered battlefield, tossing frozen bodies in the back of wagons drawn by mule teams. They found Chief Bigfoot, wrapped in a thick coat and head scarf, propped up beside the blown-out remains of his army tent, his body frozen in a half-sitting position. Not far away, inside the council circle, was the charred remains of the medicine man, Yellow Bird. Strewn along a trail more than three miles long, they found the remains of three pregnant woman riddled with bullets, another with her abdomen blown away and a young boy whose upper body had been torn apart by a cannon shell.

They also found a baby girl, covered in snow, huddled beside her dead mother. She was wrapped in a shawl, her head, hands and feet severely frostbitten, but still alive. On her head, the eight-month-old infant wore a tiny buckskin cap with a needlepoint design in the shape of an American Flag."[4] In finalizing this study it makes it obvious as to how dark men's souls can be, let alone those in power. As Abraham Lincoln stated, "Nearly all men can stand adversity, but if you want to test a man's character, give him power."[5]

Wounded Knee seems as though it was a precursor to a future of consistent adversities involving a people who just wanted to live on the prairies and be left alone. If it wasn't someone telling them how to live, it was conflict between the American government or tribal government and traditionalism.

But it was always about the land and the resources that were being discovered on that land. To the Government there wasn't a treaty they couldn't break and did. "In 1887, after years of fierce debate, Congress passed the General Allotment Act (the Dawes Act), yet another in the long series of 'reform' laws designed to assist the Indian into the American mainstream by breaking down his traditional means of existence (the act was 'a mighty pulverizing engine to break up the tribal mass,' cheered Teddy Roosevelt, who with the help of his friend J. Pierpont Morgan would later sponsor Edward Curtis's theatrical photographic portraits of "The Vanishing Redman"). Each male Indian in those tribes coerced by the Indian Bureau into accepting allotment would be given 160 acres, with any 'surplus' land to be purchased inexpensively by the government and turned over to white settlers at its own discretion, according to the rules set out by the Homestead Act of 1862. This 'surplus,' as it turned out, comprised most of the remaining Indian land.

By destroying communal guardianship of land, the Dawes Act—first aimed at tribes in Western Indian Territory but eventually affecting more than one hundred Indian groups—destroyed not only the unity of Indian nations but the people's tradition of generosity and total sharing for the common good. Since according to their sacred instructions the Indians could never 'own' a Mother Earth of which they felt themselves to be a part, and since even those willing to go against the Indian life-way—*wouncage*, 'our way of doing,' as the Lakota say—had no experience of the white economy, most of those who tried to adjust to the new system were sooner or later relieved of their land due to innocence, drink, inability to pay off mortgages and taxes, and finally, the hard exigencies of starvation; for by the time the people had been reduced to irregular handouts of flour and lard, the ration of which depended largely on their willingness to cooperate with the agents sent out by the Indian Bureau and their accomplices in the reservation missions. In short the Dawes Act legalized an

---

[4] The Dull Knives of Pine Ridge; Pg. 128-129 Para. 1-5
[5] forbes.com/quotes/76/

arrangement in which, during the next half century, the native people all across the country would lose two thirds of their remaining lands by sale and swindle.

Until World War I, the Lakota managed to resist allotment, but in 1889—the year of the great Oklahoma land rush inspired by the Dawes Act—General Crook was dispatched to his old foes with the proposal that 9 million acres of their remaining land should be turned over to white settlement. The aging Red Cloud refused to sign such an agreement, and so did Sitting Bull, who had returned from political asylum in Canada in 1881 (for a time he appeared in "Wild West" shows with the old railroad hunter Buffalo Bill Cody) and was living at Standing Rock on the Grand River, not far from the place where he was born:

Friends and Relatives: Our minds are again disturbed by the Great Father's representatives, the Indian Agent, the squaw-men, the mixed-bloods, the interpreters, and the favorite-ration-chiefs. What is it they want of us at this time? They want us to give up another chunk of our tribal land. This is not the first time nor the last time. They will try to gain possession of the last piece of ground we possess. They are again telling us what they intend to do if we agree to their wishes. Have we ever set a price on our land and received such a value? No, we never did. What we got under the former treaties were promises of all sorts. They promised how we are going to live peaceably on the land we still own and how they are going to show us the new ways of living, even told us how we can go to heaven when we die....

When the white people invaded our Black Hills country our treaty agreements were still in force but the Great Father ignored it.... Therefore I do not wish to consider any proposition to cede any portion of our tribal holdings to the Great Father.... My friends and relatives, let us stand as one family as we did before the white people led us astray.

Due mostly to the stubborn resistance of Sitting Bull and Red Cloud, the signatures required for the cession of Indian land were not obtained, and as in the seizure of the Black Hills, it was recommended to the government that it simply ignore the 1868 Treaty, which it did. A few months later President Benjamin Harrison proclaimed an act that dismantled the Great Sioux Reservation, established at Fort Laramie and created the seven reservations that exist today; the Oglala band, which had been the most hostile, was given the dry rolling hill country between the Dakota Badlands and the Sand Hills of Nebraska, now known as the Pine Ridge Reservation."[6]

But in modern times on a positive note, "In 1971 the tribe founded the Oglala Lakota College, one of the earliest tribal colleges in the nation, and part of Native American institution building of the last 40 years. First started as a two-year community college, it has expanded to offer four-year baccalaureate degrees, as well as a master's in Lakota leadership. It is operated by tribal people, with a tribal board. In 2011, it had an enrollment of 1,400."[7]

---

[6] In The Spirit of Crazy Horse; Pg. 18-19 Para. 1-6
[7] Pine Ridge Indian Reservation; Wikipedia

This new 1932 Pine Ridge Oglala Sioux Census contains over 8000 names listing sex, date of birth and age at last birthday, degree of blood, marital status (in most cases giving the wife's maiden name) and relationship to head of family along with the jurisdiction where they were enrolled and if they were a ward to the head of household. Also included is the allotment and annuity numbers.

In 1996, the 1924 to 1932 Oglala Sioux Pine Ridge Birth and Death rolls were published by this author which has long been out of print. This new 1932 Census has been transcribed as *Book I* that will go along with the original Birth and Death Records covering over 4500 names to be re-published as *Book II*. In addition to this census and the forthcoming Birth and Death Rolls you will find a few early pre-1932 photographs from the Pine Ridge Reservation included in both books. You can actually find a few of the names mentioned either in the introduction or on a picture within this 1932 census and possibly the births and deaths.

Also I wanted to thank the authors who worked so long and hard to give me the ability to dig out the facts and circumstances mentioned in this introduction. Without them searching out these materials before us we would have nothing. They give me inspiration to continue while sometimes feeling the tears of so many that didn't want and never asked for such anguish.

The 1932 Census for *Book I* has been transcribed from National Archives film NATIVE AMERICAN CENSUS ROLLS 1885-1940; Pine Ridge (Oglala Sioux Indians): M-595 roll number 378. For *Book II*, the (Oglala Sioux Indians) 1924-1932 with Birth and Death rolls was also transcribed from Indian Census Rolls 1885-1940; M-595 roll number 379.

It is the hope that this work helps many find their ancestors and that it will honor those both past and present.

Jeff Bowen
Gallipolis, Ohio
NativeStudy.com

Census Instructions

INSTRUCTIONS

(A) A separate roll is to be made of each reservation; also, of each *rancheria* or reserve, and a separate roll of Indians allotted on the public domain or homesteading. The roll is to be based on enrollment and not on residence.

(B) Persons are to be listed by families alphabetically; that is, not only by the first letter of the surname, but also by the second and subsequent letters, when the first letter or letters are the same. For example: Abalon, Abbott, Abcou, Abend, Abict; Boll, Bell, Bill, Boll, Ball; Carley, Carmen, Carton, etc. Families having the same surname are also to be listed in this way, e. g.: Brown, Anson; Brown, *Bill*; Brown, Charles; Brown, David. In the case of English translations of Indian names, such as John *Flying-Elk*, Flying-Elk is the surname and is to be listed under F. In such cases the first word of the translated Indian name determines the alphabetical position. The best way to accomplish this will be to write the names of each family group on a separate card; then, arrange the cards alphabetically and type the names therefrom onto the census roll.

Members of a family are to be listed in the following order: Head, first; wife second; then children, whether sons or daughters, *in the order of their ages;* and lastly, all other relatives and persons living with the family who do not constitute another family group.

Annuity and per capita payment rolls are also to be prepared in the same manner.

(C) A family is composed of the following members:

    1. Both parents and their unmarried children, if any, living with them; all other relatives and persons living with the family who do not constitute another family group.

    2. Either parent and the unmarried children, if the other parent is dead; all other relatives and persons living with the family who do not constitute another family group.

    3. A single person over 21 years of age, not living with a relative.

(D) For each person the following information is to be furnished:

    1. NUMBER.—A number is to be assigned in serial order. Thus, the first person listed is to be numbered as "1," the second, as "2," and so on until the census is completed.

    2. NAME.—If there are both an Indian and an English name, the allotment or annuity roll name is to be given. First, the last or surname; then, the given name in full. Ditto marks are to be used under the surname of the head for the surnames of the other members of one family.

    3. SEX.—"M," for male; "F," for female.

    4. AGE AT LAST BIRTHDAY.—Age in completed years at last birthday is to be shown. For infants under 1 year, age in completed months, expressed as twelfths of a year. Thus, 3 months as ³⁄₁₂ yr.

    5. TRIBE.—Care is to be taken that tribe, not band or local name, is given. Thus, Ute tribe, not Pahvant, which is a band of Ute. Likewise, Hupa tribe, not Bear River, which is a local name for the members of the Hupa tribe living near Bear River.

    6. DEGREE OF BLOOD.—"F," for full blood: "¼ +," for one-fourth or more Indian blood; "– ¼," for less than one-fourth Indian blood.

    7. MARITAL STATUS.—"S," for a single or unmarried person: "M," for a married person; and "Wd," for widowed of either sex.

    8. RELATIONSHIP TO HEAD OF FAMILY.—The head, whether husband or father, widow or unmarried person of either sex, is to be designated as such. For the other members, the appropriate term which designates the particular relationship the person bears to the head is to be used.

    9. RESIDENCE.—

        (a) At *jurisdiction* where enrolled: Yes or no. The term jurisdiction includes all reservations and public domain allotments under the agency.

        (b) Or at another jurisdiction. The name of the jurisdiction is to be given.

        (c) Or elsewhere:

            1. Post office: Both the proper name of the post office and the class by which it is known (city, town, village, etc.) are to be given. Thus, Lewiston, city.

            2. County.

            3. State.

    10. WARD.—Yes or no. Wardship depends primarily upon the ownership of individual property held in trust or upon membership in a tribe living on a Federal reservation. See Circular 2145.

    11. ALLOTMENT, ANNUITY, AND IDENTIFICATION NUMBERS.—"Al," for allotment; "An," for annuity; and "Id," for identification, before the appropriate number or numbers. All numbers are to be shown.

(E) Rolls not prepared in strict conformity with the above instructions will be returned for correction.

U. S. GOVERNMENT PRINTING OFFICE: 1935   06—7970

LIVE BIRTHS

1925
(July 1, 1924 - June 30, 1925)

PINE RIDGE RESERVATION
PINE RIDGE SOUTH DAKOTA

State **South Dakota** Reservation **Pine Ridge** Agency or jurisdiction
Pine Ridge Office of Indian Affairs

Key: 1925 Census Roll Number; Surname, Given; Date of Birth (Year-Month-Day); Live Births (Yes/No);
Still Births (blank unless otherwise given); Sex; Tribe (Oglala Sioux unless given otherwise); Ward (Yes/No);
Degree of Blood (Father; Mother; Child); At Jurisdiction Where Enrolled (Yes/No); (If no – Where)

Births Occurring Between July 1, 1924 and June 30, 1925 to Parents Enrolled at Jurisdiction

20; Addison, Raymond; 1925-1-10; Yes; M; Sioux & Cheyenne; Yes; F; F; F; Yes
25; Afraid Of Bear, Chester; 1924-8-21; Yes; M; Yes; F; F; F; Yes
71; Allen, Hilda Elizabeth; 1924-8-28; Yes; F; Yes; 1/8; 1/4; 3/16; Yes
73; Allen, Norman Edgar; 1924-12-7; Yes; M; Yes; 3/16; W; 3/32; Yes
81; Allman, Archie Leroy; 1924-10-19; Yes; M; Yes; 1/4; 3/4; 1/2; Yes
93; Allman, Cornelia; 1925-4-1; Yes; F; Yes; 1/4; 1/2; 3/8; Yes
127; American Horse, Martha; 1924-8-9; Yes; F; Yes; F; F; F; Yes
167; Apple, Marie Elizabeth; 1924-11-9; Yes; F; Yes; 3/4; 3/4; 3/4; Yes
220; Babby, Faith Lorraine; 1924-9-2; Yes; F; Yes; 1/8; 3/8; 1/4; Yes
249; Badger, Myrtle; 1924-12-12; Yes; F; Yes; 3/4; 3/4; 3/4; Yes
277; Bad Wound, Lavina Edith; 1925-2-3; Yes; F; Yes; 3/4; 3/8; 9/16; Yes
306; Bald Eagle Bear, Lorine E; 1924-12-30; Yes; F; Yes; F; F; F; Yes
322; Bartlett, Althia; 1924-9-1; Yes; F; Yes; 1/2; 1/2; 1/2; Yes
---; Bear Eagle, Lawrence E; 1925-5-17; Yes; M; Yes; F; F; F; Yes
---; Bear Killer, Sampson; 1925-5-19; Yes; M; Yes; F; F; F; Yes
358; Bear Nose, Arnold; 1925-2-13; Yes; M; Yes; F; F; F; Yes
----; Bear Robe, David; 1925-1-5; Yes; M; Yes; F; F; F; Yes
---; Bear Robe, Rose Victoria; 1925-1-22; Yes; F; Yes; F; 3/4; 7/8; Yes
404; Bear Shield, Jessie; 1925-3-20; Yes; F; Yes; F; F; F; Yes
---; Bettelyoun, Waldron Jerome; 1924-8-2; Yes; M; Yes; 1/2; 5/8; 9/16; Yes
582; Bissonette, Melvin Garrette; 1925-3-22; Yes; M; Yes; 3/8; F; 11/16; Yes
623; Black Bear, Esther; 1925-4-2; Yes; F; Yes; F; F; F; Yes
632; Black Bear, Lillie; 1924-9-24; Yes; F; Yes; F; F; F; Yes
686; Black Crow, Catherine Lucille; 1924-12-27; Yes; F; Oglala & Rose.; Yes; F; F; F; Yes
719; Black Feather, Lema; 1924-8-11; Yes; F; Yes; 3/4; F; 7/8; Yes
---; Black Road, Jennie; 1924-10-6; Yes; F; Yes; F; F; F; Yes
770; Black Wolf, Tresa R; 1924-9-4; Yes; F; Yes; F; F; F; Yes
796; Blue Bird, James Theodore; 1924-10-31; Yes; M; Yes; F; 7/8; 15/16; Yes
859; Brafford, Robert Levi; 1925-4-10; Yes; M; Yes; 1/4; 1/2; 3/8; Yes
874; Brave, Robert; 1924-11-18; Yes; M; Yes; F; F; F; Yes
---; Brewer, Charles; 1925-3-30; Yes; M; Yes; 1/4; 5/8; 7/16; Yes
959; Broken Leg, Peter; 1924-7-17; Yes; N; Yes; F; F; F; Yes
---; Brown, Irma Irene; 1924-8-21; Yes; F; Yes; 3/16; 1/4; 7/32; Yes
1012; Brown, Ollie Norma; 1925-3-30; Yes; F; Yes; 3/8; 1/2; 7/16; Yes
----; Brown Bull, Chester; 1924-11-9; Yes; M; Yes; F; 1/2; 3/4; Yes
1062; Brown Eyes, Wanza; 1924-11-23; Yes; F; Yes; 3/4; F; 7/8; Yes
1083; Buchman, Edith Louise; 1925-1-25; Yes; F; Yes; 3/4; 7/8; 13/16; Yes
1121; Bull Bear, Edward; 1924-10-8; Yes; M; Yes; F; 3/4; 7/8; Yes
----; Bush, Louis; 1925-1-12; Yes; M; Yes; 3/4; F; 7/8; Yes
1170; Bush, Maggie; 1925-3-9; Yes; F; Yes; 3/4; 3/4; 3/4; Yes
----; Bushy Top Pine, Isaac; 1925-5-29; Yes; M; Yes; F; F; F; Yes

3

State__ **South Dakota** ___Reservation___ **Pine Ridge** ___Agency or jurisdiction
___**Pine Ridge**___ Office of Indian Affairs

Key: 1925 Census Roll Number; Surname, Given; Date of Birth (Year-Month-Day); Live Births (Yes/No);
Still Births (blank unless otherwise given); Sex; Tribe (Oglala Sioux unless given otherwise); Ward (Yes/No);
Degree of Blood (Father; Mother; Child); At Jurisdiction Where Enrolled (Yes/No); (If no – Where)

Births Occurring Between July 1, 1924 and June 30, 1925 to Parents Enrolled at Jurisdiction

3800 Catches, Everett Bernard; 1924-6-12; Yes; M; Yes; 3/4; F; 7/8; Yes
                 Do not count
---- Catches, Everett Floyd; 1925-1-27; Yes; M; Yes; F; F; F; Yes
---- Cedar Face, Lucy; 1925-6-5; Yes; F; Yes; F; F; F; Yes
1226; Center, DeWitte; 1925-1-2; Yes; M; Yes; F; F; F; Yes
---- Chase In Morning, Grace; 1925-6-22; Yes; F; Yes; F; F; F; Yes
---- Chief, Myrtle R; 1925-6-15; Yes; F; Yes; F; F; F; Yes
1316; Chief Bear, Jennie; 1925-4-5; Yes; F; Yes; W; F; 1/2; Yes
1337 Chips, Dallas; 1925-4-20; Yes; M; Yes; F; F; F; Yes
---- Clifford, Lovelle Alice; 1925-6-25; Yes; F; Yes; 1/4; 3/16; 7/32; Yes
---- Clown Horse, Ellen; 1924-11-26; Yes; F; Yes; F; F; F; Yes
---- Coates, George Milton; 1925-3-4; Yes; M; Yes; W; 1/16; 1/32; Yes
1457; Colhoff, Ira James; 1924-11-6; Yes; M; Yes; 5/16; 3/4; 17/32; Yes
1529; Conroy, Mercy Juanita; 1925-1-14; Yes; F; Yes; 1/2; 3/4; 5/8; Yes
1562; Cottier, Eleanor; 1925-3-27; Yes; F; Yes; 1/2; 1/2; 1/2; Yes
---- Cottier, Mary Jane; 1925-2-2; Yes; F; Oglala & Muncie; Yes; 1/2; 1/2; 1/2;
      No; Tulsa, Okla
1577; Cottier, Vivian Dorothy; 1924-10-23; Yes; F; Yes; 5/8; F; 13/16; Yes
---- Crazy Thunder, Irene; 1925-6-28; Yes; F; Yes; F; F; F; Yes
---- Crooked Eyes, Ethel; 1925-2-12; Yes; F; Yes; F; F; F; Yes
1678; Cuny, Beulah Mary; 1924-10-12; Yes; F; Yes; 3/8; W; 3/16; Yes
---- Cuny, Peter; 1924-10-1; Yes; M; Yes; 3/8; 1/2; 7/16; Yes
---- Cuny, Paul Twiss; 1924-10-1; Yes; M; Yes; 3/8; 1/2; 7/16; Yes
1696; Cuny, Vernon Joseph; 1924-10-25; Yes; M; Yes; 3/8; 1/4; 5/16; Yes
1727; Curtis, Alice Emma; 1924-11-13; Yes; F; Yes; W; 3/8; 3/16; Yes
---- Cut Nose, Imogene; 1924-8-4; Yes; F; Sioux & Cheyenne; Yes; F; 5/8; 13/16;
      No; Cheyenne & Arap., Okla.
---- Dickinson, Donald Keith; 1924-9-25; Yes; M; Yes; W; 1/8; 1/16; No; Bertha,
      Wyo.
---- Dixon, Mildred Y; 1924-10-28; Yes; F; Yes; 1/4; 1/2; 3/8; Yes
1810; Dixon, Vesla I; 1924-12-9; Yes; F; Yes; 1/4; 1/4; 1/4; Yes
1820; Dog, Winnadel May; 1924-11-17; Yes; F; Yes; F; F; F; Yes
---- Dubrey, Margaret E; 1925-1-9; Yes; F; Yes; 1/2; 3/16; 11/32; Yes
1857; Dubrey, James Charles; 1925- 6-16; Yes; M; Yes; 1/2; 13/16; 21/32; Yes
1887; Eagle Bull, Mercy; 1925-3-15; Yes; F; Yes; F; F; F; Yes
1981; Evans, Myrtle Ardell; 1924-10-26; Yes; F; Yes; W; 1/2; 1/4; Yes
1999; Fast Horse, Lawrence; 1924-7-24; Yes; M; Yes; 3/4; F; 7/8; Yes
2000; Fast Horse, Lucinda; 1925-6-3; Yes; F; Yes; 3/4; F; 7/8; Yes
2051; Featherman, Zona; 1925-5-6; Yes; F; Yes; F; F; F; Yes
---- Fights Bear, Nellie; 1924-9-1; Yes; F; Yes; F; F; F; Yes
~~2120; Fire Thunder, Irene; 1925-12-5; Yes; F; Yes; 3/4; F; 7/8; Yes~~
      Transferred to Roll 1926
2134; Flesh, Cecelia May; 1924-11-28; Yes; F; Yes; F; W; 1/2; Yes

4

Key: 1925 Census Roll Number; Surname, Given; Date of Birth (Year-Month-Day); Live Births (Yes/No); Still Births (blank unless otherwise given); Sex; Tribe (Oglala Sioux unless given otherwise); Ward (Yes/No); Degree of Blood (Father; Mother; Child); At Jurisdiction Where Enrolled (Yes/No); (If no – Where)

Births Occurring Between July 1, 1924 and June 30, 1925 to Parents Enrolled at Jurisdiction

2147; Flying Hawk, Nancy; 1924-12-17; Yes; F; Yes; 7/8; F; 15/16; Yes

2170; Fool Crow, Mary; 1925-5-20; Yes; F; Yes; F; F; F; Yes (twins)
2171; "   "   Mattie; 1925-5-20; Yes; F; Yes; F; F; F; Yes
2220; Frog, Edith; 1924-11-5; Yes; F; Yes; F; F; F; Yes
2298; Ghost, Curtis Henry; 1924-12-19; Yes; M; Yes; F; F; F; Yes
2323; Ghost Dog, Theophila; 1925-3-9; Yes; F; Yes; F; F; F; Yes
2331; Giago, Sophia Marie; 1925-6-28; Yes; F; Yes; 1/4; 1/4; 1/4; Yes
~~2382; Goes In Center, May; 1925-8-8; Yes; F; Yes; F; F; F; Yes~~
       Transferred to 1926 Roll
2406; Goings, Lessanes; 1925-4-6; Yes; F; Yes; 3/8; 3/4; 9/16; Yes
2430; Good Buffalo, Grace; 1925-6-28; Yes; F; Yes; F; F; F; Yes
---- Good Lance, E. Joseph; 1924-8-30; Yes; M; Yes; F; F; F; Yes
2545; Good Plume, Lizzie; 1925-1-15; Yes; F; Yes; F; F; F; Yes
---- Good Shield, Matthew; 1924-7-30; Yes; M; Yes; F; F; F; Yes
2457; Good Shield, Theresa; 1925-4-4; Yes; F; Yes; F; F; F; Yes
2475; Good Voice Elk, May; 1924-8-5; Yes; F; Yes; F; F; F; Yes
2486; Good Voice Flute, Alexander; 1924-8-8; Yes; M; Yes; F; F; F; Yes
2525; Grass, Catherine K; 1925-4-9; Yes; F; Yes; F; F; F; Yes
---- Grass, Evaline Virginia; 1925-4-5; Yes; F; Yes; F; F; F; Yes
---- Grass, May Greda; 1925-1-4; Yes; F; Yes; F; F; F; Yes
---- Ground Spider, Noah; 1925-1-31; Yes; M; Yes; F; F; F; Yes
2649; Hawkwing, Owen; 1924-8-30; Yes; M; Yes; F; F; F; Yes
2700; Herman, Grace Marie; 1924-8-15; Yes; F; Yes; 1/2; 3/8; 7/16; Yes
2780; Hill, Evelyn Maxine; 1924-9-18; Yes; F; Yes; W; 3/8; 3/16; Yes
---- Hodge, Flossie Fae; 1925-1-28; Yes; F; Yes; W; 1/8; 1/16; No; Bono, Ark.
---- Hollow Head, Benjamin; 1924-7-16; Yes; M; Yes; F; F; F; Yes
---- Hollow Head, Levi; 1924-8-24; Yes; M; Yes; F; F; F; Yes
---- Hollow Horn, Adeline; 1924-9-8; Yes; F; Yes; F; F; F; Yes
---- Hollow Horn, Pearl; 1924-7-15; Yes; F; Yes; F; F; F; Yes
2837; Holy Eagle, Elizah Gustavus; 1924-10-13; Yes; M; Yes; F; F; F; Yes
2843; Holy Elk, Joseph; 1925-3-7; Yes; M; Yes; F; F; F; Yes
2829; Holy Dance, Rita Regina; 1925-5-25; Yes; F; Yes; F; 1/2; 3/4; Yes
2888; Horse, Eva; 1924-12-22; Yes; F; Yes; F; F; F; Yes
----- Hudspeth, Lela May; 1924-11-14; Yes; 1/2; F; 3/4; Yes
2949; Ice, Bernard; 1925-5-26; Yes; M; Yes; F; F; F; Yes
3025; Iron Heart, Calvin; 1924-9-7; Yes; M; Yes; 1/2; F; 3/4; Yes
3027; Iron Heart, Clara; 1925-4-2; Yes; F; Yes; F; 3/4; 7/8; Yes
3044; Iron Rope, Ambrose; 1924-12-1; Yes; M; Yes; F; F; F; Yes
3035; Iron Rope, Annie; 1925-3-18; Yes; F; Yes; F; F; F; Yes
3117; Janis, Geraldine; 1925-3-8; Yes; F; Yes; 1/2; 5/8; 9/16; Yes
---- Janis, Jerome; 1924-11-3; Yes; M; Yes; 1/2; 1/2; 1/2; Yes
---- Janis, Ralph Earl; 1924-9-23; Yes; M; Yes; 1/2; 3/16; 11/32; Yes

Key: 1925 Census Roll Number; Surname, Given; Date of Birth (Year-Month-Day); Live Births (Yes/No); Still Births (blank unless otherwise given); Sex; Tribe (Oglala Sioux unless given otherwise); Ward (Yes/No); Degree of Blood (Father; Mother; Child); At Jurisdiction Where Enrolled (Yes/No); (If no – Where)

Births Occurring Between July 1, 1924 and June 30, 1925 to Parents Enrolled at Jurisdiction

3232; Jones, Loren; 1925-2-3; Yes; F; Yes; 5/16; 1/2; 13/32; Yes

3240; Jumping Bull, Chris Provost; 1925-1-18; Yes; M; Yes; 3/4; 3/4; 3/4; Yes

---- Keester, Gilbert; 1925-2-24; Yes; M; Yes; W; 1/2; 1/4; Yes

3264; Keith, Ethel M; 1925-2-19; Yes; F; Oglala & Yankton; Yes; 1/8; 3/8; 7/8; Yes

3317; Kills Crow Indian, Viola; 1925-1-22; Yes; F; Yes; F; F; F; Yes

3352; Kills On Horseback, Andrew; 1925-2-13; Yes; M; Yes; F; 3/4; 7/8; Yes

3369; Kills Small, Loran; 1924-12-27; Yes; M; Yes; F; F; F; Yes

3460; Ladeaux, Thomas James; 1924-10-1; Yes; M; Sioux & Cherokee; Yes; 7/16; 3/8; 13/32; Yes

3501; Lamont, Eugene Francis; 1925-1-14; Yes; M; Yes; 1/2; F; 3/4; Yes

3540; Larabee, Pearl Olive; 1924-8-4; Yes; F; Yes; 1/2; 1/4; 3/8; Yes

~~---- Larvie, Wallace; 1925-9-10; Yes; M; Yes; 1/2; F; 3/4; Yes~~
  Transferred to 1926 Roll

---- Lays Hard, Dorothy; 1925-1-12; Yes; F; Yes; F; 1/2; 3/4; Yes

3588; Lays Hard, Verine; 1925-5-30; Yes; F; Yes; F; F; F; Yes

3601; Lee, Mary Rosalind; 1925-5-10; Yes; F; Yes; 1/2; 1/2; 1/2; Yes

3677; Little, Nadine Elizabeth; 1924-10-15; Yes; F; Yes; 3/4; 5/16; 17/32; Yes

3796; Little Moon, Raymond; 1925-6-13; Yes; M; Yes; F; 3/4; 7/8; Yes

---- Little War Bonnet, Charles; 1924-11-7; Yes; M; Yes; F; F; F; Yes

---- Little War Bonnet, James; 1924-11-7; Yes; M; Yes; F; F; F; Yes

3849; Little White Man, Aloysius; 1925-6-20; Yes; M; Yes; F; F; F; Yes

---- Livermont, Juanita Joy; 1925-5-20; Yes; F; Oglala & Chippewa; Yes; 3/16; 1/4; 7/32; Yes

3883; Livermont, Lorrain W; 1925-6-13; Yes; F; Oglala & Chippewa; Yes; 3/16; 1/4; 7/32; Yes

3908; Living Outside, Magdalen; 1915-6-5; Yes; F; Yes; F; F; F; Yes

3931; Lone Bear, Peter; 1924-10-16; Yes; M; Yes; F; F; F; No; Uintah & Oray[sic], Utah

---- Lone wolf, Evelyn; 1924-12-12; Yes; F; Yes; F; F; F; Yes

3975; Lone Wolf, George; 1925-4-30; Yes; M; Yes; F; F; F; Yes

4037; Long Woman, Steven; 1925-2-2; Yes; M; Yes; F; F; F; Yes

---- Looks Twice, Adolph; 1924-10-1; Yes; M; Yes; F; F; F; Yes

4069; Lowry, Regina; 1925-5-16; Yes; F; Yes; F; 3/4; 7/8; Yes

---- Loafer Joe, Paul; 1924-10-4; Yes; M; Yes; F; F; F; Yes

4161; Martinez, Melby; 1925-1-10; Yes; M; Yes; 1/2; 1/2; 1/2; Yes

---- McGrew, Virginia Elizabeth; 1924-10-15; Yes; F; Yes; F; 1/4; 1/8; Yes

4197; Meat, Nelson Joseph; 1925-2-16; Yes; M; Yes; F; F; F; Yes

4214; Mendenhall, Howard Harry; 1924-9-15; Yes; M; Yes; W; 1/4; 1/8; Yes

4231; Mesteth, Olive; 1925-1-18; Yes; F; Yes; 3/4; 1/2; 5/8; Yes

4244; Mesteth, Rita Geneva; 1925-4-25; Yes; F; Yes; 1/2; 1/2; 1/2; Yes

4325; Mills, Estelle Marcelleen; 1924-7-2; Yes; F; Yes; 3/4; 1/4; 1/2; Yes

4313; Mills, Ethel Norma; 1924-7-28; Yes; F; Yes; 1/2; 3/4; 5/8; Yes

4305; Mills, Kenneth James; 1925-1-29; Yes; M; Yes; 3/4; 3/4; 3/4; Yes

Key: 1925 Census Roll Number; Surname, Given; Date of Birth (Year-Month-Day); Live Births (Yes/No); Still Births (blank unless otherwise given); Sex; Tribe (Oglala Sioux unless given otherwise); Ward (Yes/No); Degree of Blood (Father; Mother; Child); At Jurisdiction Where Enrolled (Yes/No); (If no – Where)

Births Occurring Between July 1, 1924 and June 30, 1925 to Parents Enrolled at Jurisdiction

4385; Morrison, Roy George; 1925-1-6; Yes; M; Yes; 3/4; F; 7/8; Yes

---- Mousseau, Raymond; 1925-6-20; Yes; M; Yes; 1/2; F; 3/4; Yes

---- Nelson, Thomas Jr; 1924-11-11; Yes; M; Yes; 5/8; F; 13/16; Yes

---- Old Horse, Christina; 1925-1-2; Yes; F; Yes; F; F; F; Yes

4585; Oney, Maxine Elaine; 1924-12-6; Yes; F; Yes; W; 1/2; 1/4; Yes

4610; O'Rourke, Kermit; 1924-12-12; Yes; M; Yes; 1/4; 5/8; 7/16; Yes

4629; Packed, Bertha; 1925-3-4; Yes; F; Yes; F; F; F; Yes

---- Palmier, Maynard Gregory; 1925-5-17; Yes; M; Yes; 1/4; 1/2; 3/8; Yes

4639; Palmer, Helen Marie; 1925-1-17; Yes; F; Yes; W; 1/4; 1/8; Yes

4652; Palmier, Wonder Geraldine; 1924-11-3; Yes; F; Yes; 1/4; 1/4; 1/4; Yes

---- Parker, Rhoda Marie; 1924-8-24; Yes; F; Yes; W; 5/8; 5/16; Yes

---- Parkhurst, Elizabeth Ann; 1925-6-12; Yes; F; Oglala & Oneida; Yes;
1/4; 1/2; 3/8; Yes

4692; Pawnee Leggins, Mary; 1925-4-14; Yes; F; Yes; F; F; F; Yes

4708; Peterson, Virginia Mae; 1924-11-19; Yes; F; [blank]; W; 5/16; 5/32; Yes

4728; Pipe on Head, Virginia; 1925-1-6; Yes; F; Yes; F; F; F; Yes

4733; Plenty Arrows, Irene; 1925-3-6; Yes; F; Yes; F; F; F; Yes

4771; Plenty Wounds, William; 1925-4-28; Yes; M; Yes; F; F; F; Yes

~~4799; Poor Bear, Anderson; 1925-12-30; Yes; M; Yes; F; F; F; Yes~~
     On 1926 Roll

4809; Poor Thunder, Evylain; 1925-5-10; Yes; F; Yes; F; F; F; Yes

4805; Poor Thunder, Lillian Eloise; 1925-2-11; Yes; Yes F; Yes; F; F; F; Yes

4854; Pourier, Calvin; 1925-2-8; Yes; M; Yes; 3/16; 1/4; 7/32; Yes

4835; Pourier, Crispeen; 1924-12-10; Yes; F; Yes; 1/8; 1/2; 5/16; Yes

4862; Pourier, Stanley; 1924-12-28; Yes; M; Yes; 1/8; 1/2; 516; Yes

4870; Powder Woman, Daid; 1925-1-1; Yes; M; Yes; F; F; F; Yes

4924; Provost, Alfred Jos; 1924-11-11; Yes; M; Yes; 1/4; W; 1/8; Yes

4943; Provost, Pelhomine; 1925-6-5; Yes; F; Yes; 7/16; 1/2; 15/32; Yes

4963; Pulliam, James Jr; 1923-11-27; Yes; M; Yes; 1/2; 1/2; 1/2; Yes

4993; Pumpkin Seed, Madeline; 1925-1-25; Yes; F; Yes; F; 1/2; 3/4; Yes

4996; Quick Bear, Joan Virginia; 1924-8-25; Yes; F; Yes; Oglala & Rosebud; Yes;
F Roseb; 3/4; 7/8; Yes

5161; Quiver, Eva; 1925-4-4; Yes; F; Yes; F; F; F; Yes
     1928-[typed above 1925 Census Roll Number]

5059; Randall, Cordellia W; 1924-12-29; Yes; F; Oglala & River S. Cheyenne; Yes;
3/4; 1/2; 5/8; Yes

5096; Red Bow, Katherine; 1924-12-22; Yes; F; Yes; F; F; F; Yes

5114; Red Cloud, Alice; 1925-5-18; Yes; F; Yes; F; F; F; Yes

5121; Red Cloud, Cecelia; 1924-11-1; Yes; F; Yes; 7/8; 7/8; 7/8; Yes

5127; Red Cloud, Evelyn Jeanette; 1925-3-19; Yes; F; Yes; F; F; F; Yes

5111; Red Cloud, Gladys Ruby; 1925-12-30; Yes; F; Yes; F; F; F; Yes

5149; Reddy, William; 1924-10-27; Yes; M; Yes; W; 3/8; 3/16; Yes

5154 Red Eagle, Nora; 1925-3-2; Yes; F; Yes; F; F; F; Yes

7

Key: 1925 Census Roll Number; Surname, Given; Date of Birth (Year-Month-Day); Live Births (Yes/No);
Still Births (blank unless otherwise given); Sex; Tribe (Oglala Sioux unless given otherwise); Ward (Yes/No);
Degree of Blood (Father; Mother; Child); At Jurisdiction Where Enrolled (Yes/No); (If no – Where)

Births Occurring Between July 1, 1924 and June 30, 1925 to Parents Enrolled at Jurisdiction

5157; Red Ear Horse, Eva; 1924-10-4; Yes; F; Yes; F; F; F; Yes
----- Red Cloud, Lavina; 1924-12-26; Yes; F; Yes; F; F; F; Yes
5179; Red Elk, Catherine M; 1925-2-17; Yes; F; Yes; F; F; F; Yes
5334; Red Wing, Sarah E; 1924-8-29; Yes; F; Yes; F; 3/6; 11/16; Yes
5262; Red Paint, Amos; 1924-7-6; Yes; M; Yes; F; F; F; Yes
5306; Red Shirt, Joseph; 1925-3-18; Yes; M; Yes; F; F; F; Yes
5356; Returns From Scout, Stephen; 1924-11-28; Yes; M; Yes; F; F; F; Yes
5393; Richard, Albert V; 1923-10-7; Yes; M; Yes; 3/8; 3/4; 9/16; Yes
5439; Richard, Carolyn Mary; 1925-4-15; Yes; F; Yes; 9/16; 1/4; 13/32; Yes
5412; Richard, Laverne J; 1925-4-16; Yes; F; Yes; 7/16; W; 7/32; Yes
---- Richard, Laverne; 1924-2-22; Yes; F; Yes; 3/4; 5/8; 11/16; Yes
        Do not count
5441; Richard, Pearl; 1923-12-4; Yes; F; Yes; 9/16; 5/8; 19/32; Yes
5402; Richard, Theresa Marie; 1924-11-2; Yes; F; Yes; 1/4; 5/8; 7/16; Yes
5470; Robinson, Joan Adele; 1924-10-24; Yes; F; Yes; W; 1/8; 1/16; Yes
5480; Rock, Wayne; 1924-9-6; Yes; M; Yes; F; 3/4; 7/8; Yes
---- Rooks, Elane Ruby; 1925-3-16; Yes; F; Yes; 1/4; 1/2; 3/8; Yes
5520; Rooks, Timothy; 1924-11-23; Yes; M; Yes; F; 7/8; 15/16; Yes
---- Rose, Richard Morris; 1925-5-19; Yes; M; Yes; W; 3/16; 3/32; Yes
5581; Ruff, Emma Grace; 1924-11-5; Yes; F; Yes; 1/4; 3/4; 1/2; Yes
---- Running Bear, Emerson; 1925-1-11; Yes; M; Yes; F; F; F; Yes
5618; Running Eagle, Florie; 1925-3-4; Yes; F; Yes; F; F; F; Yes
5699; Salvis, Freida; 1924-9-9; Yes; F; Yes; W; 5/8; 5/16; Yes
---- Sanders, Bettie Jean; 1924-8-14; Yes; F; Yes; W; 1/8; 1/16; Yes
---- Scabby Face, Albert; 1924-10-30; Yes; M; Yes; F; F; F; Yes
---- Schwartz, Wilma E; 1925-4-23; Yes; F; Yes; W; 1/4; 1/8; Yes
---- Scott, Lavon Marie; 1924-11-4; Yes; F; Yes; W; 1/8; 1/16; Yes
---- Sharp, Albert Lee; 1925-2-13; Yes; M; Yes; W; 1/4; 1/8; Yes
---- Short Bear, Orville; 1925-3-28; Yes; M; Yes; 5/8; F; 13/16; Yes
5908; Short Step, Isaac; 1924-7-19; Yes; M; yes; F; F; F; Yes
5975; Sioux Bob, Irene; 1925-3-12; Yes; F; Yes; F; F; F; Yes
5979; Sitting Bear, Eugene; 1925-6-18; Yes; M; Yes; F; F; F; Yes
6019; Skalander, Eldene Mae; 1924-7-31; Yes; F; Yes; 1/8; 3/16; 5/32; Yes
6028; Skenandore, Pearl Lena; 1925-3-25; Yes; F; Yes; 1/4; 3/4; 1/2; Yes
6060; Smith, Joseph Orrin; 1925-3-22; Yes; M; Yes; W; 3/16; 3/32; Yes
6095; Spider, Blanche; 1925-2-1; Yes; F; Yes; F; F; F; Yes
---- Stair, Isabel; 1925-1-0; Yes; F; Yes; W; 1/8; 1/16; Yes
6190; Standing Bear, Carmel Grace; 1924-8-29; Yes; F; Yes; 5/8; 1/4; 7/16; Yes
---- Standing Bear, Lee; 1925-5-21; Yes; M; Yes; 3/4; F; 7/8; Yes
---- Standing Soldier, Paul; 1924-10-12; Yes; M; Oglala & Cherokee; Yes;
        7/8; 1/4; 9/16; Yes
6212; Standing Soldier, Maude L; 1925-3-18; Yes; F; Yes; 7/8; 3/4; 13/16; Yes
6238; Stands, Isaac; 1924-12-13; Yes; M; Yes; F; 7/8; 15/16; Yes

Key: 1925 Census Roll Number; Surname, Given; Date of Birth (Year-Month-Day); Live Births (Yes/No); Still Births (blank unless otherwise given); Sex; Tribe (Oglala Sioux unless given otherwise); Ward (Yes/No); Degree of Blood (Father; Mother; Child); At Jurisdiction Where Enrolled (Yes/No); (If no – Where)

Births Occurring Between July 1, 1924 and June 30, 1925 to Parents Enrolled at Jurisdiction

----	Stewart, Emerson; 1924-4-13; Yes; M; Yes; F; F; F; Yes
6314;	Strikes Enemy, Leo; 1925-6-30; Yes; M; Yes; F; 3/4; 7/8; Yes
6330;	Sullivan, Raymond; 1925-5-10; Yes; M; Yes; W; 1/16; 1/32; Yes
6380;	Swallow, Helen Agnes; 1915-11-25; Yes; F; Yes; 1/4; 3/8; 5/16; Yes
6365;	Swallow, Thompson; 1925-6-7; Yes; M; Yes; F; F; F; Yes
----	Swanson, Oliver H; 1924-10-25 Yes; M; Yes; W; 1/8; 1/16; Yes
6402;	Swick, Joseph; 1925-2-24; Yes; M; Yes; W; 3/4; 3/8; Yes
----	Swift Bird, Julia; 1925-5-27; Yes; F Yes; 7/8; F; 15/16; Yes
----	Tail, Rosella; 1924-12-14; Yes; F; Yes; F; 3/4; 7/8; Yes
6433;	Tail, Victoria; 1924-12-14; Yes; F; Yes; F; 3/4; 7/8; Yes
6427;	Tail, Verne Alex; 1925-3-28; Yes; M; Yes; F; F; F; Yes
6437;	Takes The Horse, Nelson; 1925-1-27; Yes M; Oglala & River S. Cheyenne; Yes; F; F; F; Yes
6542;	Thunder Hawk, Berdena; 1925-1-24; Yes; F; Yes; 3/4; F; 7/8; Yes
6557;	Thunder Tail, Emily; 1915-5-14; Yes; F; Yes; F; F; F; Yes
6547;	Thunder Tail, Fannie; 1925-3-18; Yes; F; Yes; 3/4; F; 7/8; Yes
6551;	Thunder Horse, Ethel Evelyn; 1925-2-11; Yes; F; Yes; F; F; F; Yes
6567;	Tibbits, Arline; 1925-6-18; Yes; F; Yes; 1/4; 1/8; 3/16; Yes
6638;	Turning Holy, Moses; 1915-2-10; Yes; M; Yes; F; F; F; Yes
6644;	Tuttle, Celesta A; 1925-5-26; Yes; F; Oglala & Santee S; Yes; F; 3/4; 7/8; Yes
7317;	(Wilson) Twiss, Anna W; 1924-10-10; Yes; F; Yes; 3/8; 1/8; 1/4; Yes
6697;	Twiss, Willis Paul; 1925-1-12; Yes; M; Yes; 7/8; 7/8; 7/8; Yes
6728;	Two Bulls, Mazie Elaine; 1924-11-27; Yes; F; Yes; 7/8; F; 15/16; Yes
----	Two Eagles, Rollan; 1925-1-25; Yes; M; Yes; F; 3/4; 7/8; Yes
6821;	Two Two, Aloysius; 1924-10-11; Yes; M; Yes; 3/4; F; 7/8; Yes
----	Two Two, Spencer; 1925-4-12; Yes; M; Yes; 3/4; F; 7/8; Yes
6846;	Under The Baggage, Jessie; 1925-4-5; Yes; F; Yes; F; F; F; Yes
6853;	Valandry, Alice Stacy; 1924-7-7; Yes; F; Yes; 1/8; 1/4; 3/16; Yes
6958;	Water, Thomas; 1924-12-31; Yes; M; Yes; 3/4; F; 7/8; Yes
6967;	Weasel, Villance; 1924-10-14; Yes; F; Yes; F; F; F; Yes
6979;	Weasel Bear, Benjamin; 1925-4-3; Yes; M; Yes; F; F; F; Yes
7011;	Weston, Earl Robert; 1925-4-5; Yes; M; Oglala & Santee; Yes; F; 3/4; 7/8; Yes
----	White, Verine Velma; 1925-6-30; Yes; F; Yes; 1/2; 1/2; 1/2; Yes
----	White Bull, James Ellwyn; 1925-6-10; Yes; M; Oglala & Oneida; Yes; F; 3/4; 7/8; Yes
7122;	White Butterfly, Benjamin; 1925-1-1; Yes; M; Yes; F; F; F; Yes
7128;	White Calf, Evelyn; 1924-12-15; Yes; F; Yes; F; F; F; Yes
7141;	White Cow Killer, Thomas Jr; 1925-2-17; Yes; M; Yes; F; 3/4; 7/8; Yes
7159;	White Dress, Rosa; 1925-4-15; Yes; F; Yes; F; F; F; Yes
7181;	White Eyes, Joseph F; 1924-7-8; Yes; M; Yes; F; 3/16; 19/32; Yes
7175;	White Eyes, Myrtle J; 1925-6-20; Yes; F; Yes; F; F; F; Yes
7202;	White Face, Hattie; 1925-2-1; Yes; F; Yes; F; F; F; Yes

State **South Dakota** Reservation **Pine Ridge** Agency or jurisdiction
Pine Ridge Office of Indian Affairs

Key: 1925 Census Roll Number; Surname, Given; Date of Birth (Year-Month-Day); Live Births (Yes/No);
Still Births (blank unless otherwise given); Sex; Tribe (Oglala Sioux unless given otherwise); Ward (Yes/No);
Degree of Blood (Father; Mother; Child); At Jurisdiction Where Enrolled (Yes/No); (If no – Where)

Births Occurring Between July 1, 1924 and June 30, 1925 to Parents Enrolled at Jurisdiction

7212; WhiteHawk[sic], Lawrence; 1924-11-13; Yes; M; Yes; 7/8; F; 15/16; Yes
7237; White Magpie, Samuel; 1924-8-1; Yes; M; Yes; F; F; F; Yes
7260; White Rabbit, Phlip[sic] Jr; 1924-12-25; Yes; M; Yes; F; F; F; Yes
7288; White Wolf, Robert; 1925-3-26; Yes; M; Yes; F; F; F; Yes
7338; Winfred, Charlotte; 1925-1-1; Yes; F; Oglala & Walapai; Yes; F; 1/4; 5/8; Yes
7343; Witt, Mary; 1925-2-4; Yes; F; Oglala & Cherokee; Yes; 1/4; F; 5/8; Yes
---- Witt, Nathaniel Jr; 1925-3-16; Yes; M; Yes; 1/4; F; 5/8; Yes
7345; Wolf, Bernard; 1924-11-30; Yes; M; Yes; W; 1/2; 1/4; Yes
7355; Woman Dress, Lema; 1925-5-15; Yes; F; Yes; F; F; F; Yes
7378; Wounded, Mary; 1924-9-9; Yes; F; Yes; F; F; F; Yes
7425; Yankton, Cecelia; 1924-8-4; Yes; F; Yes; 3/4; 7/8; 13/16; Yes
7415; Yankton, Emil; 1925-4-28; Yes; M; Yes; F; F; F; Yes
7439; Yellow Bear, Francis; 1925-3-4; Yes; M; Y; F; F; F; Yes
7496; Yellow Bull, Alberta; 1925-5-16; Yes; F; Yes; F; F; F; Yes
7648; Young Dog, Irene; 1924-11-14; Yes; F; Yes; F; F; F; Yes
       Shangreau, Calvin; 1925-3-10; Yes; M; Yes; F; F; F; [blank]

LIVE BIRTHS

1926
(July 1, 1925 - June 30, 1926)

PINE RIDGE RESERVATION
PINE RIDGE SOUTH DAKOTA

Key: 1926 Census Roll Number; Surname, Given; Date of Birth (Year-Month-Day); Live Births (Yes/No); Still Births (blank unless otherwise given); Sex; Tribe (Oglala Sioux unless given otherwise); Ward (Yes/No); Degree of Blood (Father; Mother; Child); At Jurisdiction Where Enrolled (Yes/No); (If no – Where)

Births Occurring Between July 1, 1925 and June 30, 1926 to Parents Enrolled at Jurisdiction

20a; Addison, Martha; 1926-6-26; Yes; F; Yes; F; F; F; Yes
39; Afraid Of Hawk, Adile Jane; 1926-3-3; Yes; F; Yes; F; F; F; Yes
31; Afraid Of Hawk, Martha Bessie; 1926-4-20; Yes; F; Yes; F; F; F; Yes
---; Allen, Maxwell James; 1926-2-10; Yes; M; Yes; 3/16; W; 3/32; Yes
156; Amiotte, Delbert Levi; 1925-8-18; Yes; M; Yes; 1/4; 1/2; 3/8; Yes
191; Apple, Anthony George; 1925-10-13; Yes; M; Yes; 3/4; 1/2; 5/8; Yes
----; Apple, Sterling; 1925-10-11; Yew; M; Yes; 3/4; 1/2; 5/8; Yes
----; Backward, Russell; 1925-10-30; Yes; M; Yes; F; F; F; Yes
246; Bad Cob, Christina; 1926-2-18; Yes; F; Yes; F; F; F; Yes
----; Bad Heart Bull, Susanna; 1926-3-3; Yes; F; Yes; F; F; F; Yes
283; Bad Wound, Leroy Spencer; 1926-4-24; Yes; M; Yes; 3/4; 1/2; 5/8; Yes
----; Bad Wound, Robert Edison; 1926-4[6?]-26; Yes; M; Yes; F; 1/2; 3/4; Yes
----; Bank, Caroline; 1926-1-25; Yes; F; Yes; F; F; F; Yes
----; Bauman, Frank G. Jr; 1925-11-15; Yes; M; Yes; W; 3/8; 3/16; Yes
384; Bear Robe, Margaret; 1925-12-9; Yes; F; Yes; F; F; F; Yes
441; Bent, Mollie Lucille; 1926-6-6; Yes; F; Yes; 5/8; 3/4; 11/16; Yes
445; Bergen, Minnie E; 1925-10-25; Yes; F; Yes; 1/4; 1/2; 3/8; Yes
----; Bettelyoun, Glen Chris; 1925-8-17; Yes; M; Yes; 3/8; 1/4; 5/16; Yes
468; Bettelyoun, Prudie Hattie; 1926-2-16; Yes; F; Yes; 3/8; 3/8; 3/8; Yes
509; Big Crow, Francis; 1926- 4-22; Yes; M; Yes; 1/2; 1/4; 3/8; Yes
548; Bird Head, Lorinda; 1926-4-1; Yes; F; Yes; F; F; F; Yes
569; Bissonette, Jackson Vern; 1926-6-15; Yes; M; Yes; 3/4; 7/8; 13/16; Yes
586; Bissonette, Lucy; 1926-4-14; Yes; F; Yes; 3/8; F; 11/16; Yes
----; Black Bear, William; 1925-11-27; Yes; M; Yes; F; F; F; Yes
----; Black Bear, Vivian; 1925-8-4; Yes; F; Yes; F; F; F; Yes
660; Black Bird, Jessie; 1926-3-10; Yes; F; Yes; F; F; F; Yes
---; Black Horse, David H; 1925-8-4; Yes; M; Yes; F; 1/2; 3/4; Yes
761; Black Wolf, Eugene; 1926-1-14; Yes; M; Yes; F; F; F; Yes
765; Black tail Deer, Andrew; 1925-8-8; Yes; M; Yes; F; F; F; Yes
777; Blind Man, Bertha Rose; 1926-4-14; Yes; F; Yes; F; F; F; Yes
801; Blue Bird, Curtis; 1925-12-27; Yes; M; Yes; F; 3/4; 7/8; Yes
----; Blue Horse Owner, Moses; 1926-2-28; Yes; M; Yes; F; F; F; Yes
----; Blue Legs, Alvina; 1926-4-2; Yes; F; Yes; F; F; F; Yes
857; Brafford, Earl Patrick; 1926-3-17; Yes; M; Yes, 1/4; 1/2; 3/8; Yes
882; Brave, Elsie; 1925-10-30; Yes; F; Yes; 3/4; F; 7/8; Yes
----; Brave, Oris; 1925-8-24; Yes; M; Yes; F; F; F; Yes
915; Breast, John; 1925-7-29; Yes; M; Yes; F; F; F; Yes
941; Brewer, Sylvia; 1926-5-15; Yes; F; Yes; 1/4; 5/8; 7/16; Yes
973; Broken Nose, Christina; 1926-2-5; Yes; F; Yes; F; F; F; Yes
----; Broken Rope, Sylvester; 1925-7-27; Yes; M; Yes; F; 3/4; 7/8; Yes
1045; Brown Bull, Thompson, Jr; 1926-5-16; Ye; M; Yes; F; 1/2; 3/4; Yes
1065; Brown Eyes, Bernice; 1925-7-20; Yes; F; Yes; 3/4; F; 7/8; Yes
----; Brown Eyes, Margaret; 1925-12-18; Yes; F; Yes; 3/4; F; 7/8; Yes

13

State __**South Dakota**__ Reservation___ **Pine Ridge** ___Agency or jurisdiction
_____ **Pine Ridge** _____ Office of Indian Affairs

Key: 1926 Census Roll Number; Surname, Given; Date of Birth (Year-Month-Day); Live Births (Yes/No);
Still Births (blank unless otherwise given); Sex; Tribe (Oglala Sioux unless given otherwise); Ward (Yes/No);
Degree of Blood (Father; Mother; Child); At Jurisdiction Where Enrolled (Yes/No); (If no – Where)

Births Occurring Between July 1, 1925 and June 30, 1926 to Parents Enrolled at Jurisdiction

1122; Bull Bear, Ida May; 1926-5-23; Yes; F; Yes; F; 3/4; 7/8; Yes
1133; Bull Bear, Loraine Sophia; 1926-5-4; Yes; F; Yes; F; F; F; Yes
----   Bull Bear, Lucy; 1926-4-7; Yes; F; Yes; F; F; F; Yes
1150; Bull Man, Laura; 1926-3-5; Yes; F; Yes; F; F; F; Yes
----   Burns Prairie, Clement; 1926-4-10; Yes; M; Yes; F; F; F; Yes
----   Carlow, Byrd Spencer; 1926-5-26; Yes; M; Yes; 1/4; W; 1/8; Yes
1200; Carlow, David Louis; 1926-3-1; Yes; M; Yes; 1/4; 1/2; 3/8; Yes
1211; Catches, Adeline; 1925-12-17; Yes; F; Yes; F; F; F; Yes
1271; Chase Alone, Agnes; 1925-10-17; Yes; F; Yes; F; F; F; Yes
1256; Charging Crow, Eva; 1926-1-27; Yes; F; Yes; F; F; F; Yes
1297; Chief, Douglas; 1925-10-30; Yes; M; Yes; F; F; F; Yes
----   Clifford, Helena; 1925-11-4; Yes; F; Yes; 1/2; 1/2; 1/2; Yes
1355   Clifford, Jeanette Gloried; 1925-12-19; Yes; F; Yes; 1/4; 1/1; 3/8; Yes
----   Clifford, Owen Stephen; 1926-6-12; Yes; M; Yes; 1/2; 3/4; 5/8; Yes
----   Clincher, Matthew; 1925-8-12; Yes; M; Yes; F; F; F; Yes
----   Cook, Stanley; 1926-3-18; Yes; M; Yes; W; 1/2; 1/4; Yes
1532; Conroy, Norma Ruby; 1925-7-5; Yes; F; Yes; 1/2; 1/2; 1/2; Yes
1511; Conquering Bear, Dawson; 1926-3-20; Yes; M; Yes; F; F; F; Yes
----   Crazy Ghost, Zack; 1926-2-10; Yes; M; Yes; F; F; F; Yes
----   Crooked Eyes, Malinda; 1926-6-26; Yes; F; Yes; F; F; F; Yes
1665; Cross, Curtis; 1926-4-21; Yes; M; Yes; 7/8; F; 15/16; Yes
1702; Cuny, Robert; 1925-11-20; Yes; M; Yes; 3/8; 1/2; 7/16; Yes
----   Clown Horse, Edison; 1925-8-18; Yes; M; Yes; F; F; F; Yes
1605; Craven, Frances Yvonne; 1925-7-30; Ye; F; Yes; 1/8; W; 1/16; Yes
3112; Deon, Leroy Curtis; 1926-2-9; Yes; M; Yes; F; 3/4; 7/8; Yes
----   DeWolf, Helen; 1925-10-5; Yes; F; Yes; W; 1/4; 1/8; Yes
----   Dismounts Thrice, Martha; 1925-10-17; Yes; F; Yes; F; F; F; Yes
----   Dismounts Thrice, Normal; 1925-7-7; Yes; M; Yes; F; F; F; Yes
1808; Distribution, George; 1925-7-2; Yes; M; Yes; F; F; F; Yes
1874; Dubray, Henry Alfred; 1925-10-9; Yes; M; Yes; 1/2; 13/16; 21/32; Yes
1906; Eagle Bull, Leo; 1925-10-30; Yes; M; Yes; F; F; F; Yes
1937; Eagle Hawk, Robert; 1926-2-2; Yes; M; Yes; F; F; F; Yes
1945; Eagle Heart, Victoria; 1926-3-28; Yes; F; Yes; F; F; F; Yes
1978; Ecoffey, Frank Robert Donald; 1926-2-8; Yes; M; Yes; 3/8; W; 3/16; Yes
2019; Fast Horse, Lucinda; 1925-7-3; Yes; F; Yes; 3/4; F; 7/8; Yes
2039; Fast Horse, Peter; 1926-3-20; Yes; M; Yes; F; 3/8; 11/16; Yes
----   Fast Wolf, Isabelle; 1926-6-25; Yes; F; Yes; 7/8; F; 15/16; Yes
2087; Feather On Head, Emma; 1925-12-23; Yes; F; Yes; F; 3/4; 7/8; Yes
2085; Feather On Head, Silas; 1925-12-23; Yes; M; Yes; F; 3/4; 7/8; Yes   Triplets
2086; Feather On Head, Susie; 1925-12-23; Yes; F; Yes; F; 3/4; 7/8; Yes
2120; Fire Place, Thomas; 1925-10-1; Yes; M; Yes; F; F; F; Yes
2143; Fire Thunder, Leona; 1916-6-23; Yes; F; Yes; 3/4; 13/16; 25/32; Yes
2221; Frazier, Calvin; 1925-7-3; Yes; M; Yes; 3/4; F; 7/8; Yes

14

Key: 1926 Census Roll Number; Surname, Given; Date of Birth (Year-Month-Day); Live Births (Yes/No);
Still Births (blank unless otherwise given); Sex; Tribe (Oglala Sioux unless given otherwise); Ward (Yes/No);
Degree of Blood (Father; Mother; Child); At Jurisdiction Where Enrolled (Yes/No); (If no – Where)

Births Occurring Between July 1, 1925 and June 30, 1926 to Parents Enrolled at Jurisdiction

2243; Frog, Minnie; 1926-4-26; Yes; F; Yes; F; F; F; Yes
2280; Garcia, Cornelia; 1925-9-1; Yes; F; Yes; 1/4; 1/2; 3/8; Yes
---- Garner, Wesley; 1926-5-25; Yes; M; Yes; 1/2; 5/8; 9/16; Yes
2375; Gibbons, Charles Joseph; 1925-7-13; Yes; M; Yes; 1/2; F; 3/4; Yes
---- Gillispie, Bettie; 1926-1-3; Yes; F; Yes; 1/2; 1/4; 3/8; Yes
2120[sic]; Fire Thunder, Irene; 1925-12-5; Yes; F; Yes; 3/4; F; 7/8; Yes
       From 1925 Roll
2428; Goings, Frank Ingraham; 1926-3-27; Yes; M; Yes; no day; 3/8; ?; Yes
2485; Good Medicine, Sallie; 1925-11-21; Yes; F; Yes; 7/8; F; 15/16; Yes
2491; Good Plume, Jennie; 1926-2-9; Yes; F; Yes; F; F; F; Yes
2519; Good voice Elk, Victoria; 1926-2-9; Yes; F; Yes; F; F; F; Yes
2535; Good Voice Flute, Louie; 1926-2-26; Yes; M; Yes; F; F; F; Yes
2539; Good Weasel, Simon; 1926-2-4; Yes; M; Yes; F; F; F; Yes
2547; Grabbing Bear, Belle; 1925-8-6; Yes; F; Yes; F; F; F; Yes
2584; Gray Grass, Mercy Esther; 1915-9-9; Yes; F; Yes; F; F; F; Yes
2605; Groaning Bear, Elsie; 1926-4-19; Yes; F; Yes; F; F; F; Yes
2613; Ground Spider, Noah; 1926-5-9; Yes; M; Yes; F; 3/4; 7/8; Yes
---- Harvey, Wilbert; 1925-8-19; Yes; M; Yes; 1/2; 1/2; 1/2; Yes
2655; Hat, Mary Elizabeth; 1926-3-29; Yes; F; Yes; F; F; F; Yes
---- Hauff, William Callie; 1925-10-26; Yes; M; Yes; W; 3/8; 3/16; Yes
2730; Hercher, John Albert; 1925-8-16; Yes; M; Yes; W; 1/4; 1/8; Yes
2749; Herman, Jacob Theodore; 1925-9-5; Yes; M; Yes; 1/2; 3/8; 7/16; Yes
2771; Hernandez, Alfonzo; 1926-6-17; Yes; M; Yes; 1/2; 3/4; 5/8; Yes
2778; Hernandez, Chauncy E; 1926-5-7; Yes; M; Yes; 1/2; 1/3; 3/8; Yes
2782; High Bull, Thomas; 1926-6-3; Yes; M; Yes; F; F; F; Yes
2791; High Crane, Cordelia Rose; 1926-5-26; Yes; F; Yes; F; F; F; Yes
2826; Hill, Frank Merrill; 1925-11-5; Yes; M; Yes; 3/4; 3/4; 3/4; Yes
----- Hollow Horn, Gilbert; 1925-11-8; Yes; M; Yes; F; F; F; Yes
2917; Hopkins, Lillian Ethel; 1925-12-2; Yes; F; Yes; F; F; F; Yes
2382; Goes in Center, May; 1925-8-8; Yes; F; Yes; F; F; F; Yes
       From 1925 Roll
2943; Horse, Daisy; 1926-6-10; Yes; F; Yes; F; F; F; Yes
2949; Horse, Mary; 1925-9-7; Yes; F; Yes; F; F; F; Yes
6280; Horse Stands In Sight, Mary Elizabeth; 1925-7-28; Yes; F; Yes; F; 3/4; 7/8;
       Yes
---- Hunter, Rebecca; 1926-5-3; Yes; F; Yes; 1/2; 1/2; 1/2; Yes
5586; Iron Bear, Beatrice; 1925-10-20; Yes; F; Yes; F; 7/8; 15/16; Yes
3039; Iron Cloud, Lavern; 1926-4-13; Yes; F; Yes; F; 7/8; 15/16; Yes
3059; Iron Crow, Morris; 1925-9-29; Yes; M; Yes; F; F; F; Yes
3064; Iron crow[sic], Noah; 1926-2-7; Yes; M; Yes; F; F; F; Yes
3068; Iron Elk, Mary Beulah; 192225-11-17; Yes; F; Yes; F; F; F; Yes
3129; Irving, Cecelia; 1925-12-28; Yes; F; Yes; 3/8; 1/2; 7/16; Yes
3133; Jack, Christianna R; 1925-7-23; Yes; F; Yes; F; F; F; Yes

15

State **South Dakota** Reservation **Pine Ridge** Agency or jurisdiction
Pine Ridge Office of Indian Affairs

Key: 1926 Census Roll Number; Surname, Given; Date of Birth (Year-Month-Day); Live Births (Yes/No); Still Births (blank unless otherwise given); Sex; Tribe (Oglala Sioux unless given otherwise); Ward (Yes/No); Degree of Blood (Father; Mother; Child); At Jurisdiction Where Enrolled (Yes/No); (If no – Where)

Births Occurring Between July 1, 1925 and June 30, 1926 to Parents Enrolled at Jurisdiction

---- Janis, Dorothy; 1926-3-25; Yes; F; Yes; 1/2; 3/8; 7/16; Yes
3195; Janis, Guy; 1925-12-1; Yes; M; Yes; 1/2; 5/8; 9/16; Yes
3235; Janis, Kenneth Matthew; 1926-5-9; Yes; M; Yes; 3/4; 3/4; 3/4; Yes
3224; Janis, Leora; 1925-7-12; Yes; F; Yes; 1/2; 3/8; 7/16; Yes
3163; Janis, Ray; 1925-7-5; Yes; M; Yes; 1/2; 1/2; 1/2; Yes
3201; Janis, Raymond Lloyd; 1926-5-16; Yes; M; Oglala & Yankton; Yes; 1/2; 1/8; 5/16; Yes
3168; Janis, Ruth; 1925-10-8; Yes; F; Yes; 1/2; W; 1/4; Yes
3240; Janis, Virgil; 1925-8-9; Yes; M; Yes; 5/8; 7/8; 3/4; Yes
---- Jones, Edward A; 1926-3-14; Yes; M; Yes; 5/16; 1/4; 9/32; Yes
3342; Kicking Bear, Adolph; 1926-4-20; Yes; M; Yes; F; F; F; Yes
3411; Kills In The Water, Elane; 1925-12-15; Yes; F; Yes; F; F; F; Yes
3405; Kills In Water, George; 1926-5-6; Yes; M; Yes; F; F; F; Yes
3430; Kills Right, Emma; 1025-8-14; Yes; F; Yes; F; F; F; Yes (twins)
3431; Kills Right, George; 1925-8-14; Yes; M; Yes; F; F; F; Yes
3474; King, Moses Bartholemew; 1926-3-22; Yes; M; Yes; F; 3/4; 7/8; Yes
3539; Lame, Leroy; 1926-4-12; Yes; M; Yes; F; F; F; Yes
3548; Lamont, Florence; 1925-8-28; Yes; F; Yes; 1/2; F; 3/4; Yes
---- LaPoint, Vera Cecelia; 1926-2-20; Yes; F; Yes; 3/4; 3/8; 9/16; Yes
3580; LaPoint, Yvonne Leah; 1925-9-25; Yes; F; Yes; 9/16; 3/8; 15/32; Yes
3612; Larabee, Alvina May; 1926-2-6; Yes; F; Yes; 1/2; 1/4; 3/8; Yes
3728; Lip, Annie; 1925-9-6; Yes; F; Yes; F; F; F; Yes
3754; Little Bear, Mamie; 1926-5-18; Yes; F; Yes; 3/4; 1/2; 5/8; Yes
---- Little Boy, Chauncey; 1925-10-6; Yes; M; Yes; F; F; F; Yes
3806; Little Crow, Laura; 1926-3-18; Yes; F; Yes; F; F; F; Yes
3813; Little Dog, Moses; 1926-3-19; Yes; M; Yes; F; F; F; Yes
3894; Little Thunder, Hattie; 1925-8-15; Yes; F; Yes; F; F; F; Yes
3885; Little Spotted Horse, Grace; 1926-2-21; Yes; F; Yes; F; F; F; Yes
3901; Little War Bonnet, Loucilia; 1926-2-11; Yes; F; Yes; F; F; F; Yes
---- Livermont, John; 1926-5-7; Yes; M; Yes; 1/8; 1/4; 3/16; Yes
---- Livermont, Marian Margaret; 1926-1-2; Yes; F; Yes; 3/16; 1/4; 7/32; Yes
3979; Loafer, Francis; 1925-12-28; Yes; M; Yes; F; F; F; Yes
3983; Loafer Joe, Leo; 1925-12-28; Yes; M; Yes; F; F; F; Yes
4016; Lone Hill, Eva; 1925-12-4; Yes; M; Yes; 3/4; F; 7/8; Yes
---- Lorrie, Wallace; 1925-9-10; Yes; M; Yes; 1/2; F; 3/4; Yes
                        From 1925 Roll
4023; Lone Hill, Mildred Pearl; 1926-5-8; Yes; F; Yes; 3/4; F; 7/8; Yes
---- Lone Wolf, Sylvia; 1926-3-2; Yes; F; Yes; F; F; F; Yes
4086; Long Soldier, Francis; 1926-1-29; Yes; M; Yes; F; F; F; Yes
4109; Looking Cloud, Martha; 1925-9-16; Yes; F; Yes; F; F; F; Yes
4125; Looks Twice, Rebecca; 1926-2-15; Yes; F; Yes; F; F; F; Yes
4137; Loves War, Clara Ruth; 1926-4-22; Yes; F; Yes; F; F; F; Yes

Key: 1926 Census Roll Number; Surname, Given; Date of Birth (Year-Month-Day); Live Births (Yes/No); Still Births (blank unless otherwise given); Sex; Tribe (Oglala Sioux unless given otherwise); Ward (Yes/No); Degree of Blood (Father; Mother; Child); At Jurisdiction Where Enrolled (Yes/No); (If no – Where)

Births Occurring Between July 1, 1925 and June 30, 1926 to Parents Enrolled at Jurisdiction

4172; ~~Marrow Bone, Ephraim; 1926-12-27; Yes; M; Yes; F; F; F; Yes~~
        Transferred to 1927
---- Marshall, Francis; 1926-5-15; Yes; M; Yes; 3/4; F; 7/8; Yes
---- Means, Lavina; 1926-2-23; Yes; F; Yes; 3/4; F; 7/8; Yes
4360; Miller, Alberta Christine; 1925-12-23; Yes; F; Oglala & OKLA; Yes; no data; 3/8; ?; Yes
4332; Mesteth, Ambrose; 19250-7-14; Yes; M; Yes; 1/2; F; 3/4; Yes
---- Mesteth, Ray; 1925-12-25; Yes; M; Yes; 1/2; 3/4; 5/8; Yes
4387; Mills, Marilyn Patricia; 1925-8-3; Yes; F; Yes; 3/4; 5/16; 17/32; Yes
4391; Mills, Sidney Leroy; 1925-12-5; Yes; M; Yes; 3/4; 1/4; 1/2; Yes
---- Moore, Norval Lamoine; 1926-5-27; Yes; M; Yes; 3/8; 1/2; 7/16; Yes
4507; Moves Camp, James; 1925-7-1; Yes; M; Yes; F; F; F; Yes
4573; New Holy, Alice; 1925-7-26; Yes; F; Yes; F; F; F; Yes
4595; No Neck, Leroy; 1925-7-2; Yes; M; Yes; F; F; F; Yes
4602; Not Help Him, Seth J; 1925-11-5; Yes; M; Yes; F; F; F; Yes
4616; Old Hair, Bernice; 1925-10-25; Yes; F; Yes; F; F; F; Yes
---- Owen, Mervin Bernard; 1026-6-20; Yes; M; Yes; white; 7/16; 7/32; Yes
4736; Patton, Grace; 1926-4-9; Yes; F; Yes; 3/8; 3/8; 3/8; Yes
4747; Patton, Norbert Lawrence; 1926-3-24; Yes; M; Yes; 1/4; 3/8; 5/16; Yes
---- Peterson, Ramon Dale; 1926-2-28; Yes; M; Yes; White; 5/16; 5/32; Yes
4783; Pine Bird, Dorothy; 1925-9-3; Yes; F; Yes; F; F; F; Yes
---- Pipe On Head, Matthew; 1926-2-3; Yes; M; Yes; F; F; F; Yes
4818; Plenty Wolf, Selvin; 1926-1-21; Yes; M; Yes; F; F; F; Yes
---- Poor Bear, Allen; 1926-2-23; Yes; M; Yes; F; F; F; Yes
---- Poor Bear, Anderson; 1925-12-30; Yes; M; Yes; F; F; F; Yes
        Also on 1925 but crossed out
4917; Pourier, Cecile Joseph; 1926-2-8; Yes; M; Yes; 3/16; 3/16; 1/4; Yes
4883; Pourier, Edward; 1925-11-19; Yes; M; Yes; 1/8; 7/16; 9/32; Yes
4913; Pourier, Verna Rose; 1925-9-10; Yes; F; Yes; 3/16; 3/8; 9/32; Yes
---- Provost, Dorothy Marie; 1925-9-15; Yes; F; Yes; 1/2; W; 1/4; Yes
5012; Pugh, Klaura[sic] Cecelia; 1926-1-4; Yes; F; Yes; 3/8; 3/16; 9/32; Yes
5166; Red Breath Bear, Myrtle; 1925-10-27; Yes; F; Yes; F; F; F; Yes
5288; Red Hawk, Ward Nelson; 1925-11-20; Yes; M; Yes; F; F; F; Yes
5322; Red Owl, Pearl; 1925-12-6; Yes; F; Yes; F; F; F; Yes
---- Red Paint, Martha; 1925-8-7; Yes; F; Yes; F; F; F; Yes
5352; Red Shirt, Ollie; 1925-11-15; Yes; F; Yes; F; F; F; Yes
5375; Red Star, Lydia; 1925-10-1; Yes; F; Yes; F; F; F; Yes
5383; Red Star, Samuel; 1925-7-16; Yes; M; Yes; F; F; F; Yes
---- Red Willow, Bertha; 1925-7-25; Yes; F; Yes; F; F; F; Yes
5413; Respects Nothing, Florine; 1926-2-25; Yes; F; Yes; F; F; F; Yes
---- Ribman, Nellie; 1926-5-17; Yes; F; Yes; F; F; F; Yes
---- Richard, Alexander Jno; 1926-6-6; Yes; M; Yes; 9/16; [?]; 19/32; Yes
---- Richard, Alfred; 1925-9-2; Yes; M; Yes; 3/4; 5/8; 11/16; Yes

Key: 1926 Census Roll Number; Surname, Given; Date of Birth (Year-Month-Day); Live Births (Yes/No); Still Births (blank unless otherwise given); Sex; Tribe (Oglala Sioux unless given otherwise); Ward (Yes/No); Degree of Blood (Father; Mother; Child); At Jurisdiction Where Enrolled (Yes/No); (If no – Where)

Births Occurring Between July 1, 1925 and June 30, 1926 to Parents Enrolled at Jurisdiction

5476; Richard, Darlene Margaret; 1925-12-4; Yes; F; Yes; 7/16; 1/16; 1/4; Yes
----- Richard, Emil; 1926-5-18; Yes; M; Yes; 3/4; F; 7/8; Yes
---- Richard, Spencer; 1926-5-21; Yes; M; Yes; 9/16; 1/4; 13/32; Yes
---- Ringing Shield, Zelma; 1926-6-9; Yes; F; Yes; F; F; F; Yes
5550; Rock, Hannah C; 1925-9-13; Yes; F; Yes; F; 3/4; 7/8; Yes
5547; Rock, Rachel; 1926-2-17; Yes; F; Yes; F; 3/4; 7/8; Yes
---- Rooks, Lucile Lydia; 1926-6-5; Yes; F; Yes; 1/4; 1/2; 3/8; Yes
5636; Ruff, William Henry; 1926-4-8; Yes; M; Yes; 1/4; 3/4; 1/2; Yes
5718; Runs Above, Lloyd Lester; 1925-10-18; Yes; M; Yes; F; W; 1/2; Yes
---- Runs Along The Edge, Lydia; 1925-10-26; Yes; F; Yes; F; 7/8; 15/16; Yes
5782; Salway, Clement Stephen; 1926-6-1; Yes; M; Yes; 5/8; 1/2; 9/16; Yes
5767; Salway, Hermus Clement; 1926-1-21; Yes; M; Yes; 5/8; 9/16; 19/32; Yes
5794; Salway, James A; 1925-10-31; Yes; M; Yes; 5/8; 7/16; 17/32; Yes
5887; Shangreau, Peter; 1925-8-3; Yes; M; Yes; 1/2; 7/8; 11/16; Yes
---- Sharp, Willard L; 1926-6-10; Yes; M; Yes; W; 1/4; 1/8; Yes
5917; She Elk Voice Walking, Margery; 1926-2-11; Yes; F; Yes; F; F; F; Yes
5934; Sherman, Rosilie[sic] Emily; 1925-9-22; Yes; F; Yes; 3/8; 1/2; 9/16; Yes
5952; Short Bear, Stanley Douglas; 1925-12-8; Yes; M; Yes; 7/8; F; 15/16; Yes
5966; Short Bull, Kerman; 1926-5-21; Yes; M; Yes; F; F; F; Yes
5983; Shot, Clement; 1926-4-6; Yes; M; Yes; F; F; F; Yes
6008; Shoulder, Stewart; 1926-4-23; Yes; M; Yes; F; F; F; Yes
6077; Sits Poor, Vincent; 1926-3-26; Yes; M; Yes; F; F; F; Yes
---- Sitting Bear, Mary; 1926-5-6; Yes; F; Yes; F; F; F; Yes
6064; Sitting Hawk, Gertrude Louise; 1926-6-12; Yes; F; Yes; F; F; F; Yes
6093; Skalander, Essie Atelia; 1925-12-19; Yes; F; Yes; 1/8; 5/16; 7/32; Yes
6089; Skalander, Lois Ilene; 1925-12-17; Yes; F; Yes; 1/8; 3/16; 5/32; Yes
6119; Slow Bear, Annie; 1926-6-24; Yes; F; Yes; F; F; F; Yes
6112; Slow Bear, Francis; 1925-9-12; Yes; M; Yes; F; F; F; Yes
6166; Spider, Avaha[sic]; 1925-7-1; Yes; F; Yes; F; F; F; Yes
6197; Spotted Eagle, Felix; 1926-1-18; Yes; M; Yes; F; F; F; Yes
6209; Spotted Elk, Philip; 1926-5-24; Yes; M; Yes; F; F; F; Yes
---- Standing Soldier, Rita Elizabeth; 1926-3-30; Yes; F; Yes; 7/8; 1/4; 9/16; Yes
6317; Stands, Jonas; 1926-5-15; Yes; M; Yes; F; 7/8; 15/16; Yes
6396; Sullivan, Frank Joshua; 1925-8-29; Yes; M; Yes; W; 1/16; 1/32; Yes
6409; Sun Bear, Randolph; 1925-10-23; Yes; M; Yes; F; F; F; Yes
---- Swallow, Armine; 1925-12-3; Yes; F; Yes; 3/8; 3/8; 3/8; Yes
6457; Swallow, Armina; 1926-1-1; Yes; F; Yes; 1/4; 1/8; 3/16; Yes
6456; Swallow, Lloyd William; 1925-7-10; Yes; M; Yes; 1/4; 1/8; 3/16; Yes
6510; Takes War Bonnet, Rena; 1925-7-29; Yes; F; Yes; F; F; F; Yes
6529; Tapia, Louis Richard; 1926-3-8; Yes; M; Yes; 1/4; 1/2; 3/8; Yes
6524; Tapia, Romania; 1926-1-1; Yes; F; Yes; 1/2; 1/2; 3/8; Yes
---- Tells His Name, Floyd; 1926-1-15; Yes; M; Yes; F; F; F; Yes
----- Terkildsen, Dahlmann William; 1925-12-10; Yes; M; Yes; W; 3/8; 3/16; Yes

18

State **South Dakota** Reservation **Pine Ridge** Agency or jurisdiction

Pine Ridge Office of Indian Affairs

Key: 1926 Census Roll Number; Surname, Given; Date of Birth (Year-Month-Day); Live Births (Yes/No); Still Births (blank unless otherwise given); Sex; Tribe (Oglala Sioux unless given otherwise); Ward (Yes/No); Degree of Blood (Father; Mother; Child); At Jurisdiction Where Enrolled (Yes/No); (If no – Where)

Births Occurring Between July 1, 1925 and June 30, 1926 to Parents Enrolled at Jurisdiction

----	Three Stars, Emily Mildred; 1925-8-8; Yes; F; Yes; 5/8; F; 13/16; Yes
----	Thunder Horse, Lucile; 1926-5-27; Yes; F; Yes; F; F; F; Yes
6638;	Tibbits, Derona; 1925-7-18; Yes; F; Yes; 1/2; 3/16; 11/32; Yes
6668;	Trimble, Ralph U; 1926-4-19; Yes; M; Yes; W; 3/4; 3/8; Yes
----	Trueblood, Richard Vincent; 1925-11-8; Yes; M; Yes; W; 1/4; 1/8; Yes
----	Twiss, Amos; 1925-12-14; Yes; M; Yes; 1/2; F; 3/4; Yes
6790;	Two Bulls, Floyd; 1926-3-2; Yes; M; Yes; 7/8; F; 15/16; Yes
6812;	Two Crow, Myrtle; 1926-1-19; Yes; F; Yes; 3/4; 3/4; 3/4; Yes
----	Two Crow, Peter; 1926-6-26; Yes; M; Yes; 3/4; F; 7/8; Yes
6857;	Two Sticks, Daisy; 1926-4-29; Yes; F; Yes; F; F; F; Yes
6888;	Two Two, Peter; 1926-2-5; Yes; M; Yes; 3/4; F; 7/8; Yes
6880;	Two Two, Veronica; 1925-10-4; Yes; F; Yes; 3/4; F; 7/8; Yes
6914;	Under The Baggage, Russell; 1926-6-6; Yes; M; Yes; F; F; F; Yes
----	Valandry, Paul Himes; 1926-6-23; Yes; M; Yes; 1/8; 1/4; 3/16; Yes
6929;	Valandry, Vesta Clara; 1926-6-12; Yes; F; Yes; 3/8; 7/16; 11/32; Yes
6074;	Walking Elk, Sarah; 1926-1-16; Yes; F; Yes; F; F; F; Yes
6999;	War Bonnet, Caroline Edna; 1926-3-28; Yes; F; Yes; F; F; F; Yes
7010;	Warrior, Irene; 1926-1-5; Yes; F; Yes; F; F; F; Yes
7045;	Weasel Bear, Alice; 1926-2-10; Yes; F; Yes; F; F; F; Yes
----	Weston, Grace; 1926-5-19; Yes; F; Yes; F; F; F; Yes
7113;	Whirlwind Horse, Raymond; 1926-3-15; Yes; M; Yes; F; 7/8; 15/16; Yes
----	White, Verina Velma; 1925-7-1; Yes; F; Yes; 1/2; 1/2; 1/2; Yes
----	White Bull, Ivan; 1925-11-12; Yes; M; Yes; F; F; F; Yes
7233;	White Eyes, Albert; 1926-1-6; Yes; M; Yes; F; 3/4; 7/8; Yes
7247;	White Eyes, Juanita Louise; 1926-1-14; Yes; F; Yes; F; 3/16; 19/32; Yes
7261;	White Face, Isaac B; 1925-11-5; Yes; M; Yes; F; F; F; Yes
7280;	White Horse, Nellie; 1926-1-22; Yes; F; Yes; F; F; F; Yes
7359;	Wilcox, Billie; 1925-8-13; Yes; M; Yes; W; F; 1/2; Yes
----	Wilson, Alice Idella; 1926-4-20; Yes; F; Yes; 1/8; W; 1/16; Yes
----	Wounded, Zona; 1925-10-28; Yes; F; Yes; F; F; F; Yes
-----	Wounded Arrow, Jene[sic] Francis; 1925-7-23; Yes; M; Yes; F; F; F; Yes
7466;	Yaeger[sic], Freda; 1925-9-16; Yes; F; Yes; W; 1/4; 1/8; Yes
7487;	Yankton, Vina; 1926-3-25; Yes; F; Yes; 3/4; 7/8; 13/16; Yes
7496;	Yellow Bear, Charles; 1926-4-1; Yes; M; Yes; F; F; F; Yes
----	Yellow Bird, Fern; 1926-2-2; Yes; F; Yes; 3/4; 1/2; 5/8; Yes
7544;	Yellow Boy, Ethel; 1925-12-22; Yes; F; Yes; 7/8; F; 15/16; Yes
7582;	Yellow Horse, Bertha; 1925-12-20; Yes; F; Yes; F; F; F; Yes
7679;	Young, Joseph Oliver; 1925-7-12; Yes; M; Yes; 3/16; 1/4; 7/32; Yes
7673;	Young, Sidney; 1926-5-15; Yes; M; Yes; 1/4; 5/8; 7/16; Yes
7696;	Young Bear, Ernest; 1925-10-19; Yes; M; Yes; F; F; F; Yes
	Fogg, Louis Jr; 1925-7-21; Yes; M; Yes; F; F; F; Yes

Authority agency verified by certificate

LIVE BIRTHS

1927
(July 1, 1926 - June 30, 1927)

PINE RIDGE RESERVATION
PINE RIDGE SOUTH DAKOTA

State__**South Dakota**__Reservation____**Pine Ridge**____Agency or jurisdiction
____**Pine Ridge**_____ Office of Indian Affairs

Key: 1927 Census Roll Number; Surname, Given; Date of Birth (Year-Month-Day); Live Births (Yes/No);
Still Births (blank unless otherwise given); Sex; Tribe (Oglala Sioux unless given otherwise); Ward (Yes/No);
Degree of Blood (Father; Mother; Child); At Jurisdiction Where Enrolled (Yes/No); (If no – Where)

Births Occurring Between July 1, 1926 and June 30, 1927 to Parents Enrolled at Jurisdiction

28; Afraid Of Bear, Joseph L; 1926-7-2; Yes; M; Yes; F; F; F; Yes
-- Adams, Virginia; 1927-6-3; Yes; F; Yes; 3/4; 3/4; 3/4; Yes
103; Allman, Mabel; 1926-7-23; Yes; F; Yes; ?; 1/4; ?; Yes
      See Census Roll
126; American Horse, Vernie; 1926-11-17; Yes; M; Yes; F; F; F; Yes
--- Ant, Hobart; 1927-5-4; Yes; M; Yes; F; 5/8; 13/16; Yes
210; Artichoker, Benjamin D; 1926-10-2; Yes; M; Oglala & Winnebago; Yes; 7/8; 1/4; 9/16; Yes
205; Around Him, Julia; 1927-2-23; Yes; F; Yes; F; F; F; Yes
234; Backward, Jessie; 1927-2-25; Yes; F; Yes; F; F; F; Yes
--- Bad Wound, Darling R; 1926-12-31; Yes; F; Yes; F; F; F; Yes
--- Bad Wound, Stella; 1927-5-29; Yes; F; Yes; 3/4; F; 7/8; Yes
311; Bald Eagle Bear, Jerome; 1926-11-25; Yes; M; Yes; F; F; F; Yes
326; Bartlett, Delphine D; 1927-2-22; Yes; F; Yes; 1/2; 1/2; 1/2; Yes
333; Bayliss, Frances E. J; 1927-6-76; Yes; M; Yes; W; 3/16; 3/32; Yes
345; Bear Eagle, Elmer; 1926-9-4; Yes; M; Yes; F; F; F; Yes
403; Bear Shield, Mathew; 1926-8-26; Yes; M; Yes; F; F; F; Yes
--- Bell, Harvey Elza; 1926-7-1; Yes; M; Yes; W; 3/8; 3/16; Yes
--- Bettelyoun, Ethel Marie; 1926-12-20; Yes; F; Oglala & Menominee; Yes; 1/2; 5/8; 9/16; Yes
511; Big Head, George; 1926-11-8; Yes; M; Yes; F; F; F; Yes
512; Big Head, Victoria; 1926-11-8; Yes; F; Yes; F; F; F; Yes
--- Black Bear, Charles; 1927-1-6; Yes; M; Yes; F; F; F; Yes
677; Black Crow, Hazel; 1927-3-22; Yes; F; Yes; F; F; F; Yes
--- Black Crow, Leona; 1927-2-28; Yes; F; Yes; F; F; F; Yes
--- Black Bear, Simon; 1927-3-19; Yes; M; Yes; F; F; F; Yes
666; Black Cat, Joseph; 1926-7-20; Yes; M; Yes; F; F; F; Yes
--- Bissonette, Lawrence F; 1926-8-11; Yes; M; Yes; 5/8; 7/8; 3/4; Yes
--- Black Elk, Charlotte R; 1926-7-14; Yes; F; Yes; F; 1/2; 3/4; Yes
689; Black Elk, Wilson; 1926-7-26; Yes; M; Yes; F; F; F; Yes
--- Black Horse, Clifford; 1926-11-1; Yes; M; Yes; F; F; F; Yes
733; Black Horse, Mildred Labelle; 1927-4-28; Yes; F; Yes; F; 1/2; 3/4; Yes
--- Blacksmith, Mathew; 1927-5-30; Yes; M; Yes; F; F; F; Yes
761; ~~Black Wolf, Eugene; 1926-1-14; Yes; M; Yes; F; F; F; Yes~~
      Transferred to 1926 roll not ver
--- Blindman, Amelia; 1926-8-31; Yes; F; Yes; F; F; F; Yes
--- Blindman, Philip; 1926-9-1; Yes; M; Yes; F; F; F; Yes
--- Blue Bird, Dorothy; 1926-7-25; Yes; F; Yes; F; 7/8; 15/16; Yes
783; Blue Bird, Florence E; 1926-8-28; Yes; F; Yes; F; 5/8; 13/16; Yes
--- Blue Legs, [No name given]; 1927-4-30; Yes; F; Yes; F; F; F; Yes
806; Blue Legs, Rebeca; 1927-2-8; Yes; F; Yes; F; F; F; Yes
828; Bores A Hole, Glenn; 1926-12-14; Yes; M; Yes; F; F; F; Yes
--- Brave, Lavern; 1927-6-15; Yes; M; Yes; F; F; F; Yes
--- Brave, Mary; 1927-4-8; Yes; F; Yes; F; F; F; Yes

23

Key: 1927 Census Roll Number; Surname, Given; Date of Birth (Year-Month-Day); Live Births (Yes/No);
Still Births (blank unless otherwise given); Sex; Tribe (Oglala Sioux unless given otherwise); Ward (Yes/No);
Degree of Blood (Father; Mother; Child); At Jurisdiction Where Enrolled (Yes/No); (If no – Where)

Births Occurring Between July 1, 1926 and June 30, 1927 to Parents Enrolled at Jurisdiction

---	Brave, Russell; 1926-10-1; Yes; ; Yes; F; F; F; Yes
894;	Brave Heart, Chris; 1926-12-10; Yes; M; Yes; F; 3/4; 7/8; Yes
---	Brewer, William L; 1926-9-7; Yes; M; Yes; 1/4; 1/2; 3/8; Yes
---	Brings Yellow, Vernon; 1926-9-6; Yes; M; Yes; F; F; F; Yes
----	Brown, Ephraim N; 1927-1-8; Yes; F[sic]; Yes; F; F; F; Yes
1007;	Brown, Joseph Jr; 1926-7-3; Yes; M; Yes; 3/8; 1/4; 5/16; Yes
----	Brown, Wm. Frederick; 1926-9-24; Yes; M; Yes; 3/16; 1/4; 7/32; Yes
----	Brown Eyes, Lena; 1927-6-24; Yes; F; Yes; 3/4; F; 7/8; Yes
----	Buckman, Verna; 1926-8-21; Yes; F; Yes; 3/4; 7/8; 13/16; Yes
1095;	Bull Bear, Norah; 1926-12-9; Yes; F; Yes; F; 7/8; 15/16; Yes
----	Bullard, Francis W; 1926-12-17; Yes; M; Yes; 1/4; W; 1/8; Yes
1153;	Bush, Vincent; 1927-6-14; Yes; M; Yes; 3/4; 3/4; 3/4; Yes
----	Bushy Top Pine, Owen; 1927-5-7; Yes; M; Yes; F; F; F; Yes
3822;	Catches, Eugene; 1927-3-29; Yes; M; Yes; ?; F; ?; Yes
1207;	Center, Kenneth P; 1927-2-15; Yes; M; Yes; F; F; F; Yes
----	Chase In Sight, Garcia; 1927-6-9; Yes; M; Yes; ?; F; ?; Yes
----	Chief, Roy; 1927-6-3; Yes; M; Yes; 1/2; 1/4; 3/8; Yes
----	Childers, Daniel Wilbur; 1926-12-10; Yes; M; Oglala & Creek; Yes; 7/8; 1/16; 15/32; Yes
----	Chips. Ethel May; 1926-8-21; Yes; F; Yes; F; F; F; Yes
1314;	Chips, Vincent; 1926-8-8; Yes; M; Yes; F; 3/4; 7/8; Yes
1368;	Clifford, Lloyd; 1926-8-5; Yes; M; Yes; 1/4; 3/16; 7/32; Yes
1367;	Clifford, Floyd; 1926-8-5; Yes; M; Yes; 1/4; 3/16; 7/32; Yes
----	Clifford, Isabelle Clara; 1926-8-22; Yes; F; Yes; 1/4; 1/2; 3/8; Yes
----	Colhoff, Frederick M; 1927-1-16; Yes; M; Yes; 1/2; 1/2; 1/2; Yes
1456;	Comes Again, Leo; 1926-9-28; Yes; M; Yes; F; F; F; Yes
----	Conroy, Vivian; 1926-11-22; Yes; F; Yes; 1/4; 1/4; 1/4; Yes
1545;	Conroy, Lola Lucille; 1927-5-15; Yes; F; Yes; 1/2; 1/2; 1/2; Yes
1491;	Conquering Bear, Ray; 1926-10-18; Yes; M; Yes; F; F; F; Yes
----	~~Cook, Stanley; 1926-3-18; Yes; M; Yes; W; 1/2; 1/4; Yes~~
	Transferred to 1926 roll not ver
1554;	Cottier, Robert; 1926-9-27; Yes; M; Yes; 1/2; 1/2; 1/2; Yes
----	~~Crooked Eyes, Malinda; 1926-8-26; Yes; F; Yes; F; F; F; Yes~~
	Transferred to 1926 rolls not ver
1668;	Crow, Alvina; 1927-5-2; Yes; F; Yes; F; F; F; Yes
----	Crow, Dorothy; 1926-10-12; Yes; F; Yes; F; F; F; Yes
	Crow, Rachel; 1927-2-27; Yes; F; Yes; ?; ?; Yes
	From 1932 roll Ok
1664;	Crow, Nelson; 1926-11-29; Yes; M; Yes; F; F; F; Yes
1742;	Cut, Irene; 1927-1-5; Yes; F; Yes; F; F; F; Yes
1750;	Cut Grass, Dora; 1926-7-21; Yes; F; Yes; F; F; F; Yes
----	Cummings, Joyce M; 1927-4-10; Yes; F; Oglala & Rosebud; Yes; 1/16; 1/16; 1/16; Yes
1702;	Cuny, Alta Marie; 1927-4-6; Yes; F; Yes; 3/8; W; 3/16; Yes

Key: 1927 Census Roll Number; Surname, Given; Date of Birth (Year-Month-Day); Live Births (Yes/No);
Still Births (blank unless otherwise given); Sex; Tribe (Oglala Sioux unless given otherwise); Ward (Yes/No);
Degree of Blood (Father; Mother; Child); At Jurisdiction Where Enrolled (Yes/No); (If no – Where)

Births Occurring Between July 1, 1926 and June 30, 1927 to Parents Enrolled at Jurisdiction

1706; Cuny, Doris Adeline; 1926-9-10; Yes; F; Yes; 3/8; 1/4; 5/16; Yes
1685; Cuny, Evelyn Patrice; 1926-8-5; Yes; F; Ya; 3/8; W; 3/16; Yes
---- Deon, Daniel Dewitt; 1926-11-30; Yes; M; Yes; 1/8; W; 1/16; Yes
---- DeSheuquette, Irene; 1927-5-31; Yes; F; Yes; 1/2; 5/8; 9/16; Yes
---- DeWolf, Vera June; 1927-6-1; Yes; F; Yes; W; 1/4; 1/8; Yes
1821; Dixon, Benjamin J; 1927-1-21; Yes; M; Yes; 1/4; 1/4; 1/4; Yes
---- Dixon, Stanley Robert; 1927-4-26; Yes; M; Yes; 1/4; 1/2; 3/8; Yes
---- Dixon, Raymond LeRoy; 1926-10-20; Yes; M; Yes; 1/4; 5/8; 7/16; Yes
        Trans from 1932 roll - not ver
1841; Dreamer, Juline Viola; 1926-12-28; Yes; F; Yes; F; F; F; Yes
1868; Dubray, Dave; 1926-8-20; Yes; M; Yes; 1/2; 13/16; 27/32; Yes
---- Dubray, Leo; 1927-5-26; Yes; M; Yes; 1/2; 5/8; 9/16; Yes
- - - Eagle Bull, Henry; 1927-2-24; Yes; M; Yes; F; F; F; Yes
---- Eagle Elk, Robert E; 1926-9-8; Yes; M; Yes; F; F; F; Yes
1992; Evans, Norman F; 1926-8-15; Yes; M; Yes; W; 1/2; 1/4; Yes
2005; Fast Eagle, Comer Paul; 1926-12-1; Yes; M; Yes; F; F; F; Yes
---- Fast Horse, Alton; 1926-11-29; Yes; M; Yes; 3/4; 3/4; 3/4; Yes
---- Feather, Leo; 1926-18-13; Yes; M; Yes; F; F; F; Yes
2058; Featherman, Douglas; 1926-9-8; Yes; M; Yes; F; F; F; Yes
2067; Featherman, Tresa; 1927-4-4; Yes; F; Yes; F; F; F; Yes
2089; Fights Bear, Lizzie; 1926-7-8; Yes; F; Yes; F; F; F; Yes
---- Fire Thunder, Annie; 1927-2-27; Yes; F; Yes; F; F; F; Yes
2166; Flying Hawk, Ernest; 1926-11-12; Yes; M; Yes; 7/8; F; 15/16; Yes
---- Fog, Bertha May; 1927-3-25; Yes; F; Yes; ?; 5/8; ?; Yes
2208; Frazier, Harold W; 1926-8-25; Yes; M; Oglala & SanteeS[sic]; Yes; 3/4; 5/8;
        11/16; Yes
2235; Frog, Ephraim; 1926-9-9; Yes; M; Yes; F; F; F; Yes
2231; Frog, Febie; 1927-4-25; Yes; F; Yes; F; F; F; Yes
2252; Galligo, Louis J; 1927-3-21; Yes; M; Yes; 3/4; 1/2; 5/8; Yes
2290; Gay, Christine; 1926-12-2; Yes; F; Yes; 3/4; F; 7/8; Yes
---- Ghost, Kiva; 1927-6-4; Yes; F; Yes; F; F; F; Yes
2334; Ghost Dog, George W; 1926-11-13; Yes; M; Yes; F; F; F; Yes
2357; Gibbons, Amelda; 1926-8-7; Yes; F; Yes; 1/2; F; 3/4; Yes
2350; Gibbons, Eugene; 1927-2-5; Yes; M; Yes; 1/2; 1/2; 1/2; Yes
2385; Glenn, Ruby Alouise; 1926-7-27; Yes; F; Yes; 1/2; 3/4; 5/8; Yes
2422; Goings, Catherine R; 1927-4-22; Yes; F; Yes; 3/8; 3/4; 9/16; Yes
2451; Good Buffalo, Peter; 1927-4-24; Yes; M; Yes; F; F; F; Yes
---- Good Crow, Zona; 1926-11-1; Yes; M; Yes; F; F; F; Yes
---- Good Soldier, Victoria; 1926-10-30; Yes; F; Yes; F; F; F; Yes
---- Good Voice Elk, Sterman[sic]; 1927-3-16; Yes; M; Yes; F; F; F; Yes
---- Good Voice Flute, Wilson; 1927-6-23; Yes; M; Yes; F; F; F; Yes
---- Grass, Carrie; 1927-5-13; Yes; F; Yes; F; F; F; Yes
2549; Grass, Kenneth J; 1927-2-24; Yes; M; Yes; F; F; F; Yes
2618; Harvey, Zella; 1927-1-29; Yes; F; Yes; 1/2; 1/2; 1/2; Yes

25

Key: 1927 Census Roll Number; Surname, Given; Date of Birth (Year-Month-Day); Live Births (Yes/No);
Still Births (blank unless otherwise given); Sex; Tribe (Oglala Sioux unless given otherwise); Ward (Yes/No);
Degree of Blood (Father; Mother; Child); At Jurisdiction Where Enrolled (Yes/No); (If no – Where)

Births Occurring Between July 1, 1926 and June 30, 1927 to Parents Enrolled at Jurisdiction

----   Hauff, Vernon Dal; 1927-2-12; Yes; M; Yes; W; 3/8; 3/16; Yes

2676;   Hawk Wing, Elsie; 1927-1-18; Yes; F; Yes; 3/4; F; 7/8; Yes

2687;   He Crow, Jefferson; 1927-3-29; Yes; M; Yes; F; F; F; Yes

2727;   Herman, Paul Joseph; 1927-5-4; Yes; M; Yes; 1/2; 3/8; 7/16; Yes

2814;   Hill, Kenneth L; 1927-1-14; Yes; M; Yes; W; 3/8; 3/16; Yes

2824;   Hodge, Guindalyne; 1927-3-2; Yes; F; Yes; W; 1/8; 1/16; Yes

2843;   Hollow Horn, Stanley; 1926-9-12; Yes; M; Yes; F; F; F; Yes

2861;   Holy Dance, Beatrice; 1927-5-12; Yes; F; Yes; F; 1/2; 3/4; Yes

----   Horse, Oliver; 1926-11-1; Yes; M; Yes; F; F; F; Yes

2951;   Huebner, Edward L; 1927-5-3; Yes; M; Yes; W; 3/8; 3/16; Yes

----   Ice, Vernie; 1927-5-1; Yes; M; Yes; F; F; F; Yes

2023;   Iron Cloud, Leo; 1926-10-16; Yes; M; Yes; F; F; F; Yes

3045;   Iron Hawk, Calvin; 1926-11-12; Yes; M; Yes; F; F; F; Yes

3058;   Iron Horse, Sally; 1926-11-28; Yes; F; Yes; F; F; F; Yes

----   Iron Rope, Joseph; 1927-3-13; Yes; M; Yes; F; F; F; Yes

----   Iron Rope, Marie; 1927-4-24; Yes; F; Yes; F; F; F; Yes

----   Janis, Catherine E; 1926-10-3; Yes; F; Yes; 3/4; F; 7/8; Yes

3152;   Janis, Emmet Everett; 1926-11-5; Yes; M; Yes; 1/2; 3/16; 11/32; Yes

3196;   Janis, Leroy Francis; 1927-2-20; Yes; M; Yes; 1/2; 3/8; 7/16; Yes

----   Janis, Norbert; 1927-5-31; Yes; M; Yes; 1/2; 1/2; 1/2; Yes

3179;   Janis, Wilson Kenneth; 1927-3-9; Yes; M; Yes; 3/4; F; 7/8; Yes

----   Jealous Of Him, Edith; 1926-11-22; Yes; F; Yes; F; F; F; Yes

3272;   Jones, Anthony; 1927-1-28; Ye; M; Yes; 5/16; 1/2; 13/32; Yes

----   Jumping Bull, Carl; 1927-4-10; Yes; M; Yes; 3/4; 3/4; 3/4; Yes

3297;   Jumping Eagle, Irene Alpha; 1927-2-28; Yes; F; Yes; F; 1/2; 3/4; Yes

3352;   Kills Crow Indian, Irene; 1927-4-30; Yes; F; Yes; F; F; F; Yes

----   Kills Enemy, Edward; 1927-4-2; Yes; M; Yes; F; F; F; Yes

3405;   Kills Small, Eugene; 1927-1-17; Yes; M; Yes; F; F; F; Yes

----   Ladeaux, Abraham Noah; 1927-5-18; Yes; M; Yes; 7/8; F; 15/16; Yes

3484;   Ladeaux, Orlando Wilson; 1927-2-11; Yes; M; Yes; 7/8; F; 15/16; Yes

----   Lang, Chas. Raymond; 1927-3-20; Yes; M; Yes; 1/8; ?; ?; Yes

----   Lays Bad, Thresa; 1927-5-4; Yes; F; Yes; F; 3/4; 7/8; Yes

3680;   Lessert, Benjamin H; 1926-8-12; Yes; M; Yes; 1/4; 1/4; 1/4; Yes

3709;   Little, Edsel Wallace; 1926-8-20; Yes; M; Yes; 4/5; 5/16; 17/32; Yes

----   Little Hawk, Richard Bennet; 1026-9-17; Yes; M; Yes; F; 1/2; 3/4; Yes

----   Livermont, Frank Lyn; 1927-6-8; Yes; M; Oglala & Chippewa; Yes; 3/16; 1/4; 7/32; Yes

3933;   Living Outside, Garfield; 1926-11-12; Yes; M; Yes; F; F; F; Yes

3941;   Loafer, Alice; 1927-1-2; Yes; F; Yes; F; F; F; Yes

----   Locke, Titus P; 1927-5-30; Yes; M; Yes; F; F; F; Yes

4056;   Long Woman, Charles; 1926-10-31; Yes; M; Yes; F; F; F; Yes

4057;   Long Woman, Eugene; 1926-10-31; Yes; M; Yes; F; F; F; Yes

4083;   Looks Twice, Angelina V; 1927-3-21; Yes; F; Yes; F; F; F; Yes

4105;   Makes Good, Lucy; 1927-4-26; Yes; F; Yes; F; F; F; Yes

26

Key: 1927 Census Roll Number; Surname, Given; Date of Birth (Year-Month-Day); Live Births (Yes/No);
Still Births (blank unless otherwise given); Sex; Tribe (Oglala Sioux unless given otherwise); Ward (Yes/No);
Degree of Blood (Father; Mother; Child); At Jurisdiction Where Enrolled (Yes/No); (If no – Where)

Births Occurring Between July 1, 1926 and June 30, 1927 to Parents Enrolled at Jurisdiction

4137; Marrow Bone, Theresa; 1927-5-14; Yes; F; Yes; F; F; F; Yes
---- Marshall, Edith Doris; 1927-4-22; Yes; F; Yes; 3/4; F; 7/8; Yes
---- Marshall, Vivian Eliza; 1926-7-23; Yes; F; Yes; 3/4; F; 7/8; Yes
4169; Martin, William W; 1926-9-17; Yes; M; Yes; 3/8; F; 11/16; Yes
---- ~~McDaniels, Frederick Jos; 1927-7-6; Yes; M; Yes; 1/2; 3/8; 7/16; Yes~~
Transferred to 1928
---- McGaa, DeWayn[sic]; 1926-10-2; Yes; M; Yes; 3/8; 1/2; 7/16; Yes
4223; Meat, Myrtle Agnes; 1927-2-27; Yes; F; Yes; F; F; F; Yes
4231; Medicine, Rosie; 1927-5-23; Yes; F; Yes; F; F; F; Yes
4245; Merrival, Dorris Jean; 1926-7-22; Yes; F; Yes; 3/8; 3/8; 3/8; Yes
4261; Mesteth, John Marquis; 1927-1-2; Yes; M; Yes; 3/4; 1/2; 5/8; Yes
4251; Mesteth, Mathew; 1926-11-16; Yes; M; Yes; 3/4; F; 7/8; Yes
4306; Mexican, Sarah Daisy; 1926-12-21; Yes; F; Yes; F; F; F; Yes
---- Mills, Katherine E; 1927-3-1; Yes; F; Yes; 3/4; 3/4; 3/4; Yes
---- Moeller, Moroni James; 1926-7-13; Yes; M; Yes; W; 1/2; 1/4; Yes
---- Morrison, Clyde; 1926-6-28; Yes; M; Yes; 3/4; F; 7/8; Yes
----- Morrison, Christensen; 1927-12-25; Yes; M; Yes; 3/4; F; 7/8; Yes
4418; Morrison, Vincent Orie; 1926-7-10; Yes; M; Yes; 3/4; 11/16; 23/32; Yes
4506; Nelson, Cecelia May; 1926-12-9; Yes; F; Yes; 5/8; F; 13/16; Yes
4512; Nelson, Narcisse; 1927-2-11; Yes; F; Yes; 5/8; F; 13/16; Yes
4516; Nelson, Truet Laverne; 1927-1-26; Yes; M; Yes; ?; 1/2; ?; Yes
---- Hew Holy, Myrle; 1927-4-23; Yes; F; Yes; F; F; F; Yes
---- No Two Horns, Luella Myrtle; 1927-3-14; Yes; F; Yes; F; F; F; Yes
---- Old Hair, Catherine; 1927-4-20; Yes; F; Yes; F; F; F; Yes
----- Old Horse, Mary; 1926-8-31; Yes; F; Yes; F; F; F; Yes
4591; Old Shield, Wilson R; 1926-12-8; Yes; M; Yes; F; 3/4; 7/8; Yes
4611; Oney, Wilmar Eugene; 1927-3-21; Yes; M; Yes; W; 1/2; 1/4; Yes
4631; O'Rourke, Eleanor; 1926-7-15; Yes; F; Yes; 1/4; 1/2; 3/8; Yes
---- O'Rourke, William Orville; 1927-5-20; Yes; M; Yes; 1/4; 5/8; 7/16; Yes
4650; Pacer, Christiana; 1926-12-13; Yes; F; Yes; F; F; F; Yes
---- Pain On Hip, Louisa; 1926-11-18; Yes; F; Yes; F; F; F; Yes
---- Palmier, Theodore; 1926-8-27; Yes; M; Yes; 1/4; 1/2; 3/8; Yes
---- Peck, Walter Jr; 1926-10-14; Yes; M; Yes; 1/4; W; 1/8; Yes
---- Perea[sic], Patsy Jean; 1927-5-2; Yes; F; Yes; W; 1/16; 1/32; Yes
---- Pflug[sic], Elaine Mary; 1927-1-18; Yes; F; Yes; W; 1/4; 1/8; Yes
4759; Plenty Arrows, Patty Jean; 1926-9-17; Yes; F; Yes; F; F; F; Yes
---- Plenty Wolf, Zack Thomas; 1926-11-6; Yes; M; Yes; F; F; F; Yes
---- Plenty Wounds, Virginia Vey; 1926-12-9; Yes; F; Yes; F; F; F; Yes
---- Poor Bear, Robert; 1926-8-10; Yes; M; Yes; F; F; F; Yes
---- Poor Bear, Weldon Lesslte; 1927-6-13; Yes; M; Yes; 7/8; F; 15/16; Yes
4813; Poor Bear, Eliza; 1927-1-19; Yes; F; Yes; 7/8; F; 15/16; Yes
4883; Pourier, Christina; 1926-11-29; Yes; F; Yes; 3/16; 1/4; 7/32; Yes
---- Pourier, Melvin Jno; 1927-3-2; Yes; M; Yes; 3/16; 3/8; 9/32; Yes
4899; Powder Woman, Eva; 1927-2-16; Yes; F; Yes; F; F; F; Yes

27

Key: 1927 Census Roll Number; Surname, Given; Date of Birth (Year-Month-Day); Live Births (Yes/No);
Still Births (blank unless otherwise given); Sex; Tribe (Oglala Sioux unless given otherwise); Ward (Yes/No);
Degree of Blood (Father; Mother; Child); At Jurisdiction Where Enrolled (Yes/No); (If no – Where)

Births Occurring Between July 1, 1926 and June 30, 1927 to Parents Enrolled at Jurisdiction

4922; Pretty Back, Oscar; 1926-8-13; Yes; M; Yes; F; F; F; Yes

4930; Pretty Bird, Viola B; 1926-7-27; Yes; F; Yes; F; F; F; Yes

4969; Provost, Alonzo Harold; 1926-7-27; Yes; M; Yes; 1/2; W; 1/4; Yes

---- Pumpkin Seed, Frances; 1926-8-28; Yes; F; Yes; F; F; F; Yes

5022; Pumpkinseed, Sophia; 1927-4-17; Yes; F; Yes; F; F; F; Yes

5016; Pumpkinseed, Winnie; 1926-7-2; Yes; F; Yes; F; F; F; Yes

---- Peterson, Maxine M. M; 1927-6-3; Yes; F; Yes; W; 5/16; 5/32; Yes

5053; Quiver, James; 1927-4-16; Yes; M; Yes; F; F; F; Yes

---- Randall, Noah; 1927-3-26; Yes; M; Yes; F; F; F; Yes

5065; Randall, Robert; 1927-4-27; Yes; M; Oglala & Rosebud Sioux; Yes; 3/4; 3/4;
       3/4; Yes

5124; Red Blanket, Walter; 1926-10-24; Yes; M; Yes; F; F; F; Yes

5140; Red Cloud, Lorene; 1927-2-18; Yes; F; Yes; F; F; F; Yes

5139; Red Cloud, Dorene; 1927-2-18; Yes; F; Yes; F; F; F; Yes

---- Red Cloud, Louisa; 1927-5-6; Yes; F; Yes; F; F; F; Yes

5156; Red Cloud, Benjamin; 1926-7-27; Yes; M; Yes; 7/8; 7/8; 7/8; Yes

5173; Red Dog, Nora; 19216-7-28; Yes; F; Yes; F; 3/4; 7/8; Yes

---- Reddy, Magdaline; 1927-3-1; Yes; F; Yes; W; 3/8; 3/16; Yes

5194; Red Ear Horse, Jacob; 1926-11-27; Yes; M; Yes; F; F; F; Yes

5211; Red Elk, James; 1927-2-24; Yes; M; Yes; F; F; F; Yes;

---- Red Feather, Bertha E; 1926-7-10; Yes; F; Yes; F; F; F; Yes

5322; Red Shirt, As; 1927-5-11; Yes; M; Yes; 3/4; F; 7/8; Yes

5331; Red Shirt, Margaret; 1926-10-15; Yes; F; Yes; F; 1/2; 3/4; Yes

---- Respects Nothing, Sylvan; 1927-5-11; Yes; F; Yes; F; F; F; Yes

5385; Returns From Scout, Edith; 1926-10-9; Yes; F; Yes; F; F; F; Yes

---- ~~Richard, Alexander Jos; 1926-6-6; Yes; M; Yes; 9/16; 5/8; 19/32; Yes~~
       Transferred to 1926 roll   not ver

---- Richard, Esther M; 1926-10-19; Yes; F; Yes; 5/8; 1/4; 7/16; Yes

---- Richard, Mervin; 1927-3-15; Yes; M; Yes; 3/8; 1/2; 7/16; Yes

5529; Romero, Leo Harris; 1927-1-7; Yes; M; Yes; ?; 3/4; ?; Yes

---- Ross, Glenn Lyle; 1927-6-18; Yes; M; Yes; 1/2; W; 1/4; Yes

5629; Ruleau, Cecelia L; 1926-11-16; Yes; F; Yes; 5/16; W; 5/32; Yes

---- Running Eagle, Samuel; 1927-5-30; Yes; M; Yes; F; F; F; Yes

5720; Salvis, Eileen; 1926-11-20; Yes; F; Yes; 5/8; 1/2; 9/16; Yes

---- Scott, Lavern Lucille; 1927-4-12; Yes; F; Yes; W; 1/8; 1/16; Yes

----- Shangreau, Helena Pearl; 1927-4-23; Yes; F; Yes; 1/2; 7/8; 11/16; Yes

5851; Shangreau, Theodore; 1926-7-28; Yes; M; Yes; 1/2; 1/4; 3/8; Yes

5828; Shangreau, Wesley Orval; 1926-10-30; Yes; M; Yes; 1/2; 5/16; 13/32; Yes

---- Short Bear, [No name given]; 1927-4-17; Yes; M; Yes; 7/8; F; 15/16; Yes

5925; Short Bear, Sylvia; 1927-4-15; Yes; F; Yes; F; 3/4; 7/8; Yes

5939; Short Horn, Gladys May; 1927-2-10; Yes; F; Yes; F; 3/4; 7/8; Yes

5993; Sierra, Howard Edward; 1927-1-24; Yes; M; Yes; 1/2; F; 3/4; Yes

---- Sierra, Loretta K; 1927-1-10; Yes; F; Yes; 1/2; F; 3/4; Yes

6006; Siers, Iola May; 1926-7-27; Yes; F; Yes; 5/8; 1/2; 9/16; Yes

Key: 1927 Census Roll Number; Surname, Given; Date of Birth (Year-Month-Day); Live Births (Yes/No); Still Births (blank unless otherwise given); Sex; Tribe (Oglala Sioux unless given otherwise); Ward (Yes/No); Degree of Blood (Father; Mother; Child); At Jurisdiction Where Enrolled (Yes/No); (If no – Where)

Births Occurring Between July 1, 1926 and June 30, 1927 to Parents Enrolled at Jurisdiction

6012; Sioux Bob, Mabel; 1926-9-28; Yes; F; Yes; F; F; F; Yes
1111; Sitting Up, Herman Jos; 1927-4-14; Yes; M; Yes; F; 7/16; 23/32; Yes
6076; Sleeps, William; 1927-5-1; Yes; M; Yes; F; F; F; Yes
**** Slow Bear, Elfreda; 1927-6-20; Yes; F; Yes; F; F; F; Yes
6104; Smith, Rose Marie; 1926-7-10; Yes; F; Yes; W; 3/16; 3/32; Yes
6127; Sounding Side, Philip; 1926-8-8; Yes; M; Yes; F; F; F; Yes
6120; Sound Sleeper, Patrick; 1926-10-20; Yes; M; Yes; F; F; F; Yes
6135; Spaulding, Evon Jean; 1926-10-11; Yes; F; Yes; F; 1/8; 1/16; Yes
6190; Spotted Elk, Jasper; 1927-3-1; Yes; M; Yes; F; F; F; Yes
6225; Standing Bear, Edsel; 1927-4-10; Yes; M; Yes; 3/4; F; 7/8; Yes
---- Standing Bear, Gladys A; 1927-1-21; Yes; F; Yes; 3/4; F; 7/8; Yes
---- Standing Soldier, Viola; 1927-3-29; Yes; F; Yes; 7/8; 3/4; 13/16; Yes
6144; Spider, Pauline; 1926-10-15; Yes; F; Yes; F; F; F; Yes
6277; Standing Soldier, Rhoda; 1926-8-1; Yes; F; Yes; F; F; F; Yes
6296; Stands, Juanita; 1926-9-10; Yes; F; Yes; F; F; F; Yes
6305; Star, Noah; 1927-1-22; Yes; M; Yes; 3/4; 1/2; 5/8; Yes
6322; Stewart, Christie; 1926-12-25; Yes; M[sic]; Yes; F; F; F; Yes
6350; Stone, Emerson Fred; 1927-3-30; Yes; M; Yes; W; 3/4; 3/8; Yes
6406; Swallow, Bernice Ione; 1926-10-1; Yes; F; Yes; 3/8; 1/2; 7/16; Yes
---- Swanson, Ruth Lillian; 1026-9-9; Yes; F; Yes; W; 1/8; 1/16; Yes
6478; Tail, Adelbert; 1927-4-10; Yes; M; Yes; F; F; F; Yes
6511; Tapio, Mercy E; 1927-3-9; Yes; F; Yes; 1/4; 1/2; 3/8; Yes
---- Tells His Name, Isabel; 1927-4-27; Yes; F; Yes; F; F; F; Yes
6535; Ten Fingers, Effy; 1926-8-18; Yes; F; Yes; F; F; F; Yes
---- Ten Fingers, Nancy; 1926-8-20; Yes; F; Yes; F; F; F; Yes
6538; Ten Fingers, Norman; 1927-1-5; Yes; M; Yes; F; F; F; Yes
---- Thunder Hawk, Martin; 1927-6-4; Yes; M; Yes; 3/4; F; 7/8; Yes
~~6603; Thunder Horse, Lucille; 1926-5-27; Yes; F; Yes; F; F; F; Yes~~
             ~~Transferred to~~ See 1926 roll not ver
6610; Thunder Tail, Edith; 1927-1-13; Yes; F; Yes; F; F; F; Yes
6569; Three Stars, Peter Paul; 1927-2-11; Yes; M; Yes; 5/8; F; 13/16; Yes
6621; Tibbets, Thressa May; 1927-5-29; Yes; F; Yes; 1/4; 1/8; 3/16; Yes
6637; Tobacco, Ethel Hermine; 1926-8-3; Yes; F; Yes; 7/8; 1/2; 11/16; Yes
6649; Trimble, John Henry Jr; 1926-8-2; Yes; M; Yes; 1/4; 1/4; 1/4; Yes
6668; Troublesome Hawk, James; 1927-4-5; Yes; M; Yes; F; F; F; Yes
6686; Turning Hawk, Vera; 1926-7-30; Yes; F; Yes; F; F; F; Yes
6702; Tuttle, Edward M; 1927-5-12; Yes M; Oglala & Santee Sioux; Yes; F; 3/4; 7/8; Yes
---- Twiss, Peter F; 1927-5-7; Yes; M; Yes; 1/2; 3/4; 5/8; Yes
6779; Two Bulls, Elizabeth; 1926-10-20; Yes; F; Yes; 7/8; F; 15/16; Yes
---- Two Crow, Hazel; 1927-3-26; Yes; F; Yes; 3/4; 3/4; 3/4; Yes
---- Two Lance, Almaria; 1926-12-1; Yes; F; Yes; F; F; F; Yes
---- Two Two, Leonard; 1927-3-21; Yes; M; Yes; 3/4; F; 7/8; Yes
----- Tyon, Louisa; 1926-9-18; Yes; F; Yes; 3/4; F; 7/8; Yes

29

State **South Dakota**_____Reservation_____**Pine Ridge**_____Agency or jurisdiction
_____**Pine Ridge**_____ Office of Indian Affairs

Key: 1927 Census Roll Number; Surname, Given; Date of Birth (Year-Month-Day); Live Births (Yes/No); Still Births (blank unless otherwise given); Sex; Tribe (Oglala Sioux unless given otherwise); Ward (Yes/No); Degree of Blood (Father; Mother; Child); At Jurisdiction Where Enrolled (Yes/No); (If no – Where)

Births Occurring Between July 1, 1926 and June 30, 1927 to Parents Enrolled at Jurisdiction

```
----   Vert, Stanley C; 1927-4-13; Yes; M; Yes; F; 1/8; 1/16; Yes
6968;  Walks Out, Blonde; 1927-4-28; Yes; F; Yes; F; F; F; Yes
7013;  Water, Katherine E; 1926-9-4; Yes; F; Yes; 3/4; F; 7/8; Yes
7068;  Weston, Harry Lincoln; 1926-10-6; Yes; M; Yes; F; 3/4; 7/8; Yes
7070;  Weston, Ray R; 1926-7-15; Yes; M; Yes; F; F; F; Yes
7087;  Whirlwind, Theodore; 1926-11-18; Yes; M; Yes; F; F; F; Yes
----   White Dress, Pearl; 1927-4-6; Yes; F; Yes; F; F; F; Yes
7254;  White Face, Rena; 1927-2-16; Yes; F; Yes; F; F; F; Yes
7247;  White Face, Salina May; 1927-5-15; Yes; F; Yes; F; F; F; Yes
----   White Hawk, Joseph; 1927-2-21; Yes; M; Yes; 7/8; F; 15/16; Yes
----   White Woman, Baptiste; 1926-7-11; Yes; M; Yes; F; F; F; Yes
----   White Woman, Catherine; 1926-7-11; Yes; F; Yes; F; F; F; Yes
7395;  Witt, Lillian; 1926-11-11; Yes; F; Yes; 1/4; F; 5/8; Yes
7412;  Woman Dress, John; 1926-7-31; Yes; M; Yes; F; F; F; Yes
----   Wounded, Stephen; 1926-8-23; Yes; M; Yes; F; F; F; Yes
7441;  Wounded Head, Robert; 1926-12-17; Yes; M; Yes; F; 3/4; 7/8; Yes
----   Yellow Bear, Johnson; 1927-6-21; Yes; M; Yes; F; F; F; Yes
7508;  Yellow Bird, Clayton K; 1926-10-24; Yes; M; Yes; 3/4; 3/16; 15/32; Yes
----   Yellow Bird, Josephine Mary; 1927-4-16; Yes; F; Yes; 3/4; 1/2; 5/8; Yes
----   Yellow Bird, Raymond J; 1927-5-6; Yes; M; Yes; 3/4; 1/2; 5/8; Yes
7527;  Yellow Boy, Raymond; 1926-10-29; Yes; M; Yes; F; F; F; Yes
----   Yellow Bull, Chester; 1927-2-23; Yes; M; Yes; F; F; F; Yes
----   Yellow Horse, Morris; 1927-1-5; Yes; M; Yes; 7/8; F; 15/16; Yes

       Running Shield, Lucile; 1927-1-16; Yes; F; Yes; F; F; F; Yes
              Authority given by agent   not ver
```

LIVE BIRTHS

1928
(July 1, 1927 - June 30, 1928)

PINE RIDGE RESERVATION
PINE RIDGE SOUTH DAKOTA

Key: 1928 Census Roll Number; Surname, Given; Date of Birth (Year-Month-Day); Live Births (Yes/No); Still Births (blank unless otherwise given); Sex; Tribe (Oglala Sioux unless given otherwise); Ward (Yes/No); Degree of Blood (Father; Mother; Child); At Jurisdiction Where Enrolled (Yes/No); (If no – Where)

Births Occurring Between July 1, 1927 and June 30, 1928 to Parents Enrolled at Jurisdiction

22; Addison, Susanna; 1927-10-8; Yes; F; Sioux & Chey; Yes; F; F; F; Yes
31; Afraid Of Bear, Francis; 1928-6-15; Yes; M; Yes; F; F; F; Yes
36; Afraid Of Hawk, Harold; 1927-8-18; Yes; M; Yes; F; F; F; Yes
79; Allen, Wendell Verne; 1927-7-31; Yes; M; Yes; 3/16; W; 3/32; Yes
88; Allman, Robert Charles; 1927-11-13; Yes; M; Yes; 1/4; 3/4; 1/2; Yes
160; Amiotte, Donald Leroy; 1927-7-7; Yes; M; Yes; 1/4; 1/2; 3/8; Yes
---; Amiotte, Gloria Joyce; 1927-7-7; Yes; F; Yes; 1/4; W; 1/8; Yes
167; Ant, Grace; 1928-5-4; Yes; F; Yes; F; 5/8; 13/16; Yes
176; Apple, Antoine Jerry; 1928-4-2; Yes; M; Yes; 3/4; 3/4; 3/4; Yes
198; Apple, Kenneth; 1928-3-15; Yes; M; Yes; 3/4; F; 7/8; Yes
201; Arapahoe, Coolidge; 1927-11-11; Yes; M; Yes; F; F; F; Yes
325; Bank, Thomas; 1927-7-27; Yes; M; Yes; F; F; F; Yes
----; Badger, Matthew; 1928-1-12; Yes; M; Yes; 3/4; 3/4; 3/4; Yes
295; Bad Wound, James; 1928-1-27; Yes; M; Yes; F; 1/2; 3/4; Yes
285; Bad Wound, Lewis; 1928-2-23; Yes; M; Yes; 3/4; 1/2; 5/8; Yes
281; Bad Wound, Leroy Albert; 1927-8-28; Yes; M; Yes; 3/4; 39; 9/16; Yes
294; Bad Wound, Susie; 1928-1-27; Yes; F; Yes; F; 1/2; 3/4; Yes
339; Bauman, Marie; 1927-7-1; Yes; F; Yes; white; 3/8; 3/16; Yes
---; Beard, Cecelia; 1927-12-2; Yes; F; Yes; F; F; F; Yes
353; Bear Eagle, Isabella; 1928-2-3; Yes; F; Yes; F; F; F; Yes
---; Bear Killer, Julia; 1927-11-14; Yes; F; Yes; F; F; F; Yes
---; Bear Nose, Phoebe; 1927-12-16; Yes; F; Yes; F; F; F; Yes
---; Bear Robe, Raymond; 1927-9-3; Yes; M; Yes; F; F; F; Yes
401; Bear Saves Life, Lavina or Alvina; 1927-9-1; Yes; F; Yes; F; F; F; Yes
414; Bear Shield, Matthew; 1927-11-14; Yes; M; Yes; F; F; F; Yes
424; Bear Tail, Regina; 1928-3-8; Yes; F; Yes; F; F; F; Yes
---; Bell, Harvey Elza; 1927-10-13; Yes; M; yes; W; 3/8; 3/16; Yes
489; Bettelyoun, Maxine May; 1928-5-18; Yes; F; Yes; 5/16; W; 5/32; Yes
513; Big Crow, Ava Marie; 1928-5-15; Yes; F; Yes; 1/2; 1/4; 3/8; Yes
---; Bissonette, Esther May; 1928-1-27; Yes; F; Yes; 3/8; F; 11/16; Yes
4271; Bissonette, Lavina; 1927-10-29; Yes; F; Yes; 7/8; 3/4; 13/16; Yes
633; Black Bear, Cecelia; 1928-2-6; Yes; F; Yes; F; F; F; Yes
657; Black Bird, Edna; 1927-11-24; Yes; F; Yes; F; F; F; Yes
687; Black Crow, Aaron; 1928-6-4; Yes; M; Yes; F; F; F; Yes
707; Black Elk, Olivia Lenora; 1927-10-10; Yes; F; Yes; F; 1/2; 3/4; Yes
750; Black Road, Catherine Rose; 1928-6-6; Yes; F; Yes; F; F; F; Yes
765; Black Tail Deer, Martha; 1927-7-8; Yes; F; Yes; F; F; F; Yes
797; Blue Bird, Chester; 1927-10-18; Yes; M; Yes; F; 3/4; 7/8; Yes
821; Blunt Horn, Levi Francis; 1928-3-7; Yes; M; Yes; F; 3/4; 7/8; Yes
858; Brafford, Marian Lousia[sic]; 1928-6-11; Yes; F; Yes; 1/4; 1/2; 3/8; Yes
901; Brave Heart, Joseph; 1927-8-12; Yes; M; Yes; F; F; F; Yes
914; Breast, Ollie Leona; 1927-10-21; Yes; F; Yes; F; F; F; Yes
929; Brewer, Madeline Ellen; 1928-3-1; Yes; F; Yes; 1/4; 1/2; 3/8; Yes

Key: 1928 Census Roll Number; Surname, Given; Date of Birth (Year-Month-Day); Live Births (Yes/No);
Still Births (blank unless otherwise given); Sex; Tribe (Oglala Sioux unless given otherwise); Ward (Yes/No);
Degree of Blood (Father; Mother; Child); At Jurisdiction Where Enrolled (Yes/No); (If no – Where)

Births Occurring Between July 1, 1927 and June 30, 1928 to Parents Enrolled at Jurisdiction

955; Brings Plenty, Leo Garfield; 1928-4-17; Yes; M; Yes; 3/4; F; 7/8; Yes
963; Brings Yellow, Theodore Ambrose; 1927-9-23; Yes; M; Yes; F; F; F; Yes
984; Broken Rope, Freedom May; 1927-7-17; Yes; F; Yes; F; 5/8; 13/16; Yes
990; Broken Rope, Mildred; 1928-2-29; Yes; F; Yes; F; F; F; Yes
1022; Brown, Archie Michael; 1927-10-21; Yes; M; Yes; 3/8; 7/8; 5/8; Yes
1046; Brown, Elsworth Clarence; 1928-4-18; Yes; M; Yes; F; 1/4; 5/8; Yes
1044; Brown, Harriett Pauline; 1927-7-21; Yes; F; Yes; F; F; F; Yes
1128; Bull Bear, Ethel May; 1928-1-12; Yes; F; Yes; F; F; F; Yes
1143; Bull Bear, Verine; 1928-3-26; Yes; F; Yes; F; F; F; Yes
--- Bull Man, (Unnamed); 1928-2-27; Yes; M; Yes; F; F; F; Yes
1173; Bush, Laurine Aloyse; 1928-5-24; Yes; F; Yes; 3/4; F; 7/8; Yes
1207; Carlow, Margaret Ann; 1928-3-12; Yes; F; Yes; 1/4; 1/2; 3/8; Yes
1219; Catches, Rose; 1928-6-25; Yes; F; Yes; F; F; F; Yes
---- Cedar Face, Annie; 1928-3-30; Yes; F; Yes; F; F; F; Yes
1261; Charging Crow, James; 1927-8-16; Yes; M; Yes; F; F; F; Yes
1276; Chase Alone, Pearl; 1928-2-8; Yes; F; Yes; F; F; F; Yes
---- Chase In Morning, Laura; 1927-12-17; Yes; F; Yes; F; F; F; Yes
1285; Chase In Winter, William Webster; 1927-8-15; Yes; M; Yes; F; F; F; Yes
1298; Cheyenne, Zona; 1927-7-27; Yes; F; Yes; F; F; F; Yes
---- Chief, William; 1928-3-1; Yes; M; Yes; 3/4; 1/2; 5/8; Yes
1344; Chips, Lillian Vivian; 1927-8-12; Yes; F; Yes; F; F; F; Yes
1347; Christensen, Vern Anthony; 1927-10-10; Yes; M; Yes; 5/16; 5/16; 5/32; Yes
1351; Clement, Dorothy May; 1927-9-26; Yes; F; Yes; W; F; 1/2; Yes
1429; Clincher, Floyd; 1927-8-24; Yes; M; Yes; F; F; F; Yes
1473; Colhoff, Norma Sophia; 1928-4-5; Yes; F; Yes; 5/16; 3/4; 17/32; Yes
1551; Conroy, Dorothy Anna; 1927-7-14; Yes; F; Yes; 1/2; 3/4; 5/8; Yes
~~1545; Conroy, Lola Lucille; 1927-5-15; Yes; F; Yes; 1/2; 1/2; 1/2; Yes~~
Trans to 1927
1567; Coryell, Paul Earl; 1928-2-27; Yes; M; Yes; W; 1/8; 1/16; Yes
1586; Cottier, Kenneth; 1928-5-5; Yes; M; Yes; 1/2; 1/2; 1/2; Yes
---- Crane, Carolyn Marie; 1927-12-15; Yes; F; Yes; W; 1/4; 1/8; Yes
1660; Crazy Thunder, Emma; 1927-12-21; Yes; F; Yes; F; 1/2; 3/4; Yes
1678; Crooked Eyes, Fern; 1928-6-7; Yes; F; Yes; F; F; F; Yes
---- Cross, Rosie Anna; 1928-2-25; Yes; F; Yes; 7/8; F; 15/16; Yes
1691; Cross Dog, Lincoln; 1928-2-12; Yes; M; Yes; F; F; F; Yes
1694; Crow, Elsie; 1928-3-23; Yes; F; Yes; F; F; F; Yes
---- Cuny, Willard; 1927-11-18; Yes; M; Yes; 3/8; 1/2; 7/16; Yes
1775; Curtis, Harry Walter; 1927-8-26; Yes; M; Yes; W; 3/8; 3/16; Yes
1791; Cut Nose, Pendleton; 1927-7-15; Yes; M; Sioux & Chey.; Yes; F; 5/8; 13/16;
No; P.O. Chey. & A
---- Deon, Nancy Juliette; 1928-5-25; Yes; F; Yes; 1/8; W; 1/16; Yes
---- Dial, Lawson Monroe, Jr; 1928-2-6; Yes; M; Sioux & Osage; Yes; 3/32; 1/4;
11/64; No; P.O. Osage

34

State **South Dakota** Reservation **Pine Ridge** Agency or jurisdiction
Pine Ridge Office of Indian Affairs

Key: 1928 Census Roll Number; Surname, Given; Date of Birth (Year-Month-Day); Live Births (Yes/No);
Still Births (blank unless otherwise given); Sex; Tribe (Oglala Sioux unless given otherwise); Ward (Yes/No);
Degree of Blood (Father; Mother; Child); At Jurisdiction Where Enrolled (Yes/No); (If no – Where)

Births Occurring Between July 1, 1927 and June 30, 1928 to Parents Enrolled at Jurisdiction

1454; Dirt Kettle, Marie; 1927-8-15; Yes; F; Yes; no data; F; ?; Yes;
---- Dixon, Doris; 1927-10-11; Yes; F; Yes; 1/4; 1/2; 3/8; Yes
1887; Dreaming Bear, Doris; 1928-3-26; Yes; F; Yes; F; F; F; Yes
---- Drury, Keith Peter William; 1927-12-5; Yes; M; Yes; W; 7/16; 7/32; Yes
1912; Dubray, Everett Eugene; 1927-11-10; Yes; M; Yes; 1/2; 13/16; 21/32; Yes
---- Eagle Bear, Zona Ethel; 1928-5-5; Yes; F; Yes; F; F; F; Yes
1947; Eagle Bull, Sarah Ellen; 1928-5-23; Yes; F; Yes; F; F; F; Yes
1963; Eagle Elk, Pearl; 1927-7-16; Yes; F; Yes; F; F; F; Yes
1958; Eagle Elk, Rosanna Norma; 1928-2-27; Yes; F; Yes; F; F; F; Yes
1968; Eagle Fox, Josephine; 1927-10-8; Yes; F; Yes; F; F; F; Yes
1986; Eagle Heart, Eddie; 1928-5-23; Yes; M; Yes; F; F; F; Yes
---- Eisenbraun, John Moreland; 1928-3-5; Yes; M; Yes; white; 1/8; 1/16; Yes
---- Fast Horse, Harry; 1927-8-27; Yes; M; Yes; 3/4; 3/4; 3/4; Yes
2098; Feather, Moses; 1927-12-9; Yes; M; Yes; F; F; F; Yes
2102; Featherman, Isabelle; 1928-3-26; Yes; F; Yes; F; F; F; Yes
---- Ferguson, Carolyn Frances; 1927-7-9; Yes; F; Yes; W; 3/8; 3/16; Yes
2187; Fire Thunder, Lillian; 1928-1-25 [or 26?]; Yes; F; Yes; F; F; F; Yes
---- Fire Thunder, Marceline Marie; 1928-5-5; Yes; F; Yes; 3/4; 9/16; 21/32; Yes
2239; Fool Head, Myrtle Gertrude; 1927-9-6; Yes; F; Yes; F; F; F; Yes
2268; Frog, Bernice; 1928-3-19; Yes; F; Yes; F; F; F; Yes
2281; Frog, Jessie; 1928-5-30; Yes; F; Yes; F; F; F; Yes
2307; Garcia, Leo; 1928-4-22; Yes; M; Yes; 1/4; 1/2; 3/8; Yes
2324; Garnier, Gladys Millie; 1927-7-12; Yes; F; Yes; 1/2; 5/8; 9/16; Yes
2344; Gerry, Benjamin Douglas; 1927-9-9; Yes; M; Yes; 1/2; F; 3/4; Yes
---- Ghost Bear, Gilbert; 1928-3-9; Yes; M; Yes; F; F; F; Yes
---- Giago, Antoine; 1927-12-22; Yes; M; Yes; 1/4; 1/4; 1/4; Yes
2405; Gibbons, Antoine Leo; 1928-3-18; Yes; M; Yes; 1/2; F; 3/4; Yes
2414; Gillispie, William Robert; 1927-9-21; Yes; M; Yes; 1/2; 3/4; 5/8; Yes
2447; Goes In Center, Veronica Eva; 1928-3-25; Yes; F; Yes; F; F; F; Yes
2455; Goings, Vincent DePaul; 1927-7-28; Yes; M; Yes; 5/8; 3/4; 11/16; Yes
---- Good Lance, Elaine; 1928-5-15; Yes; F; Yes; F; F; F; Yes
2526; Good Shield, Jeanette; 1928-4-30; Yes; F; Yes; F; F; F; Yes
2547; Good Voice Elk, Vienna; 1927-11-2; Yes; F; Yes; F; F; F; Yes
2563; Good Voice Flute, Joseph; 1927-10-12; Yes; M; Yes; F; F; F; Yes
2587; Graham, Gloria Evelyn; 1928-2-15; Yes; F; Yes; 5/8; 5/8; 5/8; Yes
2596; Grass, Elsa Virginia; 1927-7-16; Yes; F; Yes; F; F; F; Yes
2613; Gray Grass, Martha; 1928-2-7; Yes; F; Yes; F; F; F; Yes
2640; Ground Spider, Vincent Louis; 1928-5-10; Yes; M; Yes; F; 3/4; 7/8; Yes
2685; Hat, Raphael Vincent; 1928-1-18; Yes; M; Yes; F; F; F; Yes
2688; Hauff, Richard Joseph; 1928-1-13; Yes; M; Yes; W; 3/8; 3/16; Yes
2795; Hernandez, Regina; 1928-4-9; Yes; F; Yes; 1/2; 7/8; 11/16; Yes
2849; High Wolf, Geraldine Mae; 1928-5-28; Yes; F; Yes; F; 3/8; 11/16; Yes
2906; Hollow Horn, Agnes; 1927-12-22; Yes; F; Yes; F; F; F; Yes

Key: 1928 Census Roll Number; Surname, Given; Date of Birth (Year-Month-Day); Live Births (Yes/No);
Still Births (blank unless otherwise given); Sex; Tribe (Oglala Sioux unless given otherwise); Ward (Yes/No);
Degree of Blood (Father; Mother; Child); At Jurisdiction Where Enrolled (Yes/No); (If no – Where)

Births Occurring Between July 1, 1927 and June 30, 1928 to Parents Enrolled at Jurisdiction

2945; Holy Rock, Cecil Francis; 1927-11-9; Yes; M; Yes; 3/4; 5/8; 11/16; Yes
2972; Horse, Douglas; 1928-4-23; Yes; M; Yes; F; F; F; Yes
3016; Hunter, Ambrose Harlan; 1928-3-1; Yes; M; Yes; 1/2; 1/2; 1/2; Yes
3083; Iron Crow, Ida; 1928-6-4; Yes; F; Yes; F; F; F; Yes
----   Iron Crow, James; 1927-10-19; Yes; M; Yes; F; F; F; Yes
3096; Iron Hawk, Lawson Russell; 1928-5-5; Yes; M; Yes; F; F; F; Yes
3120; Iron Rope, Abel; 1928-4-1; Yes; M; Yes; F; F; F; Yes
3115; Iron Rope, Mary; 1928-5-27; Yes; F; Yes; F; F; F; Yes
3158; Jack, Irene Pauline; 1927-12-26; Yes; F; Yes; F; F; F; Yes
3222; Janis, Curtis Edward; 1928-6-16; Yes; M; Yes; 1/2; 5/8; 9/16; Yes
3229; Janis, James Lawson Edward; 1928-2-25; Yes; M; Yes; 1/2; 1/8; 5/16; Yes
----   Janis, Hermus; 1928-2-5; Yes; M; Yes; 1/2; F; 3/4; Yes
3273; Janis, Levi; 1927-12-26; Yes; M; Yes; 5/8; 7/8; 3/4; Yes
3246; Janis, Otto Charles; 1928-1-3; Yes; M; Yes; 3/8; 1/2; 7/16; Yes
3201; Janis, Willard Vincent; 1928-3-18; Yes; M; Yes; 1/2; 5/8; 9/16; Yes
3287; Jealous Of Him, Lucy; 1927-11-27; Yes; F; Yes; 7/8; F; 15/16; Yes
----   Keester, Henry; 1927-12-30; Yes; M; Yes; W; 1/2; 1/4; Yes
----   Kicking Bear, Bertha; 1928-2-18; Yes; F; Yes; F; F; F; Yes
3367; Keith, Joseph Marvin; 1927-9-8; Yes; M; Yes; 3/8; 1/8; 1/4; Yes
3434; Kills In Water, Bertha; 1928-2-9; Yes; F; Yes; F; F; F; Yes
3458; Kills Right, Neoma; 1928-3-12; Yes; F; Yes; F; F; F; Yes
6385; Kills Small, Cornelius; 1928-1-6; Yes; M; Yes; F; 3/4; 7/8; Yes
3466; Kills Small, Henry; 1927-12-26; Yes; M; Yes; F; F; F; Yes
----   Kills Warrior, Leroy; 1928-4-10; Yes; M; F; F; F; Yes
3499; King, Timothy Bartimeus; 1928-3-9; Yes; M; Yes; F; 3/4; 7/8; Yes
3577; Lame, Charles; 1927-7-30; Yes; M; Yes; F; F; F; Yes
3598; Lamont, Florentine; 1927-7-19; Yes; F; Yes; 5/8; 1/1; 13/16; Yes
3587; Lamont, Florine Catherine; 1928-5-14; Yes; F; Yes; 1/2; F; 3/4; Yes
3634; LaPoint, Cynthia; 1927-7-17; Yes; F; Yes; 7/8; 3/4; 13/16; Yes
3620; LaPoint, Richard Darl[sic]; 1927-11-20; Yes; M; Yes; 9/16; 3/8; 15/32; Yes
3680; Lays Bad, Ramsey; 1927-7-12; Yes; M; Yes; F; F; F; Yes
3691; Lays Hard, Stella; 1928-1-5; Yes; F; Yes; F; F; F; Yes
----   Little, Harson; 1928-3-23; Yes; M; Yes; 3/4; 1/4; 1/2; Yes
3781; Little, James; 1928-4-15; Yes; M; Yes; 3/4; 5/16; 7/32; Yes
----   Little Boy, Louisa; 1927-12-20; Yes; F; Yes; F; F; F; Yes
3830; Little Cloud, Gloria; 1927-8-26; Yes; F; Yes; F; F; F; Yes
----   Little Crow, Florence; 1928-1-27; Yes; F; Yes; F; F; F; Yes
3853; Little Dog, Emma; 1928-4-15; Yes; F; Yes; F; 7/8; 15/16; Yes
3864; Little Finger, Sarah Millie; 1928-5-28; Yes; F; Yes; F; F; F; Yes
----   Little Hoop, Nancy; 1928-2-26; Yes; F; Yes; F; 7/8; 15/16; Yes
3894; Little Moon, Gilbert; 1927-12-13; Yes; M; Yes; F; 3/4; 7/8; Yes
3926; Little Spotted Horse, Eleanor Inez; 1928-2-17; Yes; F; Yes; F; F; F; Yes
3942; Little War Bonnet, Oliver; 1928-4-21; Yes; M; Yes; F; F; F; Yes

Key: 1928 Census Roll Number; Surname, Given; Date of Birth (Year-Month-Day); Live Births (Yes/No);
Still Births (blank unless otherwise given); Sex; Tribe (Oglala Sioux unless given otherwise); Ward (Yes/No);
Degree of Blood (Father; Mother; Child); At Jurisdiction Where Enrolled (Yes/No); (If no – Where)

Births Occurring Between July 1, 1927 and June 30, 1928 to Parents Enrolled at Jurisdiction

4011; Livermont, Lewis; 1928-4-2; Yes; M; Yes; 1/8; 1/4; 3/16; Yes
4026; Loafer, Eunice; 1928-5-31; Yes; F; Yes; F; F; F; Yes
4061; Lone Hill, Lewellyn; 1927-10-26; Yes; M; Yes; 3/4; F; 7/8; Yes
4067; Lone Hill, Mamie Myrtle; 1928-1-14; Yes; F; Yes; 3/4; F; 7/8; Yes
4077; Lone Wolf, Laura; 1928-5-25; Yes; F; Yes; F; F; F; Yes
4109; Long Man, Stacey; 1927-11-7; Yes; M; Yes; F; F; F; Yes
4137; Long Woman, Clara; 1927-11-12; Yes; F; Yes; F; F; F; Yes
---- Little Soldier, Rebecca; 1928-3-30; Yes; F; Yes; F; F; F; Yes
4173; Makes Enemy, Jeanette Mildred; 1928-1-28; Yes; F; Yes; F; F; F; Yes
4217; Marshall, Louise Elizabeth; 1927-12-14; Yes; F; Yes; 1/2; 7/8; 11/16; Yes
4265; Martinez, Antoine; 1927-11-27; Yes; M; Yes; 1/2; 1/2; 1/2; Yes
4251; Martinez, Lyman Francis; 1928-3-20; Yes; M; Yes; 1/2; 3/4; 5/8; Yes
4558; McDaniels, Paul Alexander; 1927-9-12; Yes; M; Yes; 1/2; 3/8; 7/16; Yes
4277; Means, Josephine; 1927-12-8; Yes; F; Yes; 3/4; F; 7/8; Yes
4296; Means, Thomas David; 1927-11-16; Yes; M; Yes; 1/4; 1/2; 3/8; Yes
---- Mendenhall, Laura Norlene; 1928-1-15; Yes; F; Yes; W; 1/4; 1/8; Yes
4350; Mesteth, Francis James; 1927-10-3; Yes; M; Yes; 1/2; 3/4; 5/8; Yes (twins)
---- Mesteth, Leo Thomas; 1927-10-3; Yes; M; Yes; 1/2; 3/4; 5/8; Yes
4370; Mesteth, Nancy Dorothy; 1927-9-1; Yes; F; Yes; 12; F; 3/4; Yes
     McDaniel, Frederick Jos; 1927-7-6; Yes; M; Yes; 1/2; F; 11/16[sic]; Yes
     Tr. from 1927 roll
4430; Mills, Emma; 1927-11-20; Yes; F; Yes; 3/4; 1/4; 1/2; Yes
4461; Moore, Henry Melvin; 1928-4-23; Yes; M; Yes; 3/8; 1/2; 7/16; Yes
4474; Morgan, Duane Alex; 1928-2-27; Yes; M; Yes; W; 3/8; 3/16; Yes
4493; Morrison, Mary Ann Cecil; 1928-2-4; Yes; F; Yes; 3/4; F; 7/8; Yes
4514; Mountain, Jeanette Cynthia; 1928-2-20; Yes; F; Yes; 3/4; 3/4; 3/4; Yes
4544; Mousseau, Louis Jr; 1928-5-30; Yes; M; Yes; 7/8; 1/2; 11/16; Yes
4595; Nelson, Delbert; 1928-5-22; Yes; M; Yes; 5/8; F; 13/16; Yes
4627; New Holy, Joseph Jr; 1927-8-27; Yes; M; Yes; F; F; F; Yes
---- New Holy, Mary; 1927-8-27; Yes; F; Yes; F; F; F; Yes
4650; No Neck, Robert; 1928-1-10; Yes; M; Yes; F; 3/4; 7/8; Yes
4658; Not Help Him, Victor; 1928-6-12; Yes; M; Yes; F; F; F; Yes
4677; Old Horse, Oliver; 1927-11-11; Yes; M; Yes; F; F; F; Yes
4718; O'Rourke, Delbert Francis; 1927-12-9; Yes; M; Yes; 1/4; 1/2; 3/8; Yes
---- Pacer, Veronica; 1928-3-3; Yes; F; Yes; F; F; F; Yes
4750; Pain On Hip, Charles, Jr; 1928-1-3; Yes; M; Yes; F; F; F; Yes
4781; Parkhurst, Patrick Lloyd; 1927-9-4; Yes; M; Yes; 1/4; 1/2; 3/8; Yes
4801; Patton, Irene Marie; 1927-12-25; Yes; F; Yes; 1/4; 3/8; 5/16; Yes
4810; Pawnee Leggins, Delphine; 1928-3-9; Yes; F; Yes; F; F; F; Yes
4820; Peck, Lois Colleen; 1928-3-20; Yes; F; Yes; 1/4; 3/8; 5/16; Yes
---- Plenty Arrows, Leroyal; 1928-4-28; Yes; M; Yes; F; F; F; Yes
4864; Plenty Holes, Rosemary; 1927-12-28; Yes; F; Yes; F; 3/8; 11/16; Yes
4910; Poor Bear, Allan; 1928-3-19; Yes; M; Yes; F; F; F; Yes

Key: 1928 Census Roll Number; Surname, Given; Date of Birth (Year-Month-Day); Live Births (Yes/No);
Still Births (blank unless otherwise given); Sex; Tribe (Oglala Sioux unless given otherwise); Ward (Yes/No);
Degree of Blood (Father; Mother; Child); At Jurisdiction Where Enrolled (Yes/No); (If no – Where)

Births Occurring Between July 1, 1927 and June 30, 1928 to Parents Enrolled at Jurisdiction

4924; Poor Bear, Raymond; 1928-5-4; Yes; M; Yes; F; F; F; Yes

4932; Poor Thunder, Ruth Ione; 1928-4-3; Yes; F; Yes; F; W; 1/2; Yes

4983; Pourier, Clarence Paul; 1928-5-11; Yes; M; Yes; 3/16; 5/16; 1/4; Yes

2950; Prairie Chicken, Eva Lillian; 1928-2-11; Yes; F; Yes; No date; F; ?; Yes

5023; Pretty Back, Annie; 1928-1-13; Yes; F; Yes; F; F; F; Yes

----   Pretty Boy, Louis; 1928-3-17; Yes; M; Yes; F; F; F; Yes

5085; Pugh, Mary Louise; 1928-3-19; Yes; F; Yes; 3/8; 3/16; 9/32; Yes

----   Pulliam, Mary Ann Cecelia; 1928-5-19; Yes; F; Yes; 1/1; 5/8; 9/16; Yes

5112; Pumpkin Seed, Louis; 1928-2-7; Yes; M; Yes; F; F; F; Yes

5139; Quinn, Thomasena Ellene; 1927-10-3; Yes; F; Oglala & Sisseton; Yes; F; F; F; Yes

5201; Randall, Ramona Elsie; 1927-10-21; Yes; F; Yes; 3/4; 1/2; 5/8; Yes

----   Randall, Rebecca; 1928-6-21; Yes; Yes F; Yes; F; F; F; Yes

5239; Red Bow, Chrsitopher[sic]; 1928-2-16; Yes; M; Yes; F; F; F; Yes

5244; Red Breath Bear, Pearl; 1928-3-29; Yes; F; Yes; F; F; F; Yes

----   Red Cloud, Albert; 1927-12-3; Yes; M; Yes; F; F; F; Yes

----   Red Cloud, Vance; 1928-6-24; Yes; M; Yes; 7/8; 7/8; 7/8; Yes

5339; Red Feather, Elva Mildred; 1928-1-2; Yes; F; Yes; F; F; F; Yes

5377; Red Nest, Edson; 1927-9-9; Yes; M; Yes; F; F; F; Yes

----   Red Owl, Robert Louis; 1927-9-2; Yes; M; Yes; F; 1/2; 3/4; Yes

5403; Red Paint, Lucy; 1927-10-5; Yes; F; Yes; F; F; F; Yes

5395; Red Paint, Noah; 1927-10-20; Yes; M; Yes; F; F; F; Yes

5434; Red Shirt, Guy; 1928-6-3; Yes; M; Yes; F; 3/4; 7/8; Yes

5419; Red Shirt, Mary; 1928-6-3; Yes; F; Yes; 3/4; 3/4; 3/4; Yes

5444; Red Star, Lavinia Lydia; 1928-5-9; Yes; F; Yes; F; F; F; Yes

5449; Red Star, Merdol Newman; 1928-5-5; Yes; M; Yes; F; F; F; Yes

5581; Richard, David; 1928-3-28; Yes; M; Yes; 9/16; 34/64; 19/32; Yes

5518; Richard, Gladys; 1928-4-9; Yes; F; Yes; 3/4; F; 7/8; Yes

5576; Richard, Isabel Julia; 1927-9-20; Yes; F; Yes; 9/16; 1/4; 13/32; Yes

----   Richard, Rudolph; 1927-7-9; Yes; M; Yes; 5/8; F; 13/16; Yes

5596; Ringing Shield, Kenneth; 1928-3-30; Yes; M; Yes; F; F; F; Yes

5629; Rock, Gloria Gertrude; 1928-3-3; Yes; f; Yes; F; 3/4; 7/8; Yes

5633; Rock, Rebecca Vera; 1928-4-15; Yes; F; Yes; F; 3/4; 7/8; Yes

---   Rowland, Eugene; 1927-8-13; Yes; M; Sioux & Chey; Yes; F; F; F; Yes

5663; Rooks, Hazel Amy; 1927-8-18; Yes; F; Yes; 1/4; 1/2; 3/8; Yes

5722; Ruff, Phyllisarna; 1927-9-4; Yes; F; Yes; 1/4; 3/4; 1/2; Yes

----   Runnels, Betty Germaine; 1928-5-23; Yes; F; Yes; 3/8; 1/2; 7/16; Yes

----   Running Bear, Loranda; 1928-3-5; Yes; F; Yes; F; F; F; Yes

----   Running Bear, Richard; 1928-3-25; Yes; M; Yes; F; F; F; Yes

5807; Runs Above, George, 1928-3-16; Yes; M; Yes; F; W; 1/2; Yes

----   Runs Against, Bernice Josie; 1928-2-18; Yes; F; Yes; F; F; F; Yes

----   Russell, Shirley Aileen; 1928-1-10; Yes; F; Yes; 1/4; W; 1/8; Yes

----   Shangreau, Gertrude Rose; 1927-11-14; Yes; F; Yes; 1/2; 1/4; 3/8; Yes

38

State **South Dakota** Reservation **Pine Ridge** Agency or jurisdiction
Pine Ridge Office of Indian Affairs

Key: 1928 Census Roll Number; Surname, Given; Date of Birth (Year-Month-Day); Live Births (Yes/No); Still Births (blank unless otherwise given); Sex; Tribe (Oglala Sioux unless given otherwise); Ward (Yes/No); Degree of Blood (Father; Mother; Child); At Jurisdiction Where Enrolled (Yes/No); (If no – Where)

Births Occurring Between July 1, 1927 and June 30, 1928 to Parents Enrolled at Jurisdiction

----	Sharp, Bud Russell; 1927-11-12; Yes; M; Yes; W; 1/4; 1/8; Yes
6007;	Shell Woman, Noah; 1927-8-18; Yes; M; Yes; F; 3/4; 7/8; Yes
----	Shelton, Fredell Jean; 1927-10-1; Yes; F; Yes; W; 3/16; 3/32; Yes
----	Sherman, Caroline; 1928-6-5; Yes; F; Yes; 3/8; 3/4; 9/16; Yes (twins)
6014;	" Cornelia; 1928-6-5; Yes; F; Yes; 3/8; 3/4; 9/16; Yes
6066;	Short Step, Alma; 1927-12-25; Yes; F; Yes F; F; F; Yes
6105;	Sierro, Virginia May; 1928-5-10; Yes; F; Yes; 1/2; F; 3/4; Yes
----	Siers, John, Jr; 1928-1-6; Yes; M; Yes; 5/8; 3/4; 11/16; Yes
6158;	Sitting Up, Josephine; 1928-4-26; Yes; F; F; F; Yes
6164;	Sits Poor, Henrietta; 1927-9-24; Yes; F; Yes; F; F; F; Yes
6182;	Skalander, Mary Ann; 1928-5-4; Yes; F; Yes; 1/8; 5/16; 9/32; Yes
6197;	Sleep, Adam; 1928-5-10; Yes; M; Yes; F; F; F; Yes
6121;	Slow Bear, Irene; 1927-9-12; Yes; F; Yes; F; F; F; Yes
6267;	Spider, Adam; 1927-9-26; Yes; M; Yes; F; F; F; Yes
6285;	Spotted Bear, Emerson Leo; 1928-4-19; Yes; M; Yes; F; 3/4; 7/8; Yes
6309;	Spotted Eagle, Gladys; 1928-3-5; Yes; F; Yes; F; F; F; Yes
6325;	Spotted Elk, Mildred; 1928-3-6; Yes; F; Yes; F; F; F; Yes
6344;	Stabber, Sylvia; 1927-11-24; Yes; F; Yes; F; F; F; Yes
6402;	Standing Soldier, Joseph; 1927-10-1; Yes; M; Yes; F; 1/4; 5/8; Yes
6398;	Standing Soldier, Juliana Theresa; 1927-12-2; Yes; F; Yes; 7/8; 1/4; 9/16; Yes
6430;	Stands, Cornia; 1928-5-3; Yes; F; Yes; F; F; F; Yes
6423;	Stands, Levi Moses; 1927-11-13; Yes; M; Yes; F; 7/8; 15/16; Yes
6443;	Star Yellow Wood, Loma; 1927-10-28; Yes; F; Yes; 3/4; 1/2; 5/8; Yes
6493;	Stover, Eugene Louis; 1927-10-22; Yes; M; Yes; 1/2; W; 1/4; Yes
6499;	Strikes Enemy, Lucy; 1927-10-2; Yes; F; Yes; F; 3/4; 1/8; Yes
----	Sullivan, William Freeman; 1928-4-3; Yes; M; Yes; W; 1/16; 1/32; Yes
6521;	Sun Bear, Randolph; 1927-7-19; Yes; M; Yes; F; F; F; Yes
----	Swallow, David; 1928-3-9; Yes; M; Yes; F; F; F; Yes
----	Swallow, Lawrence; 1927-12-24; Yes; M; Yes; 3/8; 3/8; 3/8; Yes
6557;	Swallow, Melba Louise; 1927-12-21; Yes; F; Yes; 1/4; 3/16; 7/32; Yes
6597;	Swift Bird, George Jr; 1927-7-4; Yes; M; Yes; 7/8; F; 15/16; Yes
545[sic]	Tail, Lloyd Lein[sic]; 1928-3-15; Yes; M; Yes; F; F; F; Yes
6627;	Takes War Bonnet, Virginia; 1928-1-4; Yes; F; Yes; F; F; F; Yes
----	Taylor, Sarah Elizabeth; 1928-2-5; Yes; F; Yes; W; 1/8; 1/16; Yes
	Takia, Beatrice; 1928-2-14; Yes; F; Yes; 1/2; Mex; 1/4; Yes
	Trans from 1931 roll
330;	Tebo, Ona Leroy; 1927-10-26; Yes; M; Yes; No data; 1/4; ?; Yes
----	Terkildsen, Thomas George; 1928-6-24; Yes; M; Yes; W; 3/8; 3/16; Yes
----	Three Stars, Andrew; 1928-5-23; Yes; Yes M; Yes; 5/8; F; 13/16; Yes
6808;	Trueblood, Edward Sears, 1927-7-31; Yes; M; Yes; W; 1/4; 1/8; Yes
6715;	Thunder Bull, Mildred; 1927-9-26; Yes; F; Yes; F; 3/4; 7/8; Yes
6722;	Thunder Hawk, Rebecca; 1927-7-12; Yes; F; Yes; F; F; F; Yes
6737;	Thunder Horse, Dawson; 1928-6-30; Yes; M; Yes; F; F; F; Yes

State **South Dakota** Reservation **Pine Ridge** Agency or jurisdiction
Pine Ridge Office of Indian Affairs

Key: 1928 Census Roll Number; Surname, Given; Date of Birth (Year-Month-Day); Live Births (Yes/No);
Still Births (blank unless otherwise given); Sex; Tribe (Oglala Sioux unless given otherwise); Ward (Yes/No);
Degree of Blood (Father; Mother; Child); At Jurisdiction Where Enrolled (Yes/No); (If no – Where)

Births Occurring Between July 1, 1927 and June 30, 1928 to Parents Enrolled at Jurisdiction

6881; Twiss, Edith Opal; 1928-6-4; Yes; F; Yes; 7/8; 7/8; 7/8; Yes
6941; Two Crow, Idelia; 1928-3-21; Yes; F; Yes; 3/4; 3/4; 3/4; Yes
6945; Two Crow, James; 1928-5-30; Yes; M; Yes; 7/8; F; 15/16; Yes
---- Two Two, Louie; 1928-3-8; Yes; M; Yes; 3/4; F; 7/8; Yes
7002; Two Two, Mary; 1928-4-9; Yes; F; Yes; 3/4; F; 7/8; Yes
7038; Under The Baggage, Alfred; 1928-4-16; Yes; M; Yes; F; F; F; Yes
7041; Usher, Dean Emerson; 1928-5-29; Yes; M; Yes; W; 1/2; 1/4; Yes
7083; Vocu, Leo Wilfred; 1927-10-12; Yes; M; Yes; W; 1/4; 1/8; Yes
---- Walking Bull, Florance; 1927-12-28; Yes; F; Yes; F; F; F; Yes
7123; War Bonnet, Thelma Delia; 1927-10-10; Yes; F; Yes; F; F; F; Yes
---- Wartensleben, Betty Jo; 1928-1-27; Yes; F; Yes; W; 1/8; 1/16; Yes
7135; Warrior, Harvey; 1928-3-29; Yes; M; Yes; F; F; F; Yes
7157; Water, Athalia Elizabeth; 1928-2-24; Yes; F; Yes; 3/4; F; 7/8; Yes
7142; Water, Herman Norman; 1928-5-10; Yes; M; Yes; 3/4; F; 7/8; Yes
7180; Weasel Bear, Grace; 1927-7-4; Yes; F; Yes; F; F; F; Yes
---- Wellborn, Clauda; 1928-4-10; Yes; F; Yes; W; 1/8; 1/16; No;
      Noland, Ark.   (twins)
---- Wellborn, Clays; 1928-4-10; Yes; F; Yes; W; 1/8; 1/16; No
7220; Whalen, Myron Emmett; 1928-6-5; Yes; M; Yes; 1/4; 3/4; 1/2; Yes
---- Whirlwind Horse, Anthony; 1927-11-20; Yes; M; Yes; F; 1/8; 9/16; Yes
---- White, Irene Elaine Shirley; 1928-2-27; Yes; F; Yes; 1/2; 1/2; 1/2; Yes
7269; White, Neil Edward; 1927-9-28; Yes; M; Yes; W; 1/4; 1/8; Yes
---- White Bull, Isabelle; 1928-2-2; Yes; F; Yes; F; F; F; Yes
7318; White Butterfly, Leo; 1927-11-26; Yes; M; Yes; F; F; F; Yes
---- White Calf, Francis; 1927-9-24; Yes; M; Yes; F; F; F; Yes
7327; White Calf, Melba Etta; 1928-4-13; Yes; F; Yes; F; 7/8; 15/16; Yes
7370; White Eyes, Christina; 1928-1-29; Yes; F; Yes; F; F; F; Yes
7378; White Eyes, John Melvin; 1927-8-5; Yes; M; Yes; F; 3/16; 19/32; Yes
---- White Eyes, Mildred; 1928-2-6; Yes; F; Yes; F; F; F; Yes
7466; White Thunder, Pearl; 1928-3-16; Yes; F; Yes; F; F; F; Yes (twins)
7467; "   "   Pierre; 1928-3-16; Yes; M; Yes; F; F; F; Yes
7484; White Wolf, Vincent; 1927-7-16; Yes; M; Yes; F; F; F; Yes
7493; Wilcox, Zona; 1927-9-14; Yes; F; Yes; W; F; 1/2; Yes
7549; Witt, Lawrence Dewey; 1928-1-16; Yes; M; Yes; 5/8; F; 13/16; Yes
---- Woman Dress, Eldon; 1927-10-6; Yes; M; Yes; F; F; F; Yes
---- Wolf, Verna Jasper; 1927-7-17; Yes; M; Yes; W; 1/2; 1/4; Yes
7577; Wounded, Frances Clara; 1928-6-28; Yes; F; Yes; F; F; F; Yes
7573; Wounded, Maurice; 1927-8-10; Yes; M; Yes; F; F; F; Yes
7588; Wounded Head, Felix James; 1928-2-28; Yes; M; Yes; F; 5/8; 13/16; Yes
7605; Yaeger[sic], Ruth Lucy; 1927-7-17; Yes; F; Yes; W; 1/4; 1/8; Yes
7619; Yankton, Benard; 1928-1-26; Yes; M; Yes; 3/4; 7/8; 13/16; Yes
7613; Yankton, Dorothy; 1927-12-21; Yes; F; Yes; F; F; F; Yes
7631; Yellow Bear, Peter; 1928-4-2; Yes; M; Yes; F; F; F; Yes

State **South Dakota** Reservation **Pine Ridge** Agency or jurisdiction
Pine Ridge Office of Indian Affairs

Key: 1928 Census Roll Number; Surname, Given; Date of Birth (Year-Month-Day); Live Births (Yes/No); Still Births (blank unless otherwise given); Sex; Tribe (Oglala Sioux unless given otherwise); Ward (Yes/No); Degree of Blood (Father; Mother; Child); At Jurisdiction Where Enrolled (Yes/No); (If no – Where)

Births Occurring Between July 1, 1927 and June 30, 1928 to Parents Enrolled at Jurisdiction

7677; Yellow Boy, Carrie Jane; 1927-9-4; Yes; F; Yes; 7/8; F; 15/16; Yes
7690; Yellow Boy, Felix; 1928-1-28; Yes; M; Yes; F; F; F; Yes
7703; Yellow Hawk, Harlin; 1928-1-30; Yes; M; Yes; F; F; F; Yes
7715; Yellow Horse, Mary; 1927-12-21; Yes; F; Yes; F; F; F; Yes
7767; Young, Glover Calvin; 1928-7- 9- 11; Yes; M; Yes; 1/4; 1/4; 1/4; Yes
               See census roll
----; Young, Louise Della; 1927-7-7; Yes; F; Yes; No data; 3/8; ?; Yes
2930; Young, Moses Wallace; 1927-7-28; Yes; M; Yes; 1/4; 3/4; 1/2; Yes

Smith, Sylvia Freda; 1927-12-7; Yes; F; [blank]; White; F 3/16; F; [blank]
Mills, Norma Lucille; 1928-2-24; Yes; F; [blank]; 3/4; 3/4; [blank]; [blank]
Bowman, Loran; 1927-11-4; Yes; M; Yes; ?; 3/16; ?; Yes

LIVE BIRTHS

1929
(July 1, 1928 - June 30, 1929)

PINE RIDGE RESERVATION
PINE RIDGE SOUTH DAKOTA

State **South Dakota** Reservation **Pine Ridge** Agency or jurisdiction
Pine Ridge Office of Indian Affairs

Key: 1929 Census Roll Number; Surname, Given; Date of Birth (Year-Month-Day); Live Births (Yes/No);
Still Births (blank unless otherwise given); Sex; Tribe (Oglala Sioux unless given otherwise); Ward (Yes/No);
Degree of Blood (Father; Mother; Child); At Jurisdiction Where Enrolled (Yes/No); (If no – Where)

Births Occurring Between July 1, 1928 and June 30, 1929 to Parents Enrolled at Jurisdiction

36; Afraid Of Hawk, Kenneth; 1929-5-7; Yes; M; Yes; F; F; F; Yes
128; American Horse, William; 1928-7-19; Yes; M; Yes; F; F; F; Yes
178; Apple, Leroy; 1928-10-28; Yes; M; Yes; F; F; F; Yes
244; Bad Cob, Agatha; 1929-6-23; Yes; F; Yes; F; F; F; Yes
252; Badger, Rebecca; 1929-4-10; Yes; F; Yes; 3/4; 3/4; 3/4; Yes
266; Bad Heart Bull, Lucy; 1928-7-14; Yes; F; Yes; F; F; F; Yes
294; Bad Wound, Jennie; 1928-12-18; Yes; F; Yes; F; F; F; Yes
313; Bald Eagle Bear, Frederick A; 1929-6-9; Yes; M; Yes; F; F; F; Yes
----; Bayliss, Wm Arthur; 1928-10-26; Yes; M; Yes; W; 3/16; 3/32; Yes
344; Beard, Agnes; 1928-12-25; Yes; F; Yes; F; F; F; Yes
353; Bear Killer, Charles; 1929-6-9; Yes; M; Yes; F; F; F; Yes
365; Bear Nose, Orville; 1929-2-22; Yes; M; Yes; F; F; F; Yes
374; Bear Robe, Zelda Annabelle; 1928-8-17; Yes; F; Yes; F; 3/4; 7/8; Yes
---; Bear Saves Life, Charles 1928-11-22; Yes; M; Yes; F; F; F; Yes
404; Bear Shield, Lawrence; 1928-11-26; Yes; M; Yes; F; F; F; Yes
444; Belt, Jerry Fritz; 1929-1-20; Yes; M; Yes; F; 3/4; 7/8; Yes
448; Bent, Wm Henry Jr; 1929-6-2; Yes; M; Yes; 5/8; 3/4; 11/16; Yes
476; Bettelyoun, Gertrude; 1928-11-2; Yes; F; Yes; 3/8; 3/8; 3/8; Yes
539; Bird, Elmer Lloyd; 1928-10-30; Yes; M; Yes; W; 3/8; 3/16; Yes
565; Bissonette, Clement E; 1928-7-11; Yes; M; Yes; 3/4; 7/8; 13/16; Yes
---; Bissonette, Mildred Keva; 1929-6-5; Yes; F; Yes; 3/4; F; 11/16; Yes
568; Bissonette, Pearl; 1928-9-22; Yes; F; Yes; 7/8; 7/8; 7/8; Yes
610; Black Bear, Agnes; 1929-2-21; Yes; F; Yes; F; F; F; Yes
618; Black Bear, Dorothy; 1928-11-11; Yes; F; Yes; F; 7/8; 15/16; Yes
---; Black Bear, Lorna; 1928-10-14; Yes; F; Yes; F; F; F; Yes
654; Black Bird, Earl Thomas; 1929-5-9; Yes; M; Yes; F; 3/4; 7/8; Yes
686; Black Crow, Cleveland E; 1929-5-9; Yes; M; Yes; F; F; F; Yes
675; Black Cat, Florence; 1928-8-1; Yes; F; Yes; F; F; F; Yes
722; Black Feather, Geoffrey; 1928-11-17; Yes; M; Yes; F; 7/8; 13/16; Yes
735; Black Feather, Oliver; 1928-9-19; Yes; M; Yes; F; 7/8; 13/16; Yes
774; Blind Man, Helen Rita; 1929-2-10; Yes; F; Yes; F; F; F; Yes
810; Blue Legs, Armine; 1928-9-16; Yes; F; Yes; F; F; F; Yes
----; Blue Legs, Edith; 1929-3-8; Yes; F; Yes; F; F; F; Yes
883; Brave, Bessie; 1929-6-8; Yes; F; Yes; 7/8; F; 15/16; Yes
906; Brave Heart, Bertha; 1929-4-13; Yes; F; Yes; F; 3/4; 7/8; Yes
939; Brewer, Fannie E; 1929-4-13; Yes; F; Yes; 1/4; 5/8; 7/16; Yes
963; Brings Yellow, Philip; 1929-6-22; Yes; M; Yes; F; F; F; Yes
---; Broken Nose, Vivian Jane; 1929-1-16; Yes; F; Yes; F; F; F; Yes
992; Broken Rope, Florida Anna; 1929-3-25; Yes; F; Yes; F; F; F; Yes
1065; Brown Eyes, Floyd; 1929-5-24; Yes; M; Yes; 3/4; F; 7/8; Yes
1073; Brown Eyes, Joseph; 1928-8-31; Yes; M; Yes; F; F; F; Yes
1033; Brown Eyes, George R, Jr; 1928-7-12; Yes; M; Yes; 3/8; 1/2; 7/16; Yes
1089; Buckman, Wilbert C; 1928-8-25; Yes; M; Yes; 3/4; 7/8; 13/16; Yes

45

State **South Dakota** Reservation **Pine Ridge** Agency or jurisdiction
Pine Ridge Office of Indian Affairs

Key: 1929 Census Roll Number; Surname, Given; Date of Birth (Year-Month-Day); Live Births (Yes/No);
Still Births (blank unless otherwise given); Sex; Tribe (Oglala Sioux unless given otherwise); Ward (Yes/No);
Degree of Blood (Father; Mother; Child); At Jurisdiction Where Enrolled (Yes/No); (If no – Where)

Births Occurring Between July 1, 1928 and June 30, 1929 to Parents Enrolled at Jurisdiction

1113; Bullard, Virginia Claire; 1929-1-28; Yes; F; Yes; 1/4; W; 1/8; Yes
1120; Bull Bear, Theodore; 1928-8-16; Yes; M; Yes; F; 7/8; 15/16; Yes
---- Bullman, ~~Joseph~~ Raymond; 1929-5-10; Yes; M; Yes; F; F; F; Yes
1169; Burns Prairie, ~~Edward~~ Freda; 1928-8-6; Yes; ~~M~~ Fem; Yes; F; F; F; Yes
---- Bush, Theresa; 1929-2-26; Yes; F; Yes; F; F; F; Yes
---- Bushy Top Pine, Louis Allen; 1929-4-27; Yes; M; Yes; F; F; F; Yes
1262; Charging Crow, Roy; 1929-2-8; Yes; M; Yes; F; F; F; Yes
---- Chase Alone, Margaret Stella; 1929-6-4; Yes; F; Yes; F; F; F; Yes
1305; Chief, Bluche; 1928-7-16; Yes; M; Yes; F; F; F; Yes
1333; Chips, Ruby Bernice; 1928-9-16; Yes; F; Yes; F; F; F; Yes
1452; Coats, Clyde Jr; 1928-10-22; Yes; M; Yes; W; 1/16; 1/32; Yes
1458; Colhoff, Bernard Louis; 1928-12-17; Yes; M; Yes; 1/2; 1/2; 1/2; Yes
1476; Colhoff, Richard Gerald; 1928-12-8; Yes; M; Yes; 1/2; 1/4; 3/8; Yes
---- Comes From Among Them, Hermus; 1929-5-7; Yes; M; Yes; 7/8; F; 15/16; Yes
1541; Conroy, Melvin Benjamin; 1928-7-2; Yes; M; Yes; 1/2; 1/2; 1/2; Yes
1519; Conquering Bear, Stephen; 1929-4-11; Yes; M; Yes; F; F; F; Yes
1608; Cottier, Carmen Ruth; 1929-5-5; Yes; F; Yes; 1/2; 3/8; 7/16; Yes
---- Crazy Thunder, Allen; 1929-2-6; Yes; M; Yes; F; 1/2; 3/4; Yes
---- Cummings, Geraldine Minerva; 1928-12-31; Yes; F; Yes; 1/16; 1/16; 1/16; Yes
---- Cuny, Elvin; 1929-4-5; Yes; M; Yes; 3/8; 1/2; 7/16; Yes
1735; Cuny, Eleanora; 1928-9-13; Yes; F; Yes; 3/8; 1/4; 5/16; Yes
1712; Cuny, Norma Grace; 1928-8-29; Yes; F; Yes; 3/8; W; 3/16; Yes
1772; Cut, Martha; 1929-3-14; Yes; F; Yes; F; F; F; Yes
1809; Deon, Dona Lou; 1929-2-1; Yes; F; Yes; 1/8; W; 1/16; Yes
1819; Desersa, Bernice Jane; 1928-9-27; Yes; F; Yes; 1/2; F; 3/4; Yes
---- DeWolf, James Harry; 1298[sic]-12-22; Yes; M; Yes; W; 1/4; 1/8; Yes
1863; Dixon, Harold Homes; 1928-11-15; Yes; M; Yes; 1/4; 1/4; 1/4; Yes
1868; Dixon, Robert Charles; 19288-28; Yes; M; Yes; 1/4; 1/2; 3/8; Yes
1913; Dubray, Amelia Mollie; 1929-4-4; Yes; F; Yes; 1/2; 13/16; 27/32; Yes
1918; Dubray, Pauline Rose; 1928-7-30; Yes; F; Yes; 1/2; 5/8; 9/16; Yes
1980; Eagle Hawk, Lester; 1929-2-27; Yes; M; Yes; F; F; F; Yes
1998; Eagle Louse, Charley; 1929-1-12; Yes; M; Yes; F; F; F; Yes
2044; Evans, Ralph Lorane; 1928-7-9; Yes; M; Yes; W; 1/2; 1/4; Yes
2056; Fast, Phoebe; 1928-7-26; Yes; F; Yes; F; F; F; Yes
2070; Fast Horse, Beatrice; 1928-7-22; Yes; F; Yes; 3/4; 3/4; 3/4; Yes
2091; Fast Wolf, Thomas; 1928-8-11; Yes; M; Yes; 7/8; F; 15/16; Yes
2121; Feather On Head, Amelia; 1928-10-5; Yes; F; Yes; F; 3/4; 7/8; Yes
2124; Ferguson, Ethelyn; 1929-1-17; Yes; F; Yes; W; 3/8; 3/16; Yes
---- Fights Over, Rosaline; 1928-11-3; Yes; F; Yes; F; F; F; Yes
2163; Fire Thunder, Mark; 1928-10-10; Yes; M; Yes; F; F; F; Yes

Key: 1929 Census Roll Number; Surname, Given; Date of Birth (Year-Month-Day); Live Births (Yes/No);
Still Births (blank unless otherwise given); Sex; Tribe (Oglala Sioux unless given otherwise); Ward (Yes/No);
Degree of Blood (Father; Mother; Child); At Jurisdiction Where Enrolled (Yes/No); (If no – Where)

Births Occurring Between July 1, 1928 and June 30, 1929 to Parents Enrolled at Jurisdiction

2181; Fire Thunder, Mary Ora; 1929-3-15; Yes; F; Yes; 3/4; 13/16;
 25/32; Yes
2218; Flying Hawk, Stella; 1929-4-19; Yes; F; Yes; 7/8; F; 15/16; Yes
---- Fog, Emma; 1928-7-29; Yes; F; Yes; 5/8; no data; ?; Yes
2262; Frazier, Floyd Cleveland; 1928-8-7; Yes; M; Oglala & Santee; Yes;
 3/4; 5/8; 11/16; Yes
---- Garnier, Margery Theresa; 1929-1-26; Yes; F; Yes; 1/2; 5/8; 9/16; Yes
2430; Gillispie, Marian; 1928-9-2; Yes; F; Yes; 1/2; 1/4; 3/8; Yes
2443; Glenn, Cecil Alvina; 1928-8-23; Yes; F; Yes; 1/2; 3/4; 5/8; Yes
2446; Glenn, Viola Eva; 1928-9-26; Yes; F; Yes; 1/2; 7/8; 11/16; Yes
---- Goes In Center, Elizabeth; 1928-11-27; Yes; F; Yes; F; 1/2; 3/4; Yes
2467; Goings, Joseph Theodore; 1929-3-19; Yes; M; Yes; 5/8; 3/4; 11/16; Yes
2518; Good Crow, Mildred Irene 1928-7-11; Yes; F; Yes; F; F; F; Yes
2528; Good Medicine, Vivian; 1928-8-26; Yes; F; Yes; 7/8; F; 15/16; Yes
---- Good Plume, Theresa; 1929-1-4; Yes; F; Yes; F; F; F; Yes
----- Good Voice Flute, Claude; 1928-11-26; Yes; M; Yes; F; F; F; Yes
---- Good Weasel, Art Cleveland; 1928-7-15; Yes; M; Yes; F; F; F; Yes
2589; Grabbing Bear, Theresa; 1929-1-28; Yes; F; Yes; F; 3/4; 7/8; Yes
---- Grass, Raymond; 1928-9-6; Yes; M; Yes; F; 1/4; 5/8; Yes
2612; Grass, Victoria Elizabeth; 1929-6-4; Yes; F; Yes; F; F; F; Yes
2640; Gresh, Margaret Rose; 1928-12-17; Yes; F; Yes; 1/4; 1/4; 1/4; Yes
2694; Has No Horses, Arthur Douglas; 1929-1-28; Yes; M; Yes; F; F; F; Yes
2717; Hawk, Ramona May; 1928-12-1; Yes; F; Yes; F; 7/16; 23/32; Yes
---- Hawkins, Joseph Brunet; 1929-5-18; Yes; M; Yes; 5/8; 1/2; 9/16; Yes
2748; Hawk Wing, George; 1929-3-30; Yes; M; Yes; 3/4; F; 7/8; Yes
2759; He Crow, Herman; 1928-9-12; Yes; M; Yes; F; F; F; Yes
2819; Hernandez, Marie Muriel; 1929-5-6; Yes; F; Yes; 1/2; 3/4; 5/8; Yes
2841; High Crane, Frank Jacob; 1929-5-22; Yes; M; Yes; F; 7/8; 15/16; Yes
---- High Pine, Lucille; 1928-7-20; Yes; F; Yes; F; F; F; Yes
---- Hodgkinson, Frederick Eugene; 1929-3-24; Yes; M; Yes; W; 5/16; 5/32; Yes
2908; Hollow Horn, Murdie B; 1929-5-14; Yes; M; Yes; F; F; F; Yes
2936; Holy Eagle, Leroy; 1928-9-4; Yes; M; Yes; F; F; F; Yes
---- Horn Cloud, Raymond; 1928-8-10; Yes; M; Yes; F; F; F; Yes
3034; Ice, Frances Rose; 1928-9-4; Yes; F; Yes; F; F; F; Yes
5703; Iron Bear, Lincoln; 1929-2-12; Yes; M; Yes; F; 7/8; 15/16; Yes
3064; Iron Cloud, Cleveland; 1929-2-5; Yes; M; Yes; F; 7/8; 15/16; Yes
3098; Iron Hawk, Rebecca; 1929-3-31; Yes; F; Yes; F; F; F; Yes
3110; Iron Horse, Ernest; 1928-11-2; Yes; M; Yes; F; F; F; Yes;
3134; Iron White Man, Cleveland Henry; 1928-12-22; Yes; M; Yes; F; 3/4; 7/8; Yes
3164; Jacobs, Ethelyn Mae; 1929-4-3; Yes; F; Yes; 1/4; 1/2; 3/8; Yes
---- Janis, Cecelia Lavera; 1929-6-6; Yes; F; Yes; 1/2; 1/4; 3/8; Yes
3268; Janis, Dwyer Jerome Dave; 1928-8-8; Yes; M; Yes; 3/4; 3/4; 3/4; Yes
3171; Janis, Lawrence; 1929-1-7; Yes; M; Yes; 3/4; F; 7/8; Yes

State__**South Dakota**__Reservation____**Pine Ridge**____Agency or jurisdiction
_____**Pine Ridge**_____ Office of Indian Affairs

Key: 1929 Census Roll Number; Surname, Given; Date of Birth (Year-Month-Day); Live Births (Yes/No); Still Births (blank unless otherwise given); Sex; Tribe (Oglala Sioux unless given otherwise); Ward (Yes/No); Degree of Blood (Father; Mother; Child); At Jurisdiction Where Enrolled (Yes/No); (If no – Where)

Births Occurring Between July 1, 1928 and June 30, 1929 to Parents Enrolled at Jurisdiction

3256; Janis, Marian; 1929-4-28; Yes; F; Yes; 1/2; 3/8; 7/16; Yes

3193; Janis, Herbert; 1928-10-12; Yes; M; Yes; 1/2; W; 1/4; Yes

3187; Janis, Rilda Marie; 1928-12-21; Yes; F; Yes; 1/2; 1/2; 1/2; Yes

---- Jumping Bull, William Hobert; 1298[sic]-9-1; Yes; M; Yes; 3/4; 3/4; 3/4; Yes

---- Jumping Eagle, Robert Edward; 1928-12-3; Yes; M; Yes; F; 1/2; 3/4; Yes

3415; Kills Crow Indian, Tessie; 1929-6-11; Yes; F; Yes; F; F; F; Yes

3465; Kills Small, Sam; 1928-12-17; Yes; M; Yes; F; F; F; Yes

3477; Kills Warrior, Bertha; 1929-4-17; Yes; F; Yes; F; F; F; Yes

3481; Kills Warrior, Grace; 1929-5-14; Yes; F; Yes; F; F; F; Yes

3509; Knife, Maxine; 1928-7-31; Yes; F; Yes; F; F; F; Yes

3519; Knight, Richard LaRoche; 1928-11-8; Yes; M; Yes; W; 1/8; 1/16; Yes

3551; Ladeaux, Albertson; 1928-8-16; Yes; M; Yes; 7/8; F; 15/16; Yes

---- Ladeaux, Samuel Edward; 1928-9-29; Yes; M; Yes; 7/8; F; 15/16; Yes

3578; Lamb, Marlin G; 1928-8-9; Yes; M; Yes; 1/8; W; 1/16; No; Hyattville, Wyo.

3586; Lane, Wilbert; 1928-10-18; Yes; M; Yes; F; F; F; Yes

3691; Lays Bad, Francis; 1929-4-9; Yes; M; Yes; F; F; F; Yes

3722; Lee, Maxine Gayle; (1929)-8-8; Yes; F; Sioux & Cherokee; Yes; 5/16; 5/16; 5/16; No; Dead, S.D.   See Census Roll

---- Lee, Phyllis Rose; 1929-6-23; Yes; F; Yes; 1/2; 1/4; 3/8; Yes

3733; Left Hand, Eugene Valentine; 1929-2-13; Yes; M; Yes; F; 3/4; 7/8; Yes

---- Left Heron, John Verdun; 1928-8-2; Yes; M; Yes; 3/4; F; 7/8; Yes

3808; Little Bear, Evelyn Lucille; 1928-9-23; Yes; F; Yes; 5/8; 1/2; 9/16; Yes

3818; Little Boy, Helen Sylvia; 1928-12-20; Yes; F; Yes; F; 7/8; 15/16; Yes

3880; Little Hawk, Cecil Charles; 1298[sic]-9-27; Yes; M; Yes; F; 1/2; 3/4; Yes

3923; Little Soldier, Beatrice Theone; 1928-9-19; Yes; F; Yes; F; F; F; Yes

---- Little Spotted Horse, Katherine; 1929-4-18; Yes; F; Yes; No data; F; ?; Yes

3961; Little Whiteman, Bernard; 1928-9-4; Yes; M; Yes; F; 1/2; 3/4; Yes

---- Livermont, Robert Donald; 1929-1-15; Yes; M; Yes; 3/16; 1/4; 7/32; Yes

4025; Living Outside, Carl Theodore; 1929-2-10; Yes; M; Yes; F; F; F; Yes

4027; Living Outside, Nellie; 1928-8-17; Yes; F; Yes; F; F; F; Yes

4038; Loafer Joe, Annie; 1928-9-29; Yes; F; Yes; F; F; F; Yes

4126; Long Soldier, Lucile; 1929-5-28; Yes; F; Yes; F; 3/4; 7/8; Yes

4200; Makes Shine, Ida; 1928-7-18; Yes; F; Yes; F; F; F; Yes

7178; Marshall (Walks Under Ground), Antoine D; 1928-10-29; Yes; M; Yes 3/4; F; 7/8; Yes

4242; Marshall, Joy Easu[sic]; 1929-1-19; Yes M; Yes; 1/2; 7/8; 11/16; Yes

4227; Marshall, Thomas Raymond; 1929-3-15; Yes; M; Yes; 1/2; 7/8; 11/16; Yes

4220; Marrow Bone, Benedict; 1929-1-5; Yes; M; Yes; F; F; F; Yes

4257; Martin, Robert Eldon; 1929-5-30; Yes; M; Yes; 3/8; F; 11/16; Yes

---- Martinez, James Jr; 1928-11-19; Yes; M; Yes; F; F; F; Yes

---- McGaa, Aldine Deloris; 1928-11-28; Yes; F; Yes; 3/8; 1/2; 7/16; No; Rapid City, S.D.

4339; Merrival, Donroy; 1928-9-13; Yes; M; Yes; 3/9; 1/2; 7/16; Yes

48

Key: 1929 Census Roll Number; Surname, Given; Date of Birth (Year-Month-Day); Live Births (Yes/No); Still Births (blank unless otherwise given); Sex; Tribe (Oglala Sioux unless given otherwise); Ward (Yes/No); Degree of Blood (Father; Mother; Child); At Jurisdiction Where Enrolled (Yes/No); (If no – Where)

Births Occurring Between July 1, 1928 and June 30, 1929 to Parents Enrolled at Jurisdiction

4348; Mesteth, Dorothy; 1929-2-1; Yes; F; Yes; 5/8; F; 13/16; Yes

4345; Mesteth, Eva; 1928-10-20; Yes; F; Yes; 3/4; F; 7/8; Yes

4391; Mesteth, James; 1929-4-19; Yes; M; Yes; 3/4; 3/4; 3/4; Yes

---- Mesteth, Theresa; 1929-6-24; Yes; F; Yes; 3/4; 1/2; 5/8; Yes

4426; Mills, Benjamin; 1928-7-9; Yes; M; Yes; 3/4; 3/4; 3/4; Yes

---- Moore, Willard Bernard; 1929-3-17; Yes; M; Yes; 3/8; 1/2; 7/16; Yes

4532; Morrison, Clifford; 1928-7-5; Yes; M; Yes; 3/4; F; 7/8; Yes

4527; Morrison, James Jr; 1929-4-1; Yes; M; Yes; 3/4; 11/16; 23/32; Yes

6482; Nelson (Star Yellow Wood), Ramona Thea; 1928-8-19; Yes; F; Yes; 1/2; F; 3/4; Yes

4656; No Belt, Gertrude; 1928-9-17; Yes; F; Yes; F; F; F; Yes

4769; Packed, Vera Dorothy; 1929-4-17; Yes; F; Yes; F; F; F; Yes

4814; Patton, Vincent James; 1929-4-16; Yes; M; Yes; 1/4; F; 5/8; Yes

4914; Plenty Wounds, Katie; 1928-7-9; Yes; F; Yes; F; F; F; Yes

---- Plenty Wounds, Joseph; 1928-11-15; Yes; M; Yes; F; F; F; Yes

---- Plenty Wounds, Raymond; 1929-3-22; Yes; M; Yes; F; F; F; Yes

4941; Poor Bear, Raymond Leroy; 1929-5-22; Yes; M; Yes; 7/8; F; 15/16; Yes

5045; Pretty Back, Edward; 1928-9-28; Yes; M; Yes; F; F; F; Yes

5054; Pretty Bird, Ethel Esther; 1928-8-8; Yes; F; Yes; F; F; F; Yes

---- Pretty Voice Crane, John Jefferson; 1929-4-21; Yes; M; Yes; 7/8; 7/8; 7/8; Yes

5100; Provost, Howard; 1928-9-14; Yes; M; Yes; 1/4; 1/4; 1/4; Yes

5081; Provost, John William; 1928-8-29; Yes; M; Yes; 7/16; W; 7/32; Yes

5229; Randall, Jeanette; 1929-5-14; Yes; F; Yes; 3/4; 1/2; 5/8; Yes

~~5292; Randall, Marie Magdalene; 1929-8-24; Yes; F; Yes; 1/2; 3/4; 5/8; Yes~~
Trans to 1930

5261; Red Blanket, Thomas; 1928-8-22; Yes; M; Yes; F; F; F; Yes

5287; Red Cloud, Bernard; 1929-2-18; Yes; M; Yes; F; F; F; Yes

---- Red Elk, Thelma Elizabeth; 1929-4-16; Yes; F; Yes; F; F; F; Yes

5415; Red Owl, Rachel; 1928-10-10; Yes; F; Yes; F; F; F; Yes

5429; Red Paint, Flora; 1929-6-19; Yes; F; Yes; F; F; F; Yes

5459; Red Shirt, Grace; 1929-3-12; Yes; F; Yes; F; 1/2; 3/4; Yes

5486; Red Willow, Lucille; 1928-8-10; Yes; F; Yes; F; F; F; Yes

5502; Red Wolf, Timothy; 1928-7-8; Yes; M; Yes; F; F; F; Yes

5521; Returns From Scout, Katherine; 1928-7-9; Yes; F; F; F; Yes

5534; Ribman, Mary; 1928-12-19; Yes; F; Yes; F; F; F; Yes

5570; Richard, Lavern Charles; 1928-7-30; Yes; M; Yes; 7/16; 13/32; 27/64; Yes

---- Ricahrd[sic], Rosella Melissa; 1929-5-15; Yes; F; Yes; 7/16; W; 7/32; Yes (twins)

---- " Luella Minerva; 1929-5-15; Yes; F; Yes; 7/16; W; 7/32; Yes

5600; Richard, Sylvan Charles; 1929-1-21; Yes; M; Yes; Yes 9/16; W; 9/32; Yes

5574; Richard, Wildeen Irene; 1928-9-15; Yes; F; Yes; 7/16; 1/16; 1/4; Yes

5629; Ringing Shield, Ella; 1928-12-2; Yes; F; Yes; F; 3/4; 7/8; Yes

1760; Rios, Dolores; 1928-7-22; Yes; F; Yes; W; 1/2; 1/4; Yes

State **South Dakota** Reservation **Pine Ridge** Agency or jurisdiction
Pine Ridge Office of Indian Affairs

Key: 1929 Census Roll Number; Surname, Given; Date of Birth (Year-Month-Day); Live Births (Yes/No);
Still Births (blank unless otherwise given); Sex; Tribe (Oglala Sioux unless given otherwise); Ward (Yes/No);
Degree of Blood (Father; Mother; Child); At Jurisdiction Where Enrolled (Yes/No); (If no – Where)

Births Occurring Between July 1, 1928 and June 30, 1929 to Parents Enrolled at Jurisdiction

5639; Roan Eagle, Joseph; 1928-10-1; Yes; M; Yes; F; 1/2; 3/4; Yes
5680; Romero, Edward; 1929-5-31; Yes; M; Yes; No data; 3/4; ?; Yes
5744; Rowland, Mollie Pearl; 1929-1-6; Yes; F; Sioux & Chey; Yes; F; F; F; Yes
5780; Ruleau, Geraldine Laverne; 1928-7-10; Yes; F; Yes; 5/16; W; 5/32; Yes
5843; Runs Against; Claudia Lucy; 1929-1-2; Yes; F; Yes; F; F; F; Yes
5905; Salway, Vincent Wayne; 1928-10-5; Yes; M; Yes; 5/8; 1/2; 9/16; Yes
---- Sedlacek, Harriet Marie; 1928-7-1; Yes; F; Yes; W; 1/4; 1/8; Yes
6009; Shangreau, Vesta Margaret; 1929-3-26; Yes; F; Yes; 1/2; 7/8; 11/16; Yes
---- Sharp, Calvin; 1929-5-31; Yes; M; Yes; W; 1/4; 1/8; Yes
6076; Short Bear, Floyd; 1928-7-22; Yes; M; Yes; F; F; F; Yes
6097; Short Horn, Frances Alice; 1928-12-9; Yes; F; Yes; F; 3/4; 7/8; Yes
6111; Shot, Leo Charles; 1929-9-28[or 26]; Yes; M; Yes; F; F; F; Yes
          See Census Roll
6162; Siers, James Robert Charles; 1928-9-17; Yes; M; Yes; 5/8; 1/2; 9/16; Yes
6173; Sitting Bear, Aloysius; 1929-6-21; Yes; M; Yes; F; F; F; Yes
---- Six Feathers, Henry Adolph; 1928-7-18; Yes M; Yes; 7/8; 9/16; 21/32; Yes
---- Skalander, Lyle Frederick; 1929-6-15; Yes; M; Yes; 1/8; 3/16; 5/32; Yes
3686; Skinner, Benjamin; 1929-1-28; Yes; M; Yes; W; 3/4; 3/8; Yes
6310; Spider, Raymond; 1928-10-8; Yes; M; Yes; F; F; F; Yes
6332; Spotted Crow, Lena; 1928-9-11; Yes; F; Yes; F; F; F; Yes
6396; Standing Bear, Dolores Fay; 1928-10-9; Yes; F; Yes; 3/4; F; 7/8; Yes
6392; Standing Bear, Victoria; 1929-1-27; Yes; F; Yes; 3/4; F; 7/8; Yes
---- Standing Elk, Theodore; 1928-12-9; Yes; M; Yes; F; F; F; Yes
6431; Standing Soldier, Elizabeth Mary; 1928-11-14; Yes; F; Yes; F; F; F; Yes
6437; Standing Soldier, Andrew Francis; 1929-6-4; Yes; M; Yes; 7/8; 1/4; 9/16; Yes
6491; Steffensmier, Merlin Gene; 1928-9-29; Yes; M; Yes; W; 1/4; 1/8; Yes
6495; Stewart, Sifray; 1929-6-13; Yes; M; Yes; F; F; F; Yes
6582; Swallow, Marie; 1928-9-26; Yes; F; Yes; 3/8; 1/2; 7/16; Yes
---- Swanson, Mary Ann; 1929-5-18; Yes; F; Yes; W; 1/8; 1/16; No; Rapid City
6661; Tail, Cleveland James; 1929-6-8; Yes; M; Yes; F; F; F; Yes
6721; Ten Fingers, Catherine Virginia; 1929-6-17; Yes; F; Yes; F; 1/2; 3/4; Yes
6747; Three Stars, Bessie May; 1928-8-5; Yes; F; Yes; 5/8; W; 5/16; Yes
6811; Tibbits, Thomas Bennie; 1928-8-10; Yes; M; Yes; 1/2; 3/16; 11/32; Yes
---- Tobacco, Florence Louise; 1929-1-2; Yes; F; Yes;
6826; Todd, Robert Arlen; 1929-2-1; Yes; M; Yes; W; 1/8; 1/16; Yes
6844; Trimble, William Albert; 1928-8-21; Yes; M; Yes; W; 3/4; 3/8; Yes
6892; Tuttle, Marvin Nelson; 1928-7-18; Yes; M; Yes; F; 3/4; 7/8; Yes
6974; Two Bulls, Lucille Rebecca; 1928-12-6; Yes; F; Yes; 7/8; F; 15/16; Yes
6996; Two Crow, Phoebe; 1928-8-4; Yes; F; Yes; 3/4; F; 7/8; Yes
7017; Two Eagles, Lucille; 1928-7-8; Yes; F; Sioux & Yank.; Yes; F; 1/2; 3/4; Yes
7052; Two Stick, Vivian; 1929-2-14; Yes; F; Yes; F; 3/4; 11/16; Yes
7064; Two Two, John Baptiste; 1928-12-21; Yes; M; Yes; F; 3/4; 7/8; Yes
7058; Two Two, Marie Alice; 1928-12-20; Yes; F; Yes; F; F; F; Yes

50

Key: 1929 Census Roll Number; Surname, Given; Date of Birth (Year-Month-Day); Live Births (Yes/No); Still Births (blank unless otherwise given); Sex; Tribe (Oglala Sioux unless given otherwise); Ward (Yes/No); Degree of Blood (Father; Mother; Child); At Jurisdiction Where Enrolled (Yes/No); (If no – Where)

Births Occurring Between July 1, 1928 and June 30, 1929 to Parents Enrolled at Jurisdiction

7082;   Tyon, Mary; 1928-9-29; Yes; F; Yes; 3/4; F; 7/8; Yes
7111;   Valandry, Lawrence Gilbert; 1928-9-1; Yes; M; Yes; 1/8; 1/4; 3/16; Yes
7149;   Vocu, Robert Joseph; 1928-12-19; Yes; M; Yes; W; 1/4; 1/8; Yes
7152;   Wafford, Fay Gladys; 1928-10-28; Yes; F; Yes; 3/8; 1/2; 7/16; Yes
7157;   Walking Bull, Allen; 1928-12-12; Yes; M; Yes; F; F; F; Yes
7172;   Walks Out, Aurelia Lucy; 1928-11-2; Yes; F; Yes; F; F; F; Yes
7185;   Walks Under Ground, Francis; 1928-7-16; Yes; M; Yes; F; F; F; Yes
7202;   Ward, Robert Francis; 1928-12-19; Yes; M; Yes; W; 5/16; 5/32; Yes
7214;   Water, William Cleveland; 1929-5-14; Yes; M; Yes; 3/4; F; 7/8; Yes
7241;   Weasel Bear, Albert; 1928-11-30; Yes; M; Yes; F; F; F; Yes
7254;   Weber, Bonnie Lou; 1928-11-21; Yes; F; Yes; 1/8; W; 1/16; Yes
----   Weber, Jackie Blaine; 1928-6-29; Yes; M; Yes; 1/8; W; 1/16; Yes
7283;   Weston, Elnora; 1928-8-6; Yes; F; Yes; F; F; F; Yes
7280;   Weston, Laurina; 1928-8-12; Yes; F; Yes; F; 3/4; 7/8; Yes
7373;   White Bull, (Unnamed); 1929-1-18; Yes; M; Yes; F; F; F; Yes
7382;   White Bull, Keva Mary; 1928-11-8; Yes; F; Yes; F; F; F; Yes
7399;   White Calf, Lena; 1928-12-18; Yes; F; Yes; F; F; F; Yes
7467;   White Face, Clara Elizabeth; 1928-11-14; Yes; F; Yes; F; F; F; Yes
7474;   White Face, John Joseph; 1928-2-22; Yes; M; Yes; F; F; F; Yes
7531;   White Rabbit, Andrew; 1929-3-4; Yes; M; Yes; F; F; F; Yes
7562;   White Woman, Rufus; 1928-9-1; Yes; M; Yes; F; F; F Yes
7569;   Wilcox, Howard Joseph; 1928-7-17; Yes; M; Yes; W; 13/32; 13/64; Yes
----   Williams, Joseph Ward; 1928-8-21; Yes; M; Yes; W; 1/8; 1/16; Yes
6814;   Wilson, Henrietta; 1929-4-30; Yes; F; Yes; 1/2; F; 3/4; Yes
7606;   Wilson, Lyle Kenneth; 1928-8-17; Yes; M; Yes; 1/8; 1/2; 5/16; Yes
----   Witt, Nelson; 1928-11-1; Yes; M; Oglala & Cherokee; Yes; 1/4; F; 5/8; Yes
7632;   Woman Dress, Raymond Patrick; 1928-11-3; Yes; M; Yes; F; F; F; Yes
7718;   Yellow Bird, Frank Everett; 1928-9-3; Yes; M; Yes; 3/4; 1/2; 5/8; Yes
7756;   Yellow Boy, Charles; 1929-3-16; Yes; M; Yes; 7/8; F; 15/16; Yes
7759;   Yellow Boy, Winona May; 1929-3-28; Yes; F; Yes; 7/8; F; 15/16; Yes
----   Yellow Bull, Lorraine; 1928-8-9; Yes; F; Yes; F; F; F; Yes
7909;   Young Dog, Isaac; 1929-5-8; Yes; M; Yes; F; F; F; Yes

        Brown, George R; 1928-7-12; Yes; M; [blank]; 3/8; 1/2; [blank]
        Williams, Alberta Virginia; 1928-12-2; Yes; F; [blank]; [blank]; 5/16; White; [blank]
        Looks Twice, Dallas LeRoy; 1929-1-10; Yes; F; [blank]; F; F; F; [blank]
        Cut Grass, Amy; 1929-1-10; Yes; F; [blank]; F; F; F; [blank]
3141;   Iron Rope, Sophia Antonia; 1929-6-12; Yes; F; Yes; F; F; F; Yes
                Trans from 1930
4904;   Petersen, Eileen June; 1929-6-24; Yes; F; Yes; W; 5/16; 5/32; Yes
                Trans from 1930

State **South Dakota**　　Reservation　　**Pine Ridge**　　Agency or jurisdiction
　　Pine Ridge　　　Office of Indian Affairs

Key: 1929 Census Roll Number; Surname, Given; Date of Birth (Year-Month-Day); Live Births (Yes/No);
Still Births (blank unless otherwise given); Sex; Tribe (Oglala Sioux unless given otherwise); Ward (Yes/No);
Degree of Blood (Father; Mother; Child); At Jurisdiction Where Enrolled (Yes/No); (If no – Where)

Births Occurring Between July 1, 1928 and June 30, 1929 to Parents Enrolled at Jurisdiction

5833;　Ruff, Eileen Grace; 1929-5-9; Yes; F; Yes; 1/4; 1/4; 1/4; Yes ⎫
　　　　　　Trans from 1930　　　　　　　　　　　　　　　　　　　⎬ twins
5834;　Ruff, Irene Ann; 1929-5-9; Yes; F; Yes; 1/4; 1/4; 1/4; Yes ⎭
　　　　　　Trans from 1930

5933;　Salvis, Lemoyne; 1929-1-7; Yes; M; Yes; 5/8; 1/2; 9/16; Yes
　　　　　　Trans from 1930

6265;　Sitting Up, Leo Cornelius; 1929-2-6; Yes; M; Yes; F; 1/2; 3/4; Yes
　　　　　　Trans from 1930

7412;　White, Doris; 1929-4-8; Yes; F; Yes; 1/2; 5/16; 13/32; Yes
　　　　　　Trans from 1930

　　　　Randall, Julia May; 1929-4-26; Yes; F; Rosebud and Oglala Sioux; Yes;
　　　　3/4; 3/4; 3/4; Yes　　　　　　　　　Trans from 1931

LIVE BIRTHS

1930
(July 1, 1929 - June 30, 1930)

PINE RIDGE RESERVATION
PINE RIDGE SOUTH DAKOTA

Key: 1930 Census Roll Number; Surname, Given; Date of Birth (Year-Month-Day); Live Births (Yes/No);
Still Births (blank unless otherwise given); Sex; Tribe (Oglala Sioux unless given otherwise); Ward (Yes/No);
Degree of Blood (Father; Mother; Child); At Jurisdiction Where Enrolled (Yes/No); (If no – Where)

Births Occurring Between July 1, 1929 and June 30, 1930 to Parents Enrolled at Jurisdiction

27; Afraid Of Bear, Mamie; 1930-6-27; Yes; F; Yes; F; F; F; Yes

213; Artichoker, John Hobert; 1930-1-17; Yes; M; Sioux & Winnebago; Yes; 7/8;
1/4; 9/16; Yes

195; Apple, Clara; 1930-6-2; Yes; F; Yes; 3/4; 3/4; 3/4; Yes

267; Bad Heart Bull, Julius; 1930-3-14; Yes; M; Yes; F; F; F; Yes

275; Bad Wound, Fannie; 1930-3-17; Yes; F; Yes; F; 1/2; 3/4; Yes

280; Bad Wound, Noah; 1929-9-14; Yes; M; Yes; 3/4; 1/2; 5/8; Yes

290; Bad Wound, Leroy Ellis; 1930-6-21; Yes; M; Yes; F; F; F; Yes

----; Bank, Homer; 1929-7-1; Yes; M; Yes; F; F; F; Yes

359; Bear Eagle, Cora; 1930-3-16; Yes; F; Yes; F; F; F; Yes

7895; Bear Robe, Aloysius Denver; 1930-4-8; Yes; M; Yes; F; F; F; Yes

388; Bear Robe, Verne; 1929-9-18; Yes; F; Yes; F; F; F; Yes

397; Bear Robe, Wallace; 1930-6-30; Yes; M; Yes; F; F; F; Yes

441; Bell, Frances; 1929-10-16; Yes; F; Yes; W; 3/8; 3/16; Yes

506; Bettelyoun, Nance Vergil; 1930-6-9; Yes; M; Sioux & Menonune[sic]; Yes; 1/2;
5/8; 9/16; Yes

469; Bergen, Richard Darrell; 1929-9-10; Yes; M; Yes; 3/8; 1/2; 7/16; Yes

515; Between Lodges, Marie Agatha; 1930-5-8; Yes; F; Yes; F; F; F; Yes

563; Bird, Darwin Eugene; 1920-5-24; Yes; M; Yes; W; 3/8; 3/16; Yes

623; Bissonette, Bernard Francis; 1929-7-16; Yes; M; Yes; 5/8; 7/8; 3/4; Yes
622; Bissonette, Lucille Angeline; 1929-7-16; Yes; F; Yes; 5/8; 7/8; 3/4; Yes (twins)

673; Black Bear, Christina; 1929-12-14; Yes; F; Yes; F; F; F; Yes

685; Black Bird, Esther; 1929-11-6; Yes; F; Yes; F; F; F; Yes

699; Black Car, Chris; 1930-1-28; Yes; M; Yes; F; F; F; Yes

710; Black Crow, Milo; 1930-4-24; Yes; M; Yes; F; F; F; Yes

786; Black Tail Deer, Sadie; 1930-3-2; Yes; F; Yes; F; F; F; Yes

758; Black Feather, Francis Baptiste; 1930-5-25; Yes; M; Yes; 3/4; 3/4; 3/4; Yes

820; Blue Bird, Everett; 1929-12-18; Yes; M; Yes; F; 3/4; 7/8; Yes

837; Blue Legs, Emil; 1930-3-26; Yes; M; Yes; F; F; F; Yes

875; Brafford, Merle Lincoln; 1930-1-8; Yes; M; Yes; 1/4; 1/2; 3/8; Yes

927; Brave Heart, Louis; 1929-11-19; Yes; M; Yes; F; F; F; Yes

947; Brewer, Robert Jr; 1930-3-12; Yes; M; Yes; 1/4; 1/2; 3/8; Yes
946; " William; 1930-3-12; Yes; M; Yes; 1/4; 1/2; 3/8; Yes (twins)

4737; Brings, Ernestine Joyce; 1929-11-12; Yes; F; Yes; F; F; F; Yes 1059

1026; Brown, Charlotte Mary; 1930-4-10; Yes; F; Yes; 3/16; 1/4; 7/32; Yes
1025; Brown, Shirley Alice; 1930-4-10; Yes; F; Yes; 3/16; 1/4; 7/32; Yes (twins)

1059; Brown, Doris Jean; 1929-12-17; Yes; F; Yes; 3/8; 1/4; 5/16; Yes

1027; Brown, William James; 1929-11-1; Yes; M; Yes; 3/8; 7/8; 5/8; Yes

1095; Brown Eyes, Bernard; 1930-3-15; Yes; M; Yes; 3/4; 5/8; 11/16; Yes

1187; Bush, Leona Agnes; 1930-1-24; Yes; F; Yes; 3/4; F; 7/8; Yes 394

1203; Bush, Percy; 1930-4-19; Yes; M; Yes; 3/4; 3/4; 3/4; Yes

3949; Catches, Ramona; 1929-8-17; Yes; F; Yes; No data; F; ?; No; Rapid City, S[sic]

1224; Carlow, Theodore Charles; 1930-4-15; Yes; M; Yes; 1/4; 1/2; 3/8; Yes

State **South Dakota** Reservation **Pine Ridge** Agency or jurisdiction
Pine Ridge Office of Indian Affairs

Key: 1930 Census Roll Number; Surname, Given; Date of Birth (Year-Month-Day); Live Births (Yes/No);
Still Births (blank unless otherwise given); Sex; Tribe (Oglala Sioux unless given otherwise); Ward (Yes/No);
Degree of Blood (Father; Mother; Child); At Jurisdiction Where Enrolled (Yes/No); (If no – Where)

Births Occurring Between July 1, 1929 and June 30, 1930 to Parents Enrolled at Jurisdiction

1249; Cedar Face, Pearl; 1930-3-31; Yes; F; Yes; F; F; F; Yes

1292; Charging Thunder, John William; 1929-10-28; Yes; M; Yes; F; F; F; Yes

1298; Chase Alone, Anna; 1930-2-11; Yes; F; Yes; F; F; F; Yes

1312; Chase In Morning, Elizabeth; 1929-9-27; Yes; F; Yes; F; F; F; Yes

---- Chase In Winter, Madeline; 1930-4-8; Yes; F; Yes; F; F; F; Yes (twins)
---- Chase In Winter, Mary; 1930-4-8; Yes; F; Yes; F; F; F; Yes

1358; Chips, Bessie; 1930-3-27; Yes; F; Yes; F; 3/4; 7/8; Yes

1338; Chief, Yakima; 1930-6-25; Yes; M; Yes; F; F; F; Yes

---- Chips, Elizabeth; 1929-10-16; Yes; F; Yes; F; F; F; Yes

1351; Childers, Clarice Grace; 1929-7-7; Yes; F; Sioux & Creek; Yes; 7/8; 1/16; 15/32; Yes

1364; Christensen, Gene Stanley; 1929-11-22; Yes; M; Yes; W; 5/16; 5/32; Yes

1372; Clement, Rosemary; 1929-7-20; Yes; F; Yes; W; F; 1/2; Yes

1396; Clifford, Reuben Clay; 1929-8-1; Yes; M; Yes; 1/2; 1/2; 1/2; Yes

---- Coats, Hazel Ione; 1929-11-29; Yes; F; Yes; W; 1/16; 1/32; Yes

---- Comes From Among Them, Rose Marie; 1930-6-30; Yes; F; Yes; 15/16; F; 31/32; Yes

1506; Combs, Vance Shirley; 1929-11-9; Yes; M; Yes; W; 5/16; 5/32; Yes

---- Comes Last, Lorraine; 1930-6-6; Yes; F; Yes; F; F; F; Yes

1584; Conroy, Norman Stephen; 1929-12-25; Yes; M; Yes; 1/2; 3/4; 5/8; Yes

1568; Conroy, Virginia Gertrude; 1930-1-31; Yes; F; Yes; 5/8; 5/8; 5/8; Yes

1672; Crazy Ghost, Lillian; 1929-7-17; Yes; F; Yes; F; F; F; Yes

---- Crooked Eyes, Jacob; 1929-7-26; Yes; M; Yes; F; F; F; Yes

1790; Cottier, Sadie Louise; 1930-6-3; Yes; F; Yes; 1/2; 9/16; 17/32; Yes

1721; Crow, Russell; 1929-10-2; Yes; M; Yes; F; F; F; Yes 18

---- Cut Grass, Stella; 1930-4-30; Yes; F; Yes; ; F; F; F; Yes

1819; Cut Nose, Flora Ann; 1929-8-31; Yes; F; Sioux & Arap; Yes; F; 5/8; 13/16; Yes

1883; De Shenquette, Gerald Evans; 1930-6-24; Yes; M; Yes; 1/4; 5/8; 7/16; Yes

1469; Dirt Kettle, Grace; 1930-3-10; Yes; 3; 10; Yes; F; Yes; F; F; F; Yes

1913; Dog, Daniel King; 1929-11-11; Yes; M; Yes; F; F; F; Yes

4711; Dreamer, Verbena Marsland; 1929-10-3; Yes; F; Yes; F; F; F; Yes

---- Drury, Harry Ambrose; 1929-8-26; Yes; M; Yes; W; 7/16; 7/32; Yes 1954

1954; Dubray, Gordon; 1929-9-12; Yes; M; Yes; 1/2; 3/8; 7/16; Yes 1986

1995; Eagle Bear, Cornelius; 1930-6-18; Yes; M; Yes; F; F; F; Yes

1986; Eagle Bull, Chester; 1929-12-5; Yes; M; Yes; F; F; F; Yes

---- Eagle Elk, Gus; 1930-4-24; Yes; M; Yes; F; F; F; Yes (twins)
---- Eagle Elk, Guy; 1930-4-25; Yes; M; Yes; F; F; F; Yes

2016; Eagle Elk, Morris Emerson; 1930-6-19; Yes; M; Yes; F; F; F; Yes

---- Eagle Heart, (Unnamed); 1930-6-10; Yes; F; Yes; F; 7/8; 15/16; Yes

---- Ear Ring, Leon; 1929-7-2; Yes; M; Yes; F; 1/2; 3/4; Yes

---- Eisenbraun, Theodore Milton; 1929-11-27; Yes; M; Yes; W; 1/8; 1/16; Yes

2112; Fast Horse; Annie Elizabeth; 1930-3-14; Yes; F; Yes; 3/4; 3/4; 3/4; Yes 2137

State **South Dakota** Reservation **Pine Ridge** Agency or jurisdiction
Pine Ridge Office of Indian Affairs

Key: 1930 Census Roll Number; Surname, Given; Date of Birth (Year-Month-Day); Live Births (Yes/No); Still Births (blank unless otherwise given); Sex; Tribe (Oglala Sioux unless given otherwise); Ward (Yes/No); Degree of Blood (Father; Mother; Child); At Jurisdiction Where Enrolled (Yes/No); (If no – Where)

Births Occurring Between July 1, 1929 and June 30, 1930 to Parents Enrolled at Jurisdiction

2113; Fast, Gabriel; 1930-6-17; Ye; M; Yes; F; F; F; Yes
2137; Featherman, Edith; 1930-1-19; Yes; F; Yes; F; F; F; Yes
7228; Ferguson, Earl Willard; 1930-1-17; Yes; M; Yes; W; 1/4; 1/8; Yes
2170; Fights Bear, Emma; 1929-8-20; Yes; F; Yes; F; F; F; Yes
2217; Fire Thunder, Alice; 1929-8-12; Yes; F; Yes; F; F; F; Yes
2243; Flying Hawk, Lizzie; 1930-3-17; Yes; F; Yes; F; F; F; Yes
2317; Frog, Thomas; 1929-8-5; Yes; M; Yes; F; F; F; Yes
2328; Galligo, John Wesley; 1929-12-2-; Yes; M; Yes; 3/4; 1/2; 5/8; Yes
2391; Garnier, Effie; 1930-4-26; Yes; F; Yes; 1/2; F; 3/4; Yes
2356; Garnier, Sarah Jennie; 1929-12-22; Yes; F; Yes; 1/2; 5/8; 9/16; Yes
2369; Gay, Daisy; 1929-8-23; Yes; F; Yes; 3/4; F; 7/8; Yes
2432; Ghost, Malvin Pedro; 1930-6-19; Yes; M; Yes; F; F; F; Yes
2431; Giago, Ethel Lucille; 1930-2-9; Yes; F; Yes; 1/4; 1/4; 1/4; Yes
-----; Gibbons, (Unnamed); 1929-7-9; Yes; F; Yes; 1/2; F; 3/4; Yes
2510; Goings, Whitney Frank; 1929-6-26; Yes; M; Yes; 5/8; 3/4; 9/16; Yes
2529; Goes In Center, Ethel Angeline; 1930-6-16; Yes; F; Yes; F; 1/2; 3/4; Yes
2530; Good Buffalo, Charles Jr; 1929-7-17; Yes; M; Yes; F; F; F; Yes
2556; Good Plume, Graverd; 1929-11-27; Yes; M; Yes; F; F; F; Yes
2568; Good Shield, Alonzo Philip; 1929-10-23; Yes; M; Yes; F; F; F; Yes
2583; Good Voice Elk, Abel; 1929-11-5; Yes; M; Yes; F; F; F; Yes
2580; Good Voice Elk, Jeanette; 1929-7-1; Yes; F; Yes; F; F; F; Yes
2603; Good Weasel, LaVern; 1930-2-25; Yes; M; Yes; F; F; F; Yes
2620; Graham, Mary Blossom; 1930-1-11; Yes; F; Yes; 5/8; 5/8; 5/8; Yes
2641; Grass, Velma Caroline; 1929-8-7; Yes; F; Yes; F; F; F; Yes
2695; Hamernick, Mary Lucille; 1929-9-7; Yes; F; Yes; W; 7/16; 7/32; Yes
2799; Hand, Yvonne; 1930-6-21; Yes; F; Yes; F; F; F; Yes
----; Harvey, George Jr; 1929-10-13; Yes; M; Yes; 1/2; 1/2; 1/2; Yes
2724; Hat, Annie; 1930-1-26; Yes; F; Yes; F; F; F; Yes
2732; Hauff, Sylvain Racine; 1929-11-28; Yes; M; Yes; white; 3/8; 3/16; Yes
2768; Hawk Wing, Peter; 1930-2-9; Yes; M; Yes; 3/4; F; 7/8; Yes
2937; High Wolf, Leonard Earl; 1930-5-28; Yes; M; Yes; F; 3/8; 11/16; Yes
2948; Hollow Horn, Earl; 1929-11-5; Yes; M; Yes; F; F; F; Yes
2959; Holy Dance, Rex, Jr; 1929-10-26; Yes; M; Yes; F; 1/2; 3/4; Yes
3024; Holy Rock, Morris Gilbert; 1930-5-19; Yes; M; Yes; 3/4; 5/8; 11/16; Yes
3124; Iron Hawk, Clardia[sic] Lucile; 1930-3-30; Yes; F; Yes; F; F; F; Yes
3141; ~~Iron Rope, Sophia Antonia; 1929-6-18; Yes; F; Yes; F; F; F; Yes~~
        Trans to 1929
3213; Janis, Olive Marie; 1929-7-16; Yes; F; Yes; 1/2; 1/2; 1/2; Yes
3304; Janis, Ora Una; 1929-10-9; Yes; F; Yes; 3/4; F; 7/8; Yes
3223; Janis, Theresa; 1929-9-24; Yes; F; Yes; 3/8; 1/2; 7/16; Yes
3315; Jealous Of Him, Mary; 1930-2-15; Yes; F; Yes; 7/8; F; 15/16; Yes
3372; Jumping Bull, Calvin; 1929-11-9; Yes; M; Yes; 3/4; 3/4; 3/4; Yes
3395; Keester, Arthur Lee; 1929-12-12; Yes; M; Yes; W; 1/2; 1/4; Yes

57

Key: 1930 Census Roll Number; Surname, Given; Date of Birth (Year-Month-Day); Live Births (Yes/No);
Still Births (blank unless otherwise given); Sex; Tribe (Oglala Sioux unless given otherwise); Ward (Yes/No);
Degree of Blood (Father; Mother; Child); At Jurisdiction Where Enrolled (Yes/No); (If no – Where)

Births Occurring Between July 1, 1929 and June 30, 1930 to Parents Enrolled at Jurisdiction

3401; Keith, Mary Elizabeth; 1929-7-15; Yes; F; Yes; 1/8; 3/8; 1/4; Yes
3440; Kills Crow Indian, Geraldine; 1929-11-15; Yes; F; Yes; F; F; F; Yes
3473; Kills In Water, Willard; 1929-11-30; Yes; M; Yes; F; F; F; Yes
3528; Kindle, Katherine; 1929-9-1; Yes; F; Yes; F; F; F; Yes
3578; Ladeaux, Pearl Sarah; 1930-2-23; Yes; F; Yes; 7/8; F; 15/16; Yes
3652; Lamont, Verna Marie; 1929-12-12; Yes; F; Yes; 5/8; F; 13/16; Yes
3829; Little, Ernest; 1929-12-3; Yes; M; Yes; F; F; F; Yes
----; Little Bull, Leon; 1929-11-22; Yes; M; Yes; F; F; F; Yes
3944; Little Moon, Pauline; 1929-10-31; Yes; F; Yes; F; 3/4; 7/8; Yes
3968; Little Soldier, Vivian; 1929-10-7; Yes; F; Yes; F; F; F; Yes
3973; Little Spotted Horse, Lydia Lorene; 1930-3-12; Yes; F; Yes; F; F; F; Yes
3993; Little War Bonnet, Eliza; 1929-11-11; Yes; F; Yes; F; F; F; Yes
4080; Loafer, Ida; 1930-2-14; Yes; F; Yes; F; F; F; Yes
4195; Looking Cloud, Claude Leo; 1929-10-21; Yes; M; Yes; F; F; F; Yes
4199; Looking Elk, Stanley; 1929-8-10; Yes; M; Yes; F; 3/4; 7/8; Yes
4207; Looks Twice, Rose; 1930-1-4; Yes; F; Yes; F; F; F; Yes
4223; Lovelady, Kenneth Eugene; 1929-8-14; Yes; M; Yes; W; 1/8; 1/16; Yes
4622; McConnell, Clifford; 1930-1-20; Yes; M; Yes; W; 3/8; 3/16; Yes
4336; Means, Walter; 1929-9-11; Yes; M; Yes; 3/4; F; 7/8; Yes
4478; Mills, Calvin Lewis; 1929-11-12; Yes; M; Yes; 3/4; 3/4; 3/4; Yes
4485; Mills, Frederick; 1929-10-20; Yes; M; Yes; 3/4; 1/4; 1/2; Yes
4542; Morgan, Delmar William; 1929-9-17; Yes; M; Yes; W; 3/8; 3/16; Yes
4559; Morrison, Rhoda Cecelia; 1929-8-2; Yes; F; Yes; 3/4; F; 7/8; Yes
4597; Mousseau, Rebecca Jermaine; 1930-3-18; Yes; F; Yes; 7/8; 1/2; 11/16; Yes
4672; Nelson, Sophia; 1930-1-30; Yes; F; Yes; 5/8; F; 13/16; Yes
4695; New Holy, Daniel; 1929-10-28; Yes; M; Yes; F; F; F; Yes
4729; No Two Horns, Chris; 1929-10-11; Yes; M; Yes; 7/8; F; 15/16; Yes
4808; Pablo, Ramona; 1929-5-14; Yes; F; Yes; 11/16; 3/8; 17/32; Yes
4811; Pacer, Vida; 1930-3-25; Yes; F; Yes; F; F; F; Yes
4887; Peck, William Kenneth; 1929-7-26; Yes; M; Yes; 1/4; 3/8; 5/16; Yes
~~4904; Petersen, Eileen June; 1929-6-24; Yes; F; Yes; W; 5/16; 5/32; Yes~~
Trans to 1929
4921; Plenty Arrows, Sarah; 1929-11-26; Yes; F; Yes; F; F; F; Yes
4942; Plenty Wolf, Bernard; 1929-7-17; Yes; M; Yes; F; F; F; Yes
5005; Poor Thunder, Wilson; 1929-12-30; Yes; M; Yes; F; W; 1/2; Yes
5037; Pourier, Lavon; 1930-3-4; Yes; F; Yes; 3/16; 5/16; 1/4; Yes
5031; Pourier, Ramona Mae; 1930-2-17; Yes; F; Yes; 3/16; 1/4; 7/32; Yes
----; Powder Woman, Bernice; 1930-3-16; Yes; F; Yes; F; F; F; Yes
5147; Provost, Alma Jean Frances; 1929-8-24; Yes; F; Yes; 5/16; W; 5/32; Yes
5164; Pugh, George Owen; 1929-10-7; Yes; M; Yes; 3/8; 1/16; 7/32; Yes
5202; Pumpkin Seed, James; 1929-9-22; Yes; M; Yes; F; F; F; Yes
5195; Pumpkin Seed, Peter; 1930-3-16; Yes; M; Yes; F; F; F; Yes
5235; Quiver, Millie Esther; 1929-7-13; Yes; F; Yes; F; 9/16; 9/32; Yes

Key: 1930 Census Roll Number; Surname, Given; Date of Birth (Year-Month-Day); Live Births (Yes/No); Still Births (blank unless otherwise given); Sex; Tribe (Oglala Sioux unless given otherwise); Ward (Yes/No); Degree of Blood (Father; Mother; Child); At Jurisdiction Where Enrolled (Yes/No); (If no – Where)

Births Occurring Between July 1, 1929 and June 30, 1930 to Parents Enrolled at Jurisdiction

5314; Red Bow, Clarence; 1930-3-21; Yes; M; Yes; F; F; F; Yes (twins)
---- " " Lawrence; " " " Yes; M; Yes; F; F; F; Yes
---- Red Cloud, Dawson; 1930-1-30; Yes; M; Yes; F; F; F; Yes
5367; Reddy, Rose Mary; 1929-12-24; Yes; F; Yes; White; 3/8; 3/16; Yes
5409; Red Feather, Esther; 1930-3-26; Yes; F; Yes; F; F; F; Yes
5432; Red Hawk, Suey[sic] San; 1929-10-14; Yes; F; Yes; F; F; F; Yes
5466; Red Owl, Archie Lloyd; 1929-7-31; Yes; M; Yes; F; 1/2; 3/4; Yes
5470; Red Owl, Vastanna Eloise; 1929-11-16; Yes; F; Yes; F; F; F; Yes
5495; Red Shirt, Edith; 1929-11-17; Yes; F; Yes; 3/4; 3/4; 3/4; Yes
5510; Red Shirt, Esther; 1930-1-4; Yes; F; Yes; 3/4; F; 7/8; Yes
5629; Richard, Kenneth Dalbert; 1929-7-5; Yes; M; Yes; 3/4; F; 7/8; Yes
5675; Richard, Leroy; 1930-3-25; Yes; M; Yes; 7/16; 13/32; 27/64; Yes
5618; Richard, Virginia Joyce; 1930-1-25; Yes; F; Yes; 9/16; W; 9/32; Yes
5686; Ringing Shield, Zelma Una; 1930-2-12; Yes; F; Yes; F; F; F; Yes
5718; Rock, Bessie; 1929-7-15; Yes; F; Yes; F; 3/4; 7/8; Yes
5833; Ruff, Eileen Grace; 1929-5-9; Yes; F; Yes; 1/4; 1/4; 1/4; Yes
Trans to 1929 (twins)
5834;   "   Irene Ann; 1929-5-9; Yes; F; Yes; 1/4; 1/4; 1/4; Yes
Trans to 1929
3840; Ruleau, Phyllis Eileen; 1929-10-16; Yes; F; Yes; 5/16; W; 5/32; Yes
5860; Running Eagle, Hoover; 1929-8-29; Yes; M; Yes; F; F; F; Yes
5848; Runnels, Jack Ray; 1929-9-23; Yes; M; Yes; 3/8; 1/2; 7/16; Yes
5938; Salway, Iris Pauline; 1929-7-5; Yes; F; Yes; 11/16; 1/2; 19/32; Yes
5933; Salvis, Lemoyne; 1929-1-7; Yes; M; Yes; 5/8; 1/2; 9/16; Yes
Trans to 1929
5989; Sasse, Carl Jr; 1930-1-8; Yes; M; Yes; W; 1/4; 1/8; Yes
6000; Scabby Face, Victoria; 1930-3-12; Yes; F; Yes; F; F; F; Yes
---- Sedlacek, Jerald Dean; 1930-1-7; Yes; M; Yes; W; 1/4; 1/8; Yes
6042; Shald, Margaret Louise; 1929-8-18; Yes; F; Yes; W; 1/8; 1/16; Yes
6106; Shell Woman, Vivian; 1929-10-21; Yes; F; Yes; F; 3/4; 7/8; Yes
6187; Shot With Arrow, Delila; 1929-7-10; Yes; F; Yes; F; F; F; Yes
6213; Sierro, Phyllisetta; 1930-3-26; Yes; F; Yes; 1/2; F; 3/4; Yes
---- Sitting Hawk, Ethel; 1929-7-30; Yes; F; Yes; F; F; F; Yes
6270; Sitting Up, Benjamin, Jr; 1930-1-15; Yes; M; Yes; F; F; F; Yes (twins)
---- " " Richard; 1930-1-15; Yes; M; Yes; F; F; F; Yes
6265; Sitting Up, Leo Cornelius; 1929-2-6; Yes; M; Yes; F; 1/2; 3/4; Yes
Trans to 1929
6685; Sitting Up, Teresa; 1930-1-20; Yes; F; Yes; F; 3/16; 19/32; Yes
---- Sleeps, Asa Cleveland; 1930-1-11; Yes; M; Yes; F; F; F; Yes
6312; Slow Bear, Katherine; 1929-10-17; Yes; F; Yes; 7/8; F; 15/16; Yes
6320; Slow Bear, Mary Rose; 1930-1-6; Yes; F; Yes; F; F; F; Yes
6338; Smith, Dean DeCleo; 1929-8-19; Yes; M; Yes; W; 3/16; 3/32; Yes
6340; Smith, Sidney Dale; 1929-8-22; Yes; M; Yes; W; 1/8; 1/16; Yes

Key: 1930 Census Roll Number; Surname, Given; Date of Birth (Year-Month-Day); Live Births (Yes/No); Still Births (blank unless otherwise given); Sex; Tribe (Oglala Sioux unless given otherwise); Ward (Yes/No); Degree of Blood (Father; Mother; Child); At Jurisdiction Where Enrolled (Yes/No); (If no – Where)

Births Occurring Between July 1, 1929 and June 30, 1930 to Parents Enrolled at Jurisdiction

6356; Sounding Side, Jerry; 1929-10-25; Yes; M; Yes; F; F; F; Yes
6363; Sound Sleeper, Emma; 1929-8-15; Yes; F; Yes; F; F; F; Yes
6377; Spider, Lee; 1930-2-25; Yes; M; Yes; F; F; F; Yes
6398; Spotted Bear, Joseph; 1930-3-8; Yes; M; Yes; F; 3/4; 7/8; Yes
---- Standing Bear, George Eugene; 1929-10-31; Yes; M; Yes; 5/8; 5/8; 5/8; Yes
6546; Stands, Mary; 1929-7-11; Yes; F; Yes; F; 3/4; 7/8; Yes
6564; Star Comes Out, Bernard; 1930-3-14; Yes; M; Yes; No Data; F; ?; Yes
6617; Strikes Enemy, Bernard; 1930-3-3; Yes; M; Yes; F; F; F; Yes
6670; Swallow, Oliver William; 1929-12-22; Yes; M; Yes; 3/8; 3/8; 3/8; Yes
6721; Swift Bird, Leo; 1929-9-17; Yes; M; Yes; 7/8; F; 15/16; Yes
6750; Takes War Bonnet, Leo Lee; 1930-3-4; Yes; M; Yes; F; F; F; Yes
6764; Tapia, Richard Albert; 1929-8-7; Yes; M; Yes; 1/4; 1/2; 3/8; Yes
6775; Taylor, Alta Jean; 1929-4-8; Yes; F; Yes; W; 1/8; 1/16; Yes
6825; Three Stars, Jennie Irene; 1929-8-26; Yes; F; Yes; 5/8; W; 5/16; Yes
6854; Thunder Hawk, Francis; 1930-2-10; Yes; M; Yes; F; F; F; Yes
6859; Thunder Hawk, Gladys T; 1929-12-9; Yes; F; Yes; 3/4; F; 7/8; Yes
6933; Trouble In Front, Rose; 1930-1-7; Yes; F; Yes; F; F; F; Yes
6944; Trueblood, Thomas Don; 1929-12-4; Yes; M; Yes; W; 1/4; 1/8; Yes
6990; Twiss, Casper Ambrose; 1930-1-6; Yes; M; Yes; 1/2; 3/4; 5/8; Yes
7003; Twiss, Lula Jane; 1929-7-5; Yes; F; Yes; 1/2; F; 3/4; Yes
7046; Two Bulls, Fred Thomas; 1929-10-5; Yes; M; Yes; 7/8; 1/2; 11/16; Yes
7068; Two Crow, Jeanetta; 1930-2-24; Yes; F; Yes; 3/4; 3/4; 3/4; Yes
7182; Under The Baggage, William; 1930-1-30; Yes; M; Yes; F; F; F; Yes
---- War Bonnet, (Unnamed); 1929-9-20; Yes; F; Yes; F; F; F; Yes
7826; Weasel Bear, Tex; 1929-11-23; Yes; M; Yes; F; F; F; Yes
7396; Whirlwind Horse, Eugene Fay; 1929-10-22; Yes; M; Yes; F; 1/8; 9/16; Yes
~~7413; White, Doris; 1929-4-8; Yes; F; Yes; 1/2; 5/16; 16/32; Yes~~
                    Trans to 1929
7531; White Eyes, Lawrence Dole; 1929-8-8; Yes; M; Yes; F; 3/16; 19/32; Yes
7517; White Eyes, Robert; 1929-11-22; Yes; M; Yes; F; 3/4; 7/8; Yes
7486; White Cow Killer, Verene; 1930-1-30; Yes; F; Yes; F; 3/4; 7/8; Yes
---- White dress; Francis Aloysius; 1929-9-16; Yes; M; Yes; F; F; F; Yes
7617; White Thunder, Dorothy; 1929-12-28; Yes; F; Yes; F; F; F; Yes
7641; Wilcox, Amy Ollie; 1929-7-5; Yes; F; Yes; W; F; 1/2; Yes
7658; Williams, Rosemary; 1930-1-17; Yes; F; Yes; W; 1/8; 1/16; Yes
7694; Witt, Eugenia; 1929-10-4; Yes; F; Yes; 1/4; F; 5/8; Yes
7702; Wolf, Ruth M; 1929-10-13; Yes; F; Yes; W; 1/2; 1/4; Yes
7754; Wounded Horse, Ollie Pearl; 1930-1-30; Yes; F; Yes; F; 1/2; 3/4; Yes
7762; Yaeger, Mary Ann; 1930-3-14; Yes; F; Yes; W; 1/4; 1/8; Yes
7781; Yankton, Stephen; 1929-12-27; Yes; M; Yes; 3/4; 7/8; 13/16; Yes
7765; Yankton, Vina Georgette; 1930-3-5; Yes; F; Yes; 3/4; 7/8; 13/16; Yes
7787; Yellow Bear, Ryan; 1929-7-11; Yes; M; Yes; F; F; F; Yes
7801; Yellow Bird, Alex Donald; 1929-9-12; Yes; M; Yes; 3/4; 3/16; 15/32; Yes

State **South Dakota** Reservation **Pine Ridge** Agency or jurisdiction
Pine Ridge Office of Indian Affairs

Key: 1930 Census Roll Number; Surname, Given; Date of Birth (Year-Month-Day); Live Births (Yes/No);
Still Births (blank unless otherwise given); Sex; Tribe (Oglala Sioux unless given otherwise); Ward (Yes/No);
Degree of Blood (Father; Mother; Child); At Jurisdiction Where Enrolled (Yes/No); (If no – Where)

Births Occurring Between July 1, 1929 and June 30, 1930 to Parents Enrolled at Jurisdiction

7827; Yellow Boy, Antoine; 1930-3-21; Yes; M; Yes; 7/8; F; 15/16; Yes
7852; Yellow Bull, Betsey; 1930-1-17; Yes; F; Yes; F; F; F; Yes
---- Yellow Horse, (Unnamed); 1929-11-20; Yes; F; Yes; F; F; F; Yes
7886; Yellow Horse, Velma; 1929-11-23; Yes; F; Yes; 7/8; F; 15/15[sic]; Yes
---- Young, Elaine Edwin; 1929-8-8; Yes; M; Yes; 1/4; 1/8; 3/16; Yes
7967; Young, Lloyd Wayne; 1930-2-14; Yes; M; Yes; 3/16; 1/4; 7/32; Yes
7951; Young, Lyle Francis; 1929-10-17; Yes; M; Yes; 1/4; 1/4; 1/4; Yes

Colhoff, Herbert Russell; 1929-12-27; Yes; M; Yes; 5/16; 3/4; [blank]; [blank]
Rios, Frances; 1930-2-6; Yes; M; Yes; White; 1/2; [blank]; [blank]
Looks Twice, Thomasine Ann; 1930-3-31; Yes; F; Yes; F; F; F; [blank]
Merrival, Delores; 1930-6-2; Yes; F; Yes; 3/8; 3/8; [blank]; [blank]
Woodley, Beverly Jean; 1930-6-4; Yes; F; Yes; White; 1/2; 1/4; Yes
          Trans from 1931
Mesteth, Aloysius; 1930-6-25; Yes; m; Yes; 3/4; F; 7/8; Yes
5192; Randall, Marie Magdaline; 1929-8-24; Yes; F; Yes; 1/2; 3/4; 5/8; Yes
          Trans from 1931
5880; Rouillard, Peter Seymour; 1929-9-12; Yes; M; Yes; 1/4; F; 5/8; Yes
          Trans from 1931
6164; Shangreau, Willie Ann; 1930-2-18; Yes; F; Yes; 1/2; ?; ?; Yes
          Trans from 1931
6826; Takes The Horse, Max; 1930-1-13; Yes; M; Yes; F; F; F; Yes
          Trans from 1931
Peck, Mary Anne; 1930-3-28; Yes; F; Yes; 1/4; 3/16; 7/32; Yes
          Trans from 1931
Crane, Kenneth; 1929-12-6; Yes; M; Yes; W; 1/8; 1/16; Yes
          Trans from 1932
Crane, Neil A; 1929-12-6; Yes; M; Yes; W; 1/8; 1/16; Yes
          Trans from 1932
Fog, Henry; 1930-3-12; Yes; M; Crow Creek and Oglala Sioux; Yes; 5/8; F;
13/16; Yes   Trans from 1932
Hawkins, Rena Bertha; 1930-4-9; Yes; F; Rosebud and Oglala Sioux; Yes;
3/16; F; 29/32; Yes   Trans from 1932

61

LIVE BIRTHS

1931
(April 1, 1930 - March 31, 1931)

PINE RIDGE RESERVATION
PINE RIDGE SOUTH DAKOTA

State **South Dakota** Reservation **Pine Ridge** Agency or jurisdiction
Pine Ridge Office of Indian Affairs

Key: 1931 Census Roll Number; Surname, Given; Date of Birth (Year-Month-Day); Live Births (Yes/No); Still Births (blank unless otherwise given); Sex; Tribe (Oglala Sioux unless given otherwise); Ward (Yes/No); Degree of Blood (Father; Mother; Child); At Jurisdiction Where Enrolled (Yes/No); (If no – Where)

Births Occurring Between April 1, 1930 and March 31, 1931 to Parents Enrolled at Jurisdiction

18; Adams, Gerry Patrick; 1931-1-3; Yes; M; Yes; 3/4; 1/2; 5/8; Yes
27; Afraid Of Bear, Mamie; 1930-6-29; Yes; F; Yes; F; F; F; Yes
45; Afraid Of Hawk, Daniel; 1930-10-15; Yes; M; Yes; F; F; F; Yes
60; Allen, William Arthur; 1930-9-16; Yes; M; Yes; 7/16; W; 7/32; Yes
162; Amiotte, Irna[sic] Belle; 1930-11-4; Yes; F; Yes; 1/4; 1/2; 3/8; Yes
195; Apple, Clara; 1930-6-2; Yes; F; Yes; 3/4; 3/4; 3/4; Yes
227; Babby, Lois Jean; 1930-11-28; Yes; F; Yes; 1/16; W; 1/32; Yes
----; Bad Cob, Ollie; 1930-10-13; Yes; F; Yes; F; F; F; Yes
299; Bad Wound, Evelyn May; 1930-11-14; Yes; F; Yes; 3/4; 3/8; 9/16; Yes
290; Bad Wound, Leroy Ellis; 1930-6-21; Yes; M; Yes; F; F; F; Yes
314; Bald Eagle, Max, Jr; 1930-10-9; Yes; M; Yes; F; 3/4; 7/8; Yes
348; Bayliss, Betty Joan; 1930-10-3; Yes; F; Yes; W; 3/16; 3/32; Yes
356; Beard, Elizabeth Jean; 1931-3-9; Yes; F; Yes; F; F; F; Yes
7895; Bear Robe, Aloysius Denver; 1930-4-8; Yes; M; Yes; F; F; F; Yes
397; Bear Robe, Wallace; 1930-6-30; Yes; M; Yes; F; F; F; Yes
412; Bear Saves Life, Johnson; 1930-10-3; Yes; M; Yes; F; F; F; Yes
420; Bear Shield, Hazel; 1930-10-7; Yes; F; Yes; F; F; F; Yes
468; Bettelyoun, Norval Stewart; 1930-7-17; yes; M; Yes; 5/16; W; 5/32; Yes
506; Bettelyoun, Vance Vergil; 1930-6-9; Yes; M; Sioux & Menominee; Yes; 1/2; 5/8; 9/16; Yes
515; Between Lodges, Marie Agatha; 1930-5-8; Yes; F; Yes; F; F; F; Yes
525; Big Boy, Dora; 1930-9-21; Yes; F; Yes; 1/2; 1/4; 5/8; Yes
563; Bird, Darwin Eugene; 1930-5-24; Yes; M; Yes; W; 3/8; 3/16; Yes
----; Bird, Edward H; 1931-1-13; Yes; M; Yes; F; 3/4; 7/8; Yes
660; Black Bear, Iona Myrtle; 1931-2-9; Yes; F; Yes; 15/16; F; 31/32; Yes
710; Black Crow, Milo; 1930-4-24; Yes; M; Yes; F; F; F; Yes
721; Black Elk, Dolores Grace; 1930-7-14; Yes; F; Yes; F; 1/2; 3/4; Yes
758; Black Feather, Francis Baptiste; 1930-5-25; Yes; M; Yes; 3/4; 3/4; 3/4; Yes
804; Blue Bird, Beatrice Mae; 1930-12-27; Yes; F; Yes; F; 7/16; 23/32; Yes
744; Black Feather, Jessie Virginia; 1931-3-11; Yes; F; Yes; 5/8; F; 13/16; Yes
829; Blue Legs, Gladys; 1930-8-14; Yes; F; Yes; F; F; F; Yes
875; Brafford, Merle Lincoln; 1930-6-8; Yes; M; Yes; 1/4; 1/2; 3/8; Yes
931; Breast, Louise; 1930-11-1; Yes; F; Yes; F; 1/2; 3/4; Yes
963; Brings Him Back, Rose Mary; 1930-8-4; Yes; F; Yes; F; F; F; Yes
970; Brings Plenty, Vincent Ansol; 1930-8-13; Yes; M; Yes; 3/4; F; 7/8; Yes
979; Brings Yellow, John Charles; 1930-7-31; Yes; M; Yes; F; F; F; Yes
1007; Broken Rope, Esther Louise; 1931-1-22; Yes; F; Yes; F; 5/8; 13/16; Yes
1001; Broken Rope, Lucy; 1930-10-15; Yes; F; Yes; F; F; F; Yes
1026; Brown, Charlotte Mary; 1930-4-10; Yes; F; Yes; 3/16; 1/4; 7/32; Yes (twins)
1025; " Shirley Alice; " " " Yes; F; Yes; " " " "
1019; Brown, Louie Harrington; 1931-3-8; Yes; M; Yes; F; F; F; Yes
----; Brown, Theodore Edward; 1930-12-29; Yes; M; Yes; F; 1/4; 5/8; Yes
1080; Brown Ear Horse, Theresa; 1931-3-19; Yes; F; Yes; F; F; F; Yes

65

State **South Dakota** Reservation **Pine Ridge** Agency or jurisdiction **Pine Ridge** Office of Indian Affairs

Key: 1931 Census Roll Number; Surname, Given; Date of Birth (Year-Month-Day); Live Births (Yes/No); Still Births (blank unless otherwise given); Sex; Tribe (Oglala Sioux unless given otherwise); Ward (Yes/No); Degree of Blood (Father; Mother; Child); At Jurisdiction Where Enrolled (Yes/No); (If no – Where)

Births Occurring Between April 1, 1930 and March 31, 1931 to Parents Enrolled at Jurisdiction

1145; Bull Bear, Elsie Madeline; 1930-9-2; Yes; F; Yes; F; W; 1/2; Yes

1172; Bullman, Silver; 1930-5-14; Yes; M; Yes; F; F; F; Yes

1205; Bush, Lois Jean; 1930-11-17; Yes; F; Yes; W; 1/4; 1/8; No; Rapid City, S.D.

1203; Bush, Percy; 1930-4-19; Yes; M; Yes; 3/4; 3/4; 3/4; Yes

1224; Carlow, Theodore Charles; 1930-4-15; Yes; M; Yes; 1/4; 1/2; 3/8; Yes

1244; Catches, Caroline; 1930-12-27; Yes; F; Yes; F; F; F; Yes

1285; Charging Crow, Everett Isaac; 1930-12-11; Yes; M; Yes; F; F; F; Yes

----; Chase In Winter, Madeline; 1930-4-8; Yes; F; Yes; F; F; F; Yes (twins)

----; " " " Mary; " " " Yes; F; Yes; F; F; F; Yes

1348; Chief, William; 1930-7-11; Yes; M; Yes; 3/4; 1/2; 5/8; Yes

1338; Chief, Yakima; 1930-6-25; Yes; M; Yes; F; F; F; Yes

----; Chips, Inez Elaine; 1930-7-31; Yes; F; Yes; F; F; F; Yes

1373; Chips, Leona; 1930-11-20; Yes; F; Yes; F; F; F; Yes

1499; Colhoff, Luella Rose; 1930-8-20; Yes; F; Yes; 1/2; 1/2; 1/2; Yes

----; Comes From Among Them, Rose Marie; 1930-6-30; Yes; F; Yes; 15/16; F; 31/32; Yes

----; Comes Last, Lorraine; 1930-6-6; Yes; F; Yes; F; F; F; Yes

1576; Conroy, Deloris Adele; 1930-7-17; Yes; F; Yes; 1/2; 1/2; 1/2; Yes

1790; Cottier, Sadie Louise; 1930-6-3; Yes; F; Yes; 1/2; 9/16; 17/32; Yes

1738; Crow, Peter; 1931-3-31; Yes; M; Yes; F; F; F; Yes

1755; Cuny, Loretta; 1930-10-3; Yes; F; Yes; 3/8; 1/4; 5/16; Yes

1801; Cuny, Pansy; 1930-7-16; Yes; F; Yes; 3/8; 1/2; 7/16; Yes

1766; Cuny, William Joseph; 1931-3-5; Yes; M; Yes; 3/8; W; 3/16; Yes

1822; Cut, Julia Edith; 1931-1-14; Yes; F; Yes; F; F; F; Yes

----; Cut Grass, Stella; 1930-4-30; Yes; F; Yes; F; F; F; Yes

1883; DeSheuquette, Gerald Evans 1930-6-24; Yes; M; Yes; 1/4; 5/8; 7/16; Yes

1947; Dreaming Bear, Victor; 1931-2-4; Yes; M; Yes; F; F; F; Yes;

1973; Dubray, Ora Jenny; 1930-11-27; Yes; F; Yes; 1/2; 13/16; 21/32; Yes

1995; Eagle Bear, Cornelius; 1930-6-18; Yes; M; Yes; F; F; F; Yes

2009; Eagle Bull, William Jr; 1931-2-4; Yes; M; Yes; F; F; F; Yes

----; Eagle Elk, Gus; 1930-4-24; Yes; M; Yes; F; F; F; Yes (twins)

2021; " " Guy; " " " Yes; M; Yes; F; F; F; Yes

2016; Eagle Elk, Morris Emerson; 1930-6-19; Yes; M; Yes; F; F; F; Yes

----; Eagle Heart, (Unnamed); 1930-6-10; Yes; F; Yes; F; 7/8; 15/16; Yes

2073; Ecoffey, Kenneth Albert; 1930-9-4; Yes; M; Yes; 9/16; 1/4; 13/32; Yes

2113; Fast, Gabriel; 1930-6-17; Yes; M; Yes; F; F; F; Yes

2162; Featherman, Gladys; 1931-1-14; Yes; F; Yes; F; F; F; Yes

2198; Fights Bear, Jonas; 1930-7-24; Yes; M; Yes; F; F; F; Yes

2201; Fights Over, Matthew; 1930-11-16; Yes; M; Yes; F; F; F; Yes

2244; Fire Thunder, Chris Evan; 1930-11-25; Yes; M; Yes; 3/4; 3/4; 3/4; Yes

----; Frazier, Harriet Arlene; 1930-12-30; Yes; F; Yes; 1/2; F; 3/4; Yes

2328; Frazier, Jewel Sunbeam; 1930-10-7; Yes; F; Yes; 3/4; 5/8; 11/16; Yes

2348; Frog, Victoria; 1930-7-22; Yes; F; Yes; F; F; F; Yes

State **South Dakota** Reservation **Pine Ridge** Agency or jurisdiction
Pine Ridge Office of Indian Affairs

Key: 1931 Census Roll Number; Surname, Given; Date of Birth (Year-Month-Day); Live Births (Yes/No); Still Births (blank unless otherwise given); Sex; Tribe (Oglala Sioux unless given otherwise); Ward (Yes/No); Degree of Blood (Father; Mother; Child); At Jurisdiction Where Enrolled (Yes/No); (If no – Where)

Births Occurring Between April 1, 1930 and March 31, 1931 to Parents Enrolled at Jurisdiction

2391; Garnier, Effie; 1930-4-26; Yes; F; Yes; 1/2; F; 3/4; Yes
2432; Ghost, Malvin Pedro; 1930-6-19; Yes; M; Yes; F; F; F; Yes
2438; Ghost Bear, Rudy; 1930-7-1; Yes; M; Yes; F; F; F; Yes
2475; Gibbons, Orville Kenneth; 1930-8-20; Yes; M; Yes; 1/2; F; 3/4; Yes
2496; Gillispie, Jennie May; 1930-12-31; Yes; F; Yes; 1/2; 3/4; 5/8; Yes
2510; Glenn, Donald Leonard; 1931-3-16; Yes; M; Yes; 1/2; 3/4; 5/8; Yes
2514; Glenn, Flora; 1931-3-28; Yes; F; Yes; 1/2; 7/8; 11/16; Yes
2526; Goes In Center, Amos; 1931-2-27; Yes; M; Yes; F; F; F; Yes
2529; Goes In Center, Ethel Angeline; 1930-6-16; Yes; F; Yes; F; 1/2; 3/4; Yes
2592; Good Medicine, Lena; 1930-8-27; Yes; F; Yes; 7/8; F; 15/16; Yes
----; Good Shield, Moses; 1930-3-28; Yes; M; Yes; F; F; F; Yes
2653; Grabbing Bear, Emily; 1931-1-14; Yes; F; Yes; F; 3/4; 7/8; Yes
2693; Gray Grass, Kenneth; 1930-9-18; Yes; M; Yes; F; F; F; Yes
2705; Gresh, John Orlando; 1930-7-18; Yes; M; Yes; 1/4; 1/4; 1/4; Yes
2719; Ground Spider, Mary Elizabeth; 1930-9-25; Yes; F; Yes; F; F; F; Yes
2799; Hand, Yvonne; 1930-6-21; Yes; F; Yes; F; F; F; Yes
2759; Has No Horses, Ramona; 1930-10-20; Yes; F; Yes; F; F; F; Yes
2805; Hawkins, Benedict; 1930-7-22; Yes; M; Yes; 5/8; 1/4; 9/16; Yes
2831; He Crow, Francis; 1930-7-15; Yes; M; Yes; F; F; F; Yes
2880; Her Many Horses, Louie; 1930-10-2; Yes; M; Yes; F; 1/2; 3/4; Yes
2937; High Wolf, Leonard Earl; 1930-5-28; Yes; M; Yes; F; 3/8; 11/16; Yes
2953; Hill, Venus Bernice; 1931-1-14; Yes; F; Yes; W; 3/8; 3/16; Yes
2968; Hodgkinson, Rae Lucille; 1931-2-2; Yes; F; Yes; W; 5/16; 5/32; No;
       San Francisco
3024; Holy Rock, Morris Gilbert; 1930-5-19; Yes; M; Yes; 3/4; 5/8; 11/16; Yes
3046; Horse, Nancy; 1931-3-3; Yes; F; Yes; F; F; F; Yes
3052; Horse, Tex; 1930-7-5; Yes; M; Yes; F; F; F; Yes
3097; Hunter, Babe; 1931-3-19; Yes; M; Yes; 1/2; 1/2; 1/2; Yes
3110; Ice, Ellen; 1930-9-10; Yes; F; Yes; F; F; F; Yes
3149; Iron Cloud, Alice Grace; 1930-12-30; Yes; F; Yes; F; F; F; Yes
3138; Iron Cloud, Corbett; 1930-12-27; Yes; M; Yes; F; 1/2; 3/4; Yes
3200; Iron Rope, Eugene; 1931-3-5; Yes; M; Yes; F; F; F; Yes
----; Janis, Daniel; 1930-5-14; Yes; M; Yes; 1/2; F; 3/4; Yes
3354; Janis, Intha Pauline; 1930-4-9; Yes; F; Yes; 1/2; F; 3/4; Yes
3319; Janis, John; 1931-3-15; Yes; M; Yes; 1/2; 5/8; 9/16; Yes
3323; Janis, John Gilbert; 1931-1-31; Yes; M; Yes; 1/2; 3/8; 5/16; Yes
3267; Janis, Kenneth; 1931-1-7; Yes; M; Yes; 1/2; F; 3/4; Yes
3336; Janis, Lillian; 1931-1-2; Yes; F; Yes; 1/2; 1/2; 1/2; Yes
3290; Janis, Vienna Rose; 1930-8-9; Yes; F; Yes; 3/4; F; 13/16; Yes
3379; Jealous Of Him, Oscar Jr; 1931-1-27; Yes; M; Yes; F; F; F; Yes
3414; Jones, Grace Mary; 1930-10-17; Yes; F; Yes; 5/16; 1/2; 13/16; Yes
----; Kicking Bear, Angeline Lema; 1930-8-10; Yes; F; Yes; F; F; F; Yes
----; Kills Back, Andrew Vernie; 1930-5-24; Yes; M; Yes; F; F; F; Yes

State **South Dakota** Reservation **Pine Ridge** Agency or jurisdiction
Pine Ridge Office of Indian Affairs

Key: 1931 Census Roll Number; Surname, Given; Date of Birth (Year-Month-Day); Live Births (Yes/No); Still Births (blank unless otherwise given); Sex; Tribe (Oglala Sioux unless given otherwise); Ward (Yes/No); Degree of Blood (Father; Mother; Child); At Jurisdiction Where Enrolled (Yes/No); (If no – Where)

Births Occurring Between April 1, 1930 and March 31, 1931 to Parents Enrolled at Jurisdiction

7498; Kills Bad, Ranson Martin; 1930-12-5; Yes; M; Yes; F; F; F; Yes

3545; Kills Right, Ivan Simon; 1930-9-7; Yes; M; Yes; F; F; F; Yes

3646; Ladeaux, Winfred; 1930-7-15; Yes; M; Yes; 7/8; F; 15/16; Yes

3641; Ladeaux, Zona Lillie; 1930-4-10; Yes; F; Yes; 7/8; F; 15/16; Yes

---- Lakota, Walter, Jr; 1930-4-17; Yes; M; Yes; F; 7/8; 15/16; Yes

3669; Lame, Flora; 1930-10-25; Yes; F; Yes; F; F; F; Yes

3678; Lame Dog, Elmer; 1930-12-14; Yes; M; Yes; F; F; F; Yes

3704; Lamont, Alice; 1930-5-8; Yes; F; Yes; 1/2; F; 3/4; Yes

3733; LaPoint, Jacqueline Erna; 1930-10-6; Yes; F; Yes; 9/16; 3/8; 15/32; Yes

3723; LaPoint, Zeralda; 1930-9-20; Yes; F; Yes; 7/8; 3/4; 13/16; Yes

---- Lays Hard, Everett; 1930-6-10; Yes; M; Yes; F; F; F; Yes

---- Lee, Doris Marie; 1930-9-17; Yes; F; Yes; 1/2; 1/4; 3/8; Yes

3799; Lee, Yvonne Jean; 1931-3-8; Yes; F; Yes; 1/2; 3/8; 7/16; Yes

3861; Lewis, Regina Gwendolyn; 1931-2-17; Yes; F; Yes; 1/8; 1/4; 5/16; Yes

3903; Little Bear, Charles; 1930-6-3; Yes; M; Yes; 5/8; 1/2; 9/16; Yes

3931; Little Cloud, Ambrose; 1930-14-10; Yes; M; Yes; F; F; F; Yes

3954; Little Dog, Peter; 1930-4-27; Yes; M; Yes; F; F; F; Yes

3967; Little Finger, Lathel Grace; 1931-2-24; Yes; F; Yes; F; F; F; Yes

3974; Little Hawk, Muriel Stanley; 1930-12-19; Yes; M; Yes; F; 1/2; 3/4; Yes

4046; Little Thunder, Stephen; 1930-12-17; Yes; M; Yes; F; F; F; Yes

4062; Little White Man, Willard; 1930-4-8; Yes; M; Yes; F; 1/2; 3/4; Yes

---- Locke, Fay Elwood; 1930-4-9; Yes; M; Yes; F; F; F; Yes

4169; Lone Hill, Malcolm; 1930-6-12; Yes; M; Yes; 3/4; F; 7/8; Yes

4186; Lone Wolf, Dorothy Susie; 1931-1-30; Yes; F; Yes; F; 7/8; 15/16; Yes

4196; Lone Wolf, Wilbert; 1930-9-19; Yes; M; Yes; F; F; F; Yes

4227; Long Soldier, Albert; 1930-7-11; Yes; M; Yes; F; 3/4; 7/8; Yes

4233; Long Soldier, Audrey May; 1930-6-16; Yes; F; Yes; F; 3/4; 7/8; Yes

4248; Long Woman, Josephine; 1930-4-30; Yes; F; Yes; F; F; F; Yes

4280; Lovelady, George Thomas; 1930-9-10; Yes; M; Yes; W; 1/8; 1/16; Yes

4287; Makes Enemy, Thomas; 1930-12-12; Yes; M; Yes; F; F; F; Yes

4323; Marrow Bone, Rufus Jerome; 1930-9-29; Yes; M; Yes; F; F; F; Yes

7347; Marshall, Hazel Louise; 1931-3-1; Yes; f; Yes; 3/4; F; 7/8; Yes

4369; Martinez, Martin Leo; 1930-7-11; Yes; M; Yes; 1/2; 3/4; 5/8; Yes

4399; Means, Austin Eugene; 1930-7-20; Yes; M; Yes; 5/16; F; 21/32; No; Rosebush, Mich.

4433; Merdanian, Roy E Jr; 1930-5-10; Yes; M; Yes; W; 3/8; 3/16; No; Smithwick, SD

4443; Merrival, Delores; 1930-6-2; Yes; F; Yes; 3/8; 3/8; 3/8; Yes

1324; Mesteth, Aloysius; 1930-6-26; Yes; M; Yes; 3/4; F; 7/8; Yes

4461; Mesteth, Madeline; 1930-10-20; Yes; F; Yes; 3/4; F; 7/8; Yes

4488; Mesteth, Alonzo; 1930-9-1; Yes; M; Yes; 5/8; F; 13/16; Yes

---- Mexican, Ramona May; 1930-8-10; Yes; F; Yes; F; F; F; Yes

4523; Mills, Glessnor Marie; 1930-5-21; Yes; F; Yes; 5/8; 5/32; 25/64; Yes

State **South Dakota** Reservation **Pine Ridge** Agency or jurisdiction
Pine Ridge Office of Indian Affairs

Key: 1931 Census Roll Number; Surname, Given; Date of Birth (Year-Month-Day); Live Births (Yes/No);
Still Births (blank unless otherwise given); Sex; Tribe (Oglala Sioux unless given otherwise); Ward (Yes/No);
Degree of Blood (Father; Mother; Child); At Jurisdiction Where Enrolled (Yes/No); (If no – Where)

Births Occurring Between April 1, 1930 and March 31, 1931 to Parents Enrolled at Jurisdiction

4567; Monroe, Mark Wayne; 1930-10-5; Yes; M; Yes; 1/2; 1/2; 1/2; Yes
4587; Moore, Oliver D; 1930-7-25; Yes; M; Yes; 3/8; 7/16; 13/32; Yes
4639; Mountain, Joseph Ralph; 1930-9-18; Yes; M; Yes; F; 1/2; 3/4; Yes
4668; Mousseau, Mathiss; 1930-2-24; Yes; M; Yes; 5/8; F; 13/16; Yes
4731; Nelson, Daniel Jr; 1930-6-10; Yes; M; Yes; 5/8; F; 13/16; Yes
4722; Nelson, Florine; 1931-1-16; Yes; F; Yes; 5/8; F; 13/16; Yes
---- No Belt, (Unnamed); 1930-4-11; Yes; M; Yes; F; F; F; Yes
4782; No Neck, Ellen; 1931-2-11; Yes; F; Yes; F; 3/4; 7/8; Yes
4777; No Neck, John; 1930-6-11; Yes; M; Yes; F; 7/8; 15/16; Yes
4804; Old Horse, Theodore; 1930-8-28; Yes; M; yes; F; 3/4; 7/8; Yes
4851; O'Rourke, Robert Louis; 1930-12-29; Yes; M; Yes; 1/4; 1/2; 3/8; Yes
4891; Palmer, Hope Letoi; 1931-1-10; Yes; F; Yes; W; 1/4; 1/8; Yes
4917; Parkhurst, Manuel Louis; 1930-6-6; Yes; M; Yes; 1/4; 1/2; 3/8; Yes
4930; Patton, Chauncey; 1930-8-13; Yes; M; Yes; 1/4; F; 5/8; Yes
4946; Pawnee Leggins, Philip; 1930-10-9; Yes; M; Yes; F; F; F; Yes
4998; Plenty Holes, Christine; 1930-4-11; Yes; F; Yes; F; 3/8; 11/16; Yes
5025; Plenty Wounds, Moses; 1930-8-3; Yes; M; Yes; F; F; F; Yes
5016; Plenty Wounds, Raymond; 1930-6-3; Yes; M; Yes; F; F; F; Yes
---- Poor Bear, Maria; 1930-4-23; Yes; F; Yes; F; F; F; Yes (twins)
---- " " Rose; 1930-4-23; Yes; F; Yes; F; F; F; Yes
5070; Poor Thunder, Ollie Agnes; 1930-10-9; Yes; F; Yes; F; F; F; Yes
5126; Pourier, Doris Cecelia; 1930-8-21; Yes; F; Yes; 1/8; 1/2; 3/8; Yes
3035; Prairie Chicken, Zallie Eliza; 1930-10-13; Yes; F; Yes; F; F; F; Yes
5153; Pratt, Dorothy Marie; 1930-9-18; Yes; F; Sioux & Chey.; Yes; F; 5/8; 13/16;
No; Geary, Okla
5192; Pretty Voice (Crane), Mercy Julia; 1930-12-18; Yes; F; Yes; F; 3/4; 7/8; Yes
5203; Provost, Jewel; 1931-3-5; Yes; F; Yes; 7/16; 1/4; 11/32; Yes
5299; Quiver, David; 1930-5-10; Yes; M; Yes; F; F; F; Yes
5311; Quiver, Phoebe Elizabeth; 1930-8-28; Yes; F; Yes; F; 9/16; 25/32; Yes
5338; Randall, Patrick George; 1931-2-26; Yes; M; Yes; F; F; F; Yes
5333; Randall, Victoria; 1930-12-25; Yes; F; Yes; 1/2; 3/4; 5/8; Yes
5389; Red Blanket, Leslie; 1930-12-13; Yes; M; Yes; F; F; F; Yes
5413; Red Cloud, Marie; 1931-2-2; Yes; F; Yes; 7/8; 7/8; 7/8; Yes
5467; Red Elk, Aloysius; 1930-9-10; Yes; M; Yes; F; F; F; Yes
5498; Red Feather, Elizabeth; 1930-4-22; Yes; F; Yes; F; 3/4; 7/8; Yes
---- Red Shirt, Ethel Lena; 1930-6-13; Yes; F; Yes; F; 3/4; 7/8; Yes
5599; Red Star, Austin Philip; 1931-2-26; Yes; M; Yes; F; F; F; Yes
5594; Red Star, Neville Clyde; 1931-3-13; Yes; M; Yes; F; F; F; Yes
---- Red Willow, Mary; 1930-11-12; Yes; F; Yes; F; F; F; Yes
5628; Red Wolf, Chris; 1930-12-25; Yes; M; Yes; F; F; F; Yes
5624; Red Wolf, Sophia; 1930-5-8; Yes; F; Yes; F; F; F; Yes
5633; Respects Nothing, Raymond; 1931-2-21; Yes; M; Yes; F; F; F; Yes
5753; Richardson, Ase[sic] Densmore; 1930-4-24; Yes; M; Yes; W; 3/4; 3/8; Yes

Key: 1931 Census Roll Number; Surname, Given; Date of Birth (Year-Month-Day); Live Births (Yes/No); Still Births (blank unless otherwise given); Sex; Tribe (Oglala Sioux unless given otherwise); Ward (Yes/No); Degree of Blood (Father; Mother; Child); At Jurisdiction Where Enrolled (Yes/No); (If no – Where)

Births Occurring Between April 1, 1930 and March 31, 1931 to Parents Enrolled at Jurisdiction

5742;   Richard, Florence Lucille; 1930-5-5; Yes; F; Yes; 1/4; 13/16; 17/32; Yes
5671;   Richard, Rachel; 1930-11-7; Yes; F; Yes; 3/8; 3/4; 9/16; Yes
5775;   Roan Eagle, Verna May; 1930-7-4; Yes; F; Yes; F; 1/2; 3/4; Yes
5809;   Romero, Aloysius; 1930-9-25; Yes; M; Yes; 1/4; 3/4; 1/2; Yes
5878;   Rouillard, Edith Marie; 1931-1-31; Yes; F; Yes; 1/2; 1/4; 3/8; Yes
5880;   Rouillard, Peter Seymour; 1929-9-12; Yes; M; Yes; 1/4; F; 5/8; Yes
                    Trans to 1930
5882;   Rowland, Rosa May; 1930-10-7; Yes; F; Yes; 3/4; F; 7/8; Yes
5975;   Running Shield, Louis; 1931-2-18; Yes; M; Yes; 7/8; F; 15/16; Yes
6025;   Salvis, Myrtle Grace; 1931-3-29; Yes; F; Yes; 11/16; 1/2; 19/32; Yes
6142;   Shangreau, Delores; 1930-12-27; Yes; F; Yes; 1/4; W; 1/8; Yes
6164;   Shangreau, Willie Ann; 1930-2-18; Yes; F; Oglala & Osage; Yes; 1/2; ?; ?;
             Yes   Trans to 1930
6242;   Short Horn, Edna Lucille; 1930-6-5; Yes; F; Yes; F; 3/4; 7/8; Yes
6300;   Siers, Albert Henry; 1930-4-4; Yes; M; Yes; 5/8; 1/2; 9/16; Yes
6307;   Siers, Fannie; 1930-5-31; Yes; F; Yes; 5/8; 3/4; 11/16; Yes
6347;   Sitting Up, Ellen Louise; 1930-9-25; Yes; F; Yes; F; 7/16; 23/32; Yes
----   Six Feathers, Phoebe May; 1930-5-31; Yes; F; Yes; 7/8; 9/16; 21/32; Yes
6380;   Sleeps, Mary Sarah; 1930-6-5; Yes; F; Yes; F; F; F; Yes
6366;   Skalander, Margaret Katherine; 1930-8-1; Yes; F; Yes; 1/8; 5/16; 7/32; Yes
3782;   Skinner, Nellie Jule; 1930-11-3; Yes; F; Yes; W; 3/4; 3/8; Yes
6393;   Slow Bear, Roland; 1930-5-29; Yes; M; Yes; F; F; F; Yes
6456;   Speck, Eva Mary; 1930-4-14; Yes; F; Yes; W; 3/8; 3/16; Yes
6468;   Spider, Melvin; 1930-5-30; Yes; M; Yes; F; F; F; Yes
7954;   Spotted Bear, Homer Francis; 1930-10-13; Yes; M; Yes; 7/8; F; 15/16; Yes
6505;   Spotted Eagle, Agnes Ellen; 1930-6-20; Yes; F; Yes; F; 7/8; 15/16; Yes
6495;   Spotted Eagle, Lorene; 1930-12-22; Yes; F; Yes; F; F; F; Yes
4089;   Standing Bear, Mamie Fern; 1930-4-19; Yes; F; Yes; 3/4; 1/2; 5/8; Yes
                    (Adopted by Livermont)
6569;   Standing Buffalo, Purcell; 1931-1-25; Yes; M; Yes; F; F; F; Yes
6597;   Standing Soldier, Robert; 1930-10-6; Yes; M; Yes; 7/8; 3/4; 13/16; Yes
6621;   Stands, Vivian; 1930-11-1; Yes; F; Yes; F; F; F; Yes
6640;   Star Yellow Wood, Thelma Sue; 1930-6-15; Yes; F; Yes; 1/2; 3/4; 5/8; Yes
6747;   Swallow, Charles W; 1930-6-30; Yes; M; Yes; 3/8; 1/2; 7/16; Yes
6233;   Short Bull, Eastman; 1930-4-20; Yes; M; Yes; F; F; F; Yes
6820;   Tail, Lula Pauline; 1931-1-21; Yes; F; Yes; F; F; F; Yes
----   Tail, Richard Floyd; 1930-8-17; Yes; M; Yes; F; F; F; Yes
6826;   Takes The Horses, Max; 1930-1-13; Yes; M; Yes; F; F; F; Yes
                    Trans to 1930
6866;   Ten Fingers, Evelyn; 1930-6-1; Yes; F; Yes; F; F; F; Yes
6891;   Terkildsen, Raymond Lowes; 1930-12-27; Yes; M; Yes; W; 3/8; 3/16; Yes
6947;   Thunder Horse, Walter; 1930-6-15; Yes; M; Yes; Yes F; F; F; Yes
6970;   Tibbets, Sylvester Edward; 1931-3-25; Yes; M; Yes; 1/4; 1/8; 3/16; Yes

Key: 1931 Census Roll Number; Surname, Given; Date of Birth (Year-Month-Day); Live Births (Yes/No);
Still Births (blank unless otherwise given); Sex; Tribe (Oglala Sioux unless given otherwise); Ward (Yes/No);
Degree of Blood (Father; Mother; Child); At Jurisdiction Where Enrolled (Yes/No); (If no – Where)

Births Occurring Between April 1, 1930 and March 31, 1931 to Parents Enrolled at Jurisdiction

7007; Trimble, Lyel[sic] Louis; 1931-3-8; Yes; M; Yes; 1/4; 1/4; 1/4; Yes
7003; Trimble, Nelson David; 1930-5-18; Yes; M; Yes; W; 3/4; 3/8; Yes
7035; Turning Hawk, Zoey; 1930-8-24; Yes; F; Yes; F; F; F; Yes
---- Turning Holy, Kenneth; 1931-2-17; Yes; M; Yes; F; F; F; Yes
7052; Tuttle, Florence Lorene; 1930-7-5; Yes; F; Yes; F; 3/4; 7/8; Yes
7130; Two Bulls, Norene Ann; 1930-7-17; Yes; F; Yes; 7/8; F; 15/16; Yes
7164; Two Crow, Asay Marvin; 1930-7-9; Yes; M; Yes; 3/4; F; 7/8; Yes
4509; Two Elk, Collins; 1930-5-14; Yes; M; Yes; F; F; F; Yes
7181; Two Elk, Twellie[sic] Delores; 1930-7-17; Yes; F; Yes; F; F; F; Yes
7202; Two Lance, Vincent; 1931-1-31; Yes; M; Yes; F; 7/8; 15/16; Yes
7232; Tyndall, Verene Elizabeth; 1930-7-6; Yes; F; Yes; 3/4; W; 3/8; Yes
7258; Understanding Crow, Dorthia Visla; 1931-1-30; Yes; F; Yes; F; F; F; Yes
7267; Usher, Dorothy Yvonne; 1930-7-25; Yes; F; Yes; W; 1/2; 1/4; Yes
7308; Vocu, Melvin Roy; 1931-3-31; Yes; M; Yes; W; 1/4; 1/8; Yes
7318; Walking Bull, Junior Gilbert; 1930-6-19; Yes; M; Yes; F; F; F; Yes
---- Walks Under Ground, Douglas; 1931-1-4; Yes; M; Yes; F; F; F; Yes
7333; Walks Out, Hermus; 1930-11-3; Yes; M; Yes; F; F; F; Yes
7357; Ward, William Ward; 1930-7-12; Yes; M; Yes; 5/16; W; 5/32; Yes
7356; War Bonnet, Philip; 1931-1-27; Yes; M; Yes; F; F; F; Yes
7372; Warrior, Wilbur; 1930-4-15; Yes; M; Yes; F; F; F; Yes
7382; Water, Leroy Neville; 1930-5-1; Yes; M; Yes; 3/4; F; 7/8; Yes
7391; Water, Rebecca Elizabeth; 1930-5-17; Yes; F; Yes; 3/4; F; 7/8; Yes
7403; Weasel, Orla; 1931-2-15; Yes; F; Yes; F; F; F; Yes
7401; Weasel, Van; 1930-5-23; Yes; M; Yes; F; F; F; Yes
7434; Weber, Wilda Elizabeth; 1930-12-1; Yes; F; Yes; 1/8; W; 1/16; Yes
7455; Weston, Belle Lois; 1930-6-25; Yes; F; Yes; F; 3/4; 7/8; Yes
7459; Weston, Ruby Martha; 1931-2-20; Yes; F; Yes; F; F; F; Yes
7490; Whirlwind Horse, Thelma; 1931-3-31; Yes; F; Yes; F; 1/8; 9/16; Yes
7480; Whirlwind Horse, Verda; 1930-4-29; Yes; F; Yes; F; 3/4; 7/8; Yes
7509; White, Marie Elizabeth; 1930-10-24; Yes; F; Yes; 1/2; 5/16; 21/32; Yes
7566; White Calf, Lindy Laroix; 1931-1-30; Yes; M; Yes; F; 7/8; 15/16; Yes
---- White Calf, Margaret; 1930-10-7; Yes; F; Yes; F; F; F; Yes
7599; White Dress, Edward; 1931-3-25; Yes; M; Yes; F; F; F; Yes
7618; White Eyes, Claudia Fredline; 1930-5-16; Yes; F; Yes; F; F; F; Yes
7649; White Face, Hannah Berdena; 1930-11-2; Yes; F; Yes; F; F; F; Yes
7635; White Face, Susan Ellen; 1930-7-7; Yes; F; Yes; F; F; F; Yes
---- White Face, Victoria; 1930-7-25; Yes; F; Yes; F; F; F; Yes
7659; White Hawk, Rosalyn Agatha; 1930-4-18; Yes; F; Yes; 3/4; F; 7/8; Yes
---- White Wash, Ramona; 1931-2-21; Yes; F; Yes; F; F; F; Yes
7728; White Wolf, Louis; 1930-11-13; Yes; M; Yes; F; F; F; Yes
7745; Wilcox, Curtis Jerome; 1930-7-21; Yes; M; Yes; W; 13/32; 13/64; Yes
7756; Williams, Helen Jewel; 1930-4-22; Yes; F; Yes; 5/16; W; 5/32; Yes
7787; Wilson, Nadine Joy; 1930-5-28; Yes; F; Yes; 1/8; W; 1/16; Yes

71

Key: 1931 Census Roll Number; Surname, Given; Date of Birth (Year-Month-Day); Live Births (Yes/No); Still Births (blank unless otherwise given); Sex; Tribe (Oglala Sioux unless given otherwise); Ward (Yes/No); Degree of Blood (Father; Mother; Child); At Jurisdiction Where Enrolled (Yes/No); (If no – Where)

Births Occurring Between April 1, 1930 and March 31, 1931 to Parents Enrolled at Jurisdiction

7805; Witt, Delane; 1931-1-14; Yes; Yes M; Yes; 1/4; F; 5/8; Yes
7803; Witt, Milfred; 1930-6-13; Yes; M; Yes; 1/4; F; 5/8; Yes
2398; Witt, Wilbur Floyd; 1931-2-2; Yes; M; Yes; 1/3; 3/4; 1/2; Yes
7826; Woman Dress, Joseph; 1931-3-13; Yes; M; Yes; F; F; F; Yes
      Woodley, Beverly Jean; 1930-6-4; Yes; F; Yes; White; 4/4; [blank]; [blank]
7846; Wounded, Amy; 1930-10-3; Yes; F; Yes; F; F; F; Yes
7849; Wounded Arrows, Cecelia Jane; 1930-6-17; Yes; F; Yes; F; 5/8; 9/16; Yes
7924; Yellow Bird, Beulah; 1930-6-3; Yes; F; Yes; 3/4; 1/2; 5/8; Yes
7961; Yellow Bull, Isaac; 1831-1-26; Yes; M; Yes; F; F; F; Yes

      Tokio, Martha; 1931-1-4; Yes; Fem; Yes; 1/2; Mex; [blank]; [blank]
      Allman, Verna May; 1931-1-6; Yes; Fem; Yes; 1/4; 3/4; [blank]; [blank]
      Buckingham, Wm Darrell; 1930-9-29; Yes; M; Yes; white; 3/16; 3/32; Yes
               Trans from 1932
      Cottier, W^m Jr; 1931-3-30; Yes; M; Yes; white; 1/8; 1/16; Yes
               Trans from 1932
      DeWolf, Alice Marie; 1931-3-2; Yes; F; Yes; W; 1/4; 1/8; Yes
               Trans from 1932
      DeWolf, Frances Eva; 1931-3-2; Yes; F; Yes; W; 1/4; 1/8; Yes
               Trans from 1932
      Dixon, Fred Edw.; 1930-5-28; Yes; M; Yes; 1/4; 5/8; 7/16; Yes
               Trans from 1932
      Iron Bear, Madeline; 1931-3-30; Yes; F; Yes; F; 7/8; 15/16; Yes
               Trans from 1932
      Janis, Mildred Grace; 1931-2-1; Yes; Yes F; Yes; ?; 7/8; ?; Yes
               Trans from 1932
      Hawkins, Rena Bertha; 1930-4-9; Yes; F; Rosebud and Oglala Sioux; Yes;
      3/16; F; 29/32; Yes;   Trans from 1932

LIVE BIRTHS

1932
(April 1, 1931 - March 31, 1932)

PINE RIDGE RESERVATION
PINE RIDGE SOUTH DAKOTA

Key: Surname, Given; Date of Birth (Year-Month-Day); Live Births (Yes/No); Still Births (blank unless otherwise given); Sex; Tribe (Oglala Sioux unless given otherwise); Ward (Yes/No); Degree of Blood (Father; Mother; Child); At Jurisdiction Where Enrolled (Yes/No); (If no – Where)

Births Occurring Between April 1, 1931 and March 31, 1932 to Parents Enrolled at Jurisdiction

Addison, Esther Veronica; 1931-6-13; Yes; F; Arapahoe and Oglala Sioux; Yes; F; F; F; Yes

Afraid of Bear, Isaac; 1932-1-23; Yes; M; Sioux; Yes; F; F; F; Yes

Afraid of Hawk, Eldred; 1931-5-2; Yes; M; Yes; F; F; F; Yes

American Horse, David; 1931-7-3; Yes; M; Sioux; Yes; F; F; F; Yes

Amiotte, Hazel; 1931-11-26; Yes; F; Rosebud and Oglala Sioux; Yes; 3/8; F; 11/16; Yes

Amiotte, Wallace Emery; 1931-4-17; Yes; M; Yes; 1/4; W; 1/8; Yes

Apple, Francis Daniel; 1931-9-26; Yes; M; Yes; 3/4; F; 7/8; Yes

Badger, Vera; 1931-6-20; Yes; F; Yes; Yes 3/4; 3/4; 3/4; Yes

Bad Wound, Wesley; 1931-12-11; Yes; M; Yes; F; 1/2; 3/4; Yes

Bald Eagle Bear, Evangeline R; 1931-9-6; Yes; F; Yes; F; F; F; Yes

Bear Eagle, Laura; 1931-8-4; Yes; F; Yankton and Oglala Sioux; Yes; F; F; F; Yes

Bear Nose, Alvina; 1931-7-14; Yes; F; Yes; F; F; F; Yes

Bear Robe, Leo Bernard; 1931-5-13; Yes; M; Yes; F; F; F; Yes

Bear Shield, Theresa; 1931-4-10; Yes; F; Yes; F; F; F; Yes

Bear Tail, (Unnamed); 1931-12-1; Yes; F; Yes; ?; F; ?; Yes

Belt, Evelyn M; 1931-5-11; Yes; F; Yes; F; 3/4; 7/8; Yes

Bergen, Robert; 1931-6-9; Yes; M; Standing Rock and Oglala Sioux; Yes; 3/8; 1/4; 5/16; Yes

Big Crow, Leatrice C; 1931-8-26; Yes; F; Yes; 1/2; 1/4; 3/8; Yes

Bird, Raymond C; 1932-2-24; Yes; M; Yes; ?; 3/4; 7/8; Yes

Bird Head, Agnes; 1931-5-13; Yes; F; Yes; F; F; F; Yes

Bissonette, Elfreda; 1931-5-10; Yes; F; Yes; 7/8; 7/8; 7/8; Yes

Bissonette, Ethel Pearl; 1932-1-2; Yes; F; Yes; 3/8; F; 11/16; Yes

Bissonette, Mattie Marie; 1931-5-23; Yes; F; Yes; 1/2; F; 3/4; Yes

Black Bear, Aloysius; 1931-12-7; Yes; M; Yes; F; F; F; Yes

Black Crow, Frances Sallie; 1931-5-17; Yes; F; Yes; F; F; F; Yes

Black Feather, Raymond; 1931-8-8; Yes; M; Yes; 3/4; 7/8; 13/16; Yes

Blacksmith, Lucille; 1930-5-9; Yes; F; Cheyenne River & Oglala Sioux; Yes; F; F; F; Yes

Blind Man, Alfonso; 1931-8-9; Yes; M; Yes; F; F; F; Yes

Blue Bird, Florence E; 1931-4-19; Yes; F; Yes; F; 3/4; 7/8; Yes

Blue Bird, Vivian Doris; 1931-8-14; Ye; F; Yes; F; F; F; Yes

~~Bowman, Loran; 1927-11-4; Yes; M; Yes; ?; 3/16; ?; Yes~~

Brafford, Thelma; 1931-11-12; Yes; F; Yes; 1/4; 1/2; 3/8; Yes

Brave, Verne Elmer; 1931-12-19; Yes; M; Yes; F; F; F; Yes

Brave Heart, Christopher; 1932-3-5; Yes; M; Yes; F; 3/4; 7/8; Yes

Brave Heart, Lucy; 1932-1-10; Yes; F; Yes; F; F; F; Yes

Brewer, Emilene G; 1931-9-14; Yes; F; Yes; 1/4; 5/8; 7/16; Yes

Brewer, Ernest Walter; 1931-11-29; Yes; M; Yes; 1/4; 1/2; 3/8; Yes

State **South Dakota** Reservation **Pine Ridge** Agency or jurisdiction
_____**Pine Ridge**_____ Office of Indian Affairs

Key: Surname, Given; Date of Birth (Year-Month-Day); Live Births (Yes/No); Still Births (blank unless otherwise given); Sex; Tribe (Oglala Sioux unless given otherwise); Ward (Yes/No); Degree of Blood (Father; Mother; Child); At Jurisdiction Where Enrolled (Yes/No); (If no – Where)

Births Occurring Between April 1, 1931 and March 31, 1932 to Parents Enrolled at Jurisdiction

Brewer, Leona Irene; 1931-9-14; Yes; F; Yes; 1/4; 5/8; 7/16; Yes

Brings Yellow, Levi; 1931-7-21; Yes; M; Yes; F; F; F; Yes

Brings Yellow, Orva; 1931-7-21; Yes; F; Yes; F; F; F; Yes

Broken Leg, Jessie; 1931-10-2; Yes; F; Yes; F; F; F; Yes

Broken Nose, Bernard; 1932-1-11; Yes; M; Yes; F; F; F; Yes

Brown, Doloris[sic] Vivian; 1931-5-24; Yes; F; Rosebud and Oglala Sioux; Yes; ?; 3/8; ?; Yes

Brown, Imogene; 1932-1-12; Yes; F; Yes; 3/16; W; 3/32; Yes

Brown, Joyce A; 1931-4-16; Yes; F; Oneida and Oglala Sioux; Yes; 3/8; 1/2; 7/16; Yes

Brown Eyes, Virginia Mary; 1931-11-16; Yes; F; Yes; 3/4; F; 7/8; Yes

~~Buckingham, William Darrell; 1930-9-29; Yes; M; Yes; W; 3/16; 3/32; Yes~~
Trans to 1931

Bull Bear, Barbara; 1931-10-22; Yes; F; Yes; F; 7/8; 15/16; Yes

Bush, Clara; 1931-11-28; Yes; F; Yes; 3/4; F; 7/8; Yes

Bushy Top Pine, Abraham; 1931-11-27; Yes; M; Yes; F; F; F; Yes

Chase Alone, Rowland; 1931-7-28; Yes; M; Yes; F; F; F; Yes

Chase In Morning, Winifred; 1931-12-11; Yes; F; Yes; F; F; F; Yes

Chase In Winter, Alfred; 1931-7-11; Yes; M; Yes; F; F; F; Yes

Chief Eagle, Martha Wyola; 1931-10-1; Yes; F; Yes; F; F; F; Yes

Childers, Harold Clarence; 1932-1-5; Yes; M; Creek and Oglala Sioux; Yes; 7/8; 1/16; 15/32; Yes

Clement, Thomas Alfred; 1931-10-7; Yes; M; Yes; W; F; 1/2; Yes

Clifford, Esther Helen; 1931-6-3; Yes; F; Yes; 1/2; 3/16; 11/32; Yes

Clincher, George James; 1931-10-10; Yes; M; Yes; F; F; F; Yes

Coats, Eulala Eileen; 1931-7-4; Yes; F; Yes; W; 1/16; 1/32; Yes

Colhoff, Melvin John; 1931-4-8; Yes; M; Cheyenne and Oglala Sioux; Yes; 1/2; 3/4; 5/8; Yes

Colhoff, Phyllis; 1931-9-16; Yes; F; Yes; 1/2; 5/8; 9/16; Yes

Colhoff, Virgil John; 1932-3-25; Yes; M; Yes; 5/16; 3/4; 17/32; Yes

Conroy, John Orville; 1932-1-23; Yes; M; Yes; 1/2; 1/2; 1/2; Yes

Cottier, John H, Jr; 1931-5-29; Yes; M; Yes; 1/2; 1/2; 1/2; Yes

~~Cottier, William Jr; 1931-3-30; Yes; M; Yes; 1/2; 9/16; 17/32; Yes~~

Crawford, William Thos; 1931-8-3; Yes; M; Yes; W; 3/8; 3/16; Yes

Cuny, Mary Jane; 1932-1-11; Yes; F; Yes; 3/8; 1/2; 7/17[sic]; Yes

Curtis, Verna Mae; 1931-7-28; Yes; F; Yes; W; 3/8; 3/16; Yes

~~DeWolf, Alice Marie; 1931-3-2; Yes; F; Yes; W; 1/4; 1/8; Yes~~

~~" Frances Elva; 1931-3-2; Yes; F; Yes; W; 1/4; 1/8; Yes~~

Dillon, John; 1931-6-14; Yes; Rosebud and Oglala Sioux; Yes; 1/2; 1/2; 1/2; Yes

76

State **South Dakota** Reservation **Pine Ridge** Agency or jurisdiction **Pine Ridge** Office of Indian Affairs

Key: Surname, Given; Date of Birth (Year-Month-Day); Live Births (Yes/No); Still Births (blank unless otherwise given); Sex; Tribe (Oglala Sioux unless given otherwise); Ward (Yes/No); Degree of Blood (Father; Mother; Child); At Jurisdiction Where Enrolled (Yes/No); (If no – Where)

Births Occurring Between April 1, 1931 and March 31, 1932 to Parents Enrolled at Jurisdiction

Dog, Doris Lavena; 1932-1-26; Yes; F; Yes; F; F; F; Yes
Donnahue[sic], Adeline Lorrain; 1932-1-6; Yes; F; Yes; W; 9/16; 9/32; Yes
Dubray, Annie Mae; 1931-5-6; Yes; F; Yes; 1/2; 5/8; 9/16; Yes

Eagle Bear, Wilfred; 1931-12-10; Yes; M; Yes; F; F; F; Yes
Eagle Heart, John; 1931-4-5; Yes; M; Yes; F; 7/8; 15/16; Yes
"   " Joseph; 1931-4-5; Yes; M; Yes; F; 7/8; 15/16; Yes
Eisenbraun, Donald Edward; 1931-6-1; Yes; M; Yes; W; 1/8; 1/16; Yes

Fast, Joseph; 1931-4-21; Yes; M; Yes; F; F; F; Yes
Fast Wolf, James Vine; 1932-1-3; Yes; M; Yes; 7/8; 7/8; 7/8; Yes
Fast Wolf, Mary Jennie; 1931-4-17; Yes; F; Yes; 7/8; 3/4; 13/16; Yes
Fills The Pipe, Isaac Paul; 1931-8-12; Yes; M; Yes; F; 3/4; 7/8; Yes
Fire Thunder, Stephen; 1932-3-12; Yes; M; Yes; F; F; F; Yes
Flying Hawk, Madeline J; 1931-11-7; Yes; F; Yes; 15/16; F; 31/32; Yes
Fool Head, Hattie; 1932-1-12; Yes; F; Yes; F; F; F; Yes
Frog, Buster; 1931-10-2; M; Yes; F; F; F; Yes

Galligo, May Evelyn; 1931-11-11; Yes; F; Yes; 5/8; 11/16; 21/32; Yes
Garnett, Anna Elizabeth; 1931-7-3; Yes; F; Yes; 3/8; 1/4; 5/16; Yes
Garnier, Bertha; 1931-9-14; Yes; F; Yes; 1/2; F; 3/4; Yes
Garnier, John Francis; 1931-10-24; Yes; M; Yes; 1/2; 5/8; 9/16; Yes
Gay, Lavina; 1931-12-19; Yes; F; Yes; 3/4; F; 7/8; Yes
Giago, Lillian; 1931-12-19; Yes; F; Yes; 1/4; Mex; 1/4; Yes
Gibbons, Jerome Orrin; 1931-6-8; Yes; M; Yes; 1/2; 1/2; 1/2; Yes
Goings, Angelique Rose; 1932-3-7; Yes; F; Yes; 3/8; 3/4; 9/16; Yes
Good Buffalo, Minnie; 1931-6-5; Yes; F; Yes; F; F; F; Yes
Good Crow, Levi; 1931-4-30; Yes; M; Yes; F; 11/16; 27/32; Yes
Good Medicine, Velma; 1932-2-6; Yes; F; Yes; 7/8; F; 15/16; Yes
Good Shield, Grace; 1931-8-16; Yes; F; Rosebud and Oglala Sioux; Yes; F; F; F; Yes
Good Voice Elk, May; 1931-5-30; Yes; F; Yes; F; F; F; Yes
Good Voice Elk, William; 1931-9-18; Yes; M; Yes; F; F; F; Yes
Grass, Carmen; 1931-12-27; Yes; F; Yes; F; 3/4; 7/8; Yes
Green, Geraldine; 1931-9-9; Yes; F; Yes; W; 1/4; 1/8; Yes

Hamernick, Louisa; 1931-10-5; Yes; F; Yes; W; 7/16; 7/32; Yes
Hard Heart, Leona; 1932-2-23; Yes; F; Yes; F; F; F; Yes
Hawk, Michael; 1931-11-19; Yes; M; Yes; F; F; F; Yes
Hernandez, Anna May; 1931-5-21; Yes; F; Yes; 1/2; 7/8; 11/16; Yes

Key: Surname, Given; Date of Birth (Year-Month-Day); Live Births (Yes/No); Still Births (blank unless otherwise given); Sex; Tribe (Oglala Sioux unless given otherwise); Ward (Yes/No); Degree of Blood (Father; Mother; Child); At Jurisdiction Where Enrolled (Yes/No); (If no – Where)

Births Occurring Between April 1, 1931 and March 31, 1932 to Parents Enrolled at Jurisdiction

High Bull, Charles Jr; 1931-6-3; Yes; M; Rosebud and Oglala Sioux; Yes; F; F; F;
Yes
High Pine, Delbert; 1931-8-2; Yes; M; Yes; F; F; F; Yes
Hollow Horn, George; 1931-5-16; Yes; M; Yes; F; F; F; Yes
Holy Cloud, Denver; 1931-11-24; Yes; M; Yes; F; 3/4; 7/8; Yes
Holy Pipe, Jennie; 1931-8-25; Yes; F; Yes; F; F; F; Yes

~~Iron Bear, Madeline; 1931-3-30; Yes; F; Yes; F; 7/8; 15/16; Yes~~\
Trans to 1931
Iron Cloud, Martha; 1931-4-12; Yes; F; Yes; F; F; F; Yes
Iron Rope, Freda; 1931-12-8; Yes; F; Yes; F; F; F; Yes
Irving, William; 1031-7-30; Yes; M; Yes; 7/16; 7/8; 21/32; Yes

Jacobs, Caroline Rose; 1931-8-15; Yes; F; Yes; 1/4; 1/2; 3/8; Yes
Janis, Annabel; 1931-11-18; Yes; F; Yes; 3/4; F; 7/8; Yes
Janis, Aurea Faith; 1931-8-14; Yes; F; Yankton and Oglala Sioux; Yes; 3/8; 1/2; 7/16;
Yes
Janis, Donald Robert; 1931-4-2; Yes; M; Ye; 1/2; 3/8; 7/16; Yes
Janis, Godfrey Steven; 1931-12-26; Yes; M; Yes; 3/4; 7/8; 13/16; Yes
Jealous Of Him, Christina; 1931-12-25; Yes; F; Yes; 7/8; F; 15/16; Yes
Jones, Christopher C; 1931-4-15; Yes; M; Yes; F; F; F; Yes
Jumping Bull, Roselyn Louise; 1931-11-18; Yes; F; Yes; 3/4; 3/4; 3/4; Yes

Kills Back, Mowis Eugene; 1931-12-8; Yes; M; Yes; F; F; F; Yes
Kills Crow Indian, Rufus; 1931-6-11; Yes; M; Yes; F; F; F; Yes
Kills In Water, Bernard; 1931-10-20; Yes; M; Yes; F; F; F; Yes
Kills Right, Marie; 1931-4-7; Yes; F; Sisseton and Oglala Sioux; Yes; F; F; F; Yes

Ladeaux, Grace Jeannette; 1931-12-5; Yes; F; Yes; 7/8; F; 15/16; Yes
Ladeaux, Mary; 1932-3-21; Yes; F; Yes; 7/8; F; 15/16; Yes
Ladeaux, Viola Pauline; 1932-3-14; Yes; F; Yes; 7/8; F; 15/16; Yes
Lakota, Marylin[sic]; 1931-4-29; Yes; F; Yes; F; 7/8; 15/16; Yes
Lame, Matilda; 1931-12-20; Yes; F; Yes; F; F; F; Yes
Lays Bad, Pauline; 1931-7-14; Yes; F; Yes; F; F; F; Yes
Lee, Evelyn; 1932-1-31; Yes; F; Yes; 1/2; 3/8; 7/16; Yes
Left Hand, Theresa Marie; 1931-8-3; Yes; F; Yes; F; 1/4; 7/8; Yes
Little, Leroy Donald; 1931-4-27; Yes; M; Yes; 3/4; 11/16; 23/32; Yes
Little Bear, Royal Leroy; 1931-11-29; Yes; M; Yes; 5/8; 1/8; 7/16; Yes
Little Boy, Joseph Thomas; 1931-10-13; Yes; M; Yes; F; 7/8; 15/16; Yes

State **South Dakota** Reservation **Pine Ridge** Agency or jurisdiction
Pine Ridge Office of Indian Affairs

Key: Surname, Given; Date of Birth (Year-Month-Day); Live Births (Yes/No); Still Births (blank unless otherwise given); Sex; Tribe (Oglala Sioux unless given otherwise); Ward (Yes/No); Degree of Blood (Father; Mother; Child); At Jurisdiction Where Enrolled (Yes/No); (If no – Where)

Births Occurring Between April 1, 1931 and March 31, 1932 to Parents Enrolled at Jurisdiction

Little Cloud, Herbert; 1931-8-3; Yes; M; Rosebud and Oglala Sioux; Yes; F; F; F; Yes

Little Crow, Ruth; 1932-2-5; Yes; F; Yes; F; F; F; Yes

Little Wolf, Cecil Mark; 1931-8-25; Yes; M; Yes; F; F; F; Yes

Livermont, Jewel Martha; 1931-10-1; Yes; F; Yes; 3/16; W; 3/32; Yes

Livermont, Leonard Bates; 1931-8-2; Yes; M; Chippewa and Oglala Sioux; Yes; 3/16; 1/5; 7/32; Yes

Loafer, Chauncey; 1931-12-11; Yes; M; Yes; F; F; F; Yes

Makes Good, Joseph Wm; 1931-6-24; Yes; M; Yes; F; F; F; Yes

Means, Dorothy; 1932-1-21; Yes; F; Yes; 3/4; F; 7/8; Yes

Medicine, Lulu; 1931-8-8; Yes; F; Yes; F; F; F; Yes

Merrival, Barton Stephen; 1931-10-24; Yes; M; Yes; 3/8; 3/8; 3/8; Yes

Mesteth, Alvina May; 1931-7-22; Yes; F; Yes; 1/2; F; 3/4; Yes

Milk, Susan; 1931-4-21; Yes; F; Yes; F; F; F; Yes

Mills, Elizabeth Rose; 1931-12-21; Yes; F; Yes; 3/4; 3/4; 3/4; Yes

Mills, Henrietta Flo.; 1931-8-19; Yes; F; Yes; 5/8; 5/32; 25/64; Yes

Moore, Mary Anne; 1931-4-11; Yes; F; Yes; 3/8; 1/2; 7/16; Yes

Morgan, Kenneth; 1932-1-9; Yes; M; Yes; W; 3/8; 3/16; Yes

Morrisette, Lawrence; 1931-11-30; Yes; M; Yes; 3/4; F; 7/8; Yes

Morrison, Martina; 1931-12-14; Yes; F; Yes; 3/4; 11/16; 23/32; Yes

Morrison, Russell; 1931-7-1; Yes; M; Yes; 3/4; F; 7/8; Yes

Mousseau, Mary; 1931-7-17; Yes; F; Yes; 3/4; F; 7/8; Yes

Mousseau, Rose; 1931-7-17; Yes; F; Yes; 3/4; F; 7/8; Yes

Moves Camp, Marian; 1931-4-14; Yes; F; Yes; F; F; F; Yes

McConnell, Beverly Nadean; 1931-9-26; Yes; F; Yes; W; 3/8; 3/16; Yes

McGaa, Wm Denver; 1931-7-1; Yes; M; Yes; 3/8; 1/2; 7/16; Yes

McLane, Gladys Louise; 1931-4-16; Yes; Rosebud and Oglala Sioux; Yes; 1/2; 1/4; 3/8; Yes

New Holy, Virginia; 1931-9-4; Yes; F; Yes; F; F; F; Yes

No Neck, Lottie; 1932-1-21; Yes; F; Yes; 7/8; F; 15/16; Yes

Pacer, Leo Cornelius; 1931-9-24; Yes; M; Yes; F; F; F; Yes

Parts His Hair, Owen; 1931-9-15; Yes; M; Yes; F; F; F; Yes

Patton, Elizabeth L; 1931-11-12; Yes; F; Yes; 1/4; 3/8; 7/16; Yes

Peck, Marvin Wm; 1931-5-12; Yes; M; Yes; W; 1/4; 1/8; Yes

Peck, Wanda Lorraine; 1931-7-27; Yes; F; Yes; 1/4; 3/8; 7/16; Yes

Picket Pin, Susie Aurelia; 1931-10-14; Yes; F; Rosebud Sioux and Oglala Sioux; Yes; F; F; F; Yes

Key: Surname, Given; Date of Birth (Year-Month-Day); Live Births (Yes/No); Still Births (blank unless otherwise given); Sex; Tribe (Oglala Sioux unless given otherwise); Ward (Yes/No); Degree of Blood (Father; Mother; Child); At Jurisdiction Where Enrolled (Yes/No); (If no – Where)

Births Occurring Between April 1, 1931 and March 31, 1932 to Parents Enrolled at Jurisdiction

Pipe On Head, Darrell; 1931-6-19; Yes; M; Yes; F; F; F; Yes;
Plenty Arrows, Leroyal; 1932-2-10; Yes; M; Yes; F; F; F; Yes
Poor Bear, Irene; 1931-8-1; Yes; F; Yes; 7/8; F; 15/16; Yes
Poor Bear, Leona; 1931-11-14; Yes; F; Yes; F; F; F; Yes
Pourier, Lawton; 1931-9-2; Yes; M; Yes; 3/16; 1/4; 7/32; Yes
Pourier, Lester Walter; 1931-11-19; Yes; M; Yes; 3/16; 5/16; 1/4; Yes
Pourier, Lucille Madeline; 1931-7-17; Yes; F; Yes; 3/16; 3/8; 9/32; Yes
Pourier, Marlene Claire; 1931-8-16; Yes; F; Yes; 3/16; 1/2; 11/32; Yes
Pretty Back, Lorene; 1931-5-11; Yes; F; Yes; F; F; F; Yes
Pretty Bird, Bernice; 1932-3-23; Yes; F; Yes; F; F; F; Yes
Pumpkin Seed, Cora; 1931-7-31; Yes; F; Yes; F; F; F; Yes
Pumpkin Seed, Jacob; 1931-12-12; Yes; M; Yes; F; F; F; Yes

Quiver, Bernard, 1932-3-7; Yes; M; Yes; F; 9/16; 25/32; Yes

Randall, Florence Louise; 1931-4-22; Yes; F; Rosebud and Oglala Sioux; Yes; 3/4;
    3/4; 3/4; Yes
Red Bow, Wallace; 1931-7-16; Yes; M; Yes; F; F; F; Yes
Red Breath Bear, Percy; 1931-10-27; Yes; M; Rosebud and Oglala Sioux; Yes; F; F;
    F; Yes
Red Ear Horse, Melvina B; 1931-10-24; Yes; F; Yes; F; F; F; Yes
Red Owl, Elizabeth; 1931-11-1; Yes; F; Yes; F; F; F; Yes
Red Shirt, Ignitius[sic]; 1931-9-26; Yes; M; Yes; F; 1/2; 3/4; Yes
Red Shirt, Mathew; 1932-1-30; Yes; M; Yes; 3/4; F; 7/8; Yes
Respects Nothing, Hildegard B; 1932-2-4; Yes; F; Yes; F; 1/2; 3/4; Yes
Returns From Scout, Melvin; 1931-9-25; Yes; M; Yes; F; F; F; Yes
Richard, Julia; 1932-3-6; Yes; F; Yes; 9/16; 5/8; 19/32; Yes
Richard, Ramsay Ward; 1931-5-21; Yes; M; Yes; 3/4; 7/16; 19/32; Yes
Richardson, Caroline LaVern; 1931-5-2; Yes; F; Yes; W; 3/4; 3/8; Yes
Rouillard, Mary Evelyn; 1931-8-24; Yes; F; Santee and Oglala Sioux; Yes; ?; F; ?;
    Yes
Ruleau, Donald Delroy; 1931-6- 19; Yes; M; Yes; 5/16; W; 5/32; Yes
Running Eagle, Thomas; 1931-5-9; Yes; M; Yes; F; F; F; Yes
Running Horse, Hobert; 1931-11-27; Yes; M; Rosebud and Oglala Sioux; Yes; F; F;
    F; Yes

Salway, Harley Warren; 1931-10-1; Yes; M; Yes; 5/8; 7/16; 17/32; Yes
Saves Life, Earl Wayne; 1931-7-5; Yes; M; Standing Rock and Oglala Sioux; Yes;
    1/2; 5/8; 9/16; Yes
Shangreau, Richard Wm; 1931-10-11; Yes; M; Yes; 1/2; 7/8; 11/16; Yes

State **South Dakota** Reservation **Pine Ridge** Agency or jurisdiction **Pine Ridge** Office of Indian Affairs

Key: Surname, Given; Date of Birth (Year-Month-Day); Live Births (Yes/No); Still Births (blank unless otherwise given); Sex; Tribe (Oglala Sioux unless given otherwise); Ward (Yes/No); Degree of Blood (Father; Mother; Child); At Jurisdiction Where Enrolled (Yes/No); (If no – Where)

Births Occurring Between April 1, 1931 and March 31, 1932 to Parents Enrolled at Jurisdiction

Sharp, Ben Franklyn; 1931-7-16; Yes; M; Yes; W; 1/4; 1/8; Yes

Shell Woman, Lydia; 1932-2-4; Yes; F; Yes; F; 3/4; 7/8; Yes

Shelton, James Valandry; 1931-10-22; Yes; M; Yes; W; 3/16; 3/32; Yes

Sherman, Bertha Mary; 1931-12-25; Yes; F; Ponca and Oglala Sioux; Yes; 3/16; 3/4; 9/16; Yes

Short Bear, Moses; 1931-4-24; Yes; M; Yes; 7/8; F; 15/16; Yes

Shot, Anna Theresa; 1932-3-21; Yes; F; Yes; F; F; F; Yes

Shot With Arrows, Cleveland B; 1931-11-13; Yes; M; Omaha and Oglala Sioux; Yes; F; ?; ?; Yes

Siers, Victoria Mae; 1931-12-22; Yes; F; Yes; 5/8; 1/4; 7/16; Yes

Sitting Bear, Cecelia; 1931-9-15; Yes; F; Yes; F; F; F; Yes

Skalander, Velma June; 1931-11-13; Yes; F; Yes; 1/8; 3/16; 5/32; Yes

Slow Bear, Kate; 1931-7-6; Yes; F; Yes; 7/8; F; 15/16; Yes

Speck, Lola Iris; 1932-1-23; Yes; F; Yes; W; 3/8; 3/16; Yes

Spider, Florence Rose; 1931-4-3; Yes; F; Yes; F; F; F; Yes

Spotted Bear, Pearl Mary; 1932-3-25; Yes; F; Yes; 7/8; F; 15/16; Yes

Spotted Eagle, Joseph; 1931-5-24; Yes; M; Yes; F; 5/8; 13/16; Yes

Spotted Elk, Victoria; 1931-7-4; Yes; Yes F; Yes; F; F; F; Yes

Standing Soldier, Lena Mildred; 1931-9-4; Yes; F; Cherokee and Oglala Sioux; Yes; 7/8; 1/4; 9/16; Yes

Surrounded in Woods, Peter; 1931-10-26; Yes; M; Yes; F; F; F; Yes

Swallow, Thelma Dorothy; 1932-3-17; Yes; F; Yes; 3/16; 11/16; 7/16; Yes

Swick, Joseph; 1931-11-24; Yes; M; Yes; W; 3/4; 3/8; Yes

Tail, Cleveland C; 1931-8-21; Yes; M; Yes; F; F; F; Yes

Takes War Bonnet, Lottie; 1931-6-21; Yes; F; Yes; F; F; F; Yes

Ten Fingers, Helen; 1931-11-19; Yes; F; Yes; F; F; F; Yes

Tibbits, Phyllis K; 1931-6-2; Yes; F; Yes; 1/2; 3/16; 11/32; Yes

Tobacco, Leroy Stephen; 1931-6-6; Yes; M; Yes; 7/8; 1/2; 11/16; Yes

Turning Holy, Altine Mae; 1931-5-15; Yes; F; Yes; F; F; F; Yes

Twiss, George Wm; 1931-11-8; Yes; M; Yes; 3/8; 7/16; 13/32; Yes

Two Crow, Chester; 1931-7-10; Yes; M; Yes; 3/4; 3/4; 3/4; Yes

Two Lance, Christina; 1931-10-27; Yes; F; Yes; F; F; F; Yes

Two Sticks, Eleanor G; 1931-6-7; Yes; F; Yes; F; 3/8; 11/16; Yes

Tyon, Elizabeth C; 1931-6-26; Yes; F; Yes; 3/4; 1/2; 5/8; Yes

Under The Baggage, Norman; 1932-2-9; Yes; M; Yes; F; F; F; Yes

Walks Under Ground, Burdick; 1931-4-16; Yes; M; Yes; F; F; F; Yes

Water, Aloysius; 1932-1-8; Yes; M; Yes; 5/8; 3/4; 11/16; Yes

Key: Surname, Given; Date of Birth (Year-Month-Day); Live Births (Yes/No); Still Births (blank unless otherwise given); Sex; Tribe (Oglala Sioux unless given otherwise); Ward (Yes/No); Degree of Blood (Father; Mother; Child); At Jurisdiction Where Enrolled (Yes/No); (If no – Where)

Births Occurring Between April 1, 1931 and March 31, 1932 to Parents Enrolled at Jurisdiction

Water, Georgette Mae; 1931-5-12; Yes; F; Yes; 3/4; 3/4; 3/4; Yes

Water, Martha Mae; 1931-5-14; Yes; F; Yes; 3/4; F; 7/8; Yes

Weston, Samuel Chris; 1932-1-6; Yes; M; Flandreau & Oglala S.; Yes; F; F; F; Yes

Whalen, Merle Robert; 1931-6-20; Yes; M; Winnebago and Oglala Sioux; Yes; 1/4; F; 5/8; Yes

White Bear, Katie; 1931-11-6; Yes; F; Yes; F; F; F; Yes

White Bear, William D; 1931-11-25; Yes; M; Yes; F; 7/8; 15/16; Yes

White Butterfly, Paul Emmerson; 1931-11-17; Yes; M; Yes; F; F; F; Yes

White Cow Killer, Celeste Mercedes; 1932-3-23; Yes; F; Yes; F; 3/4; 7/8; Yes

White Dress, William; 1931-12-27; Yes; M; Yes; F; F; F; Yes

White Eyes, Dorothy; 1932-1-7; Yes; F; Yes; F; 3/16; 19/32; Yes

White Face, Vine Quinton; 1932-2-23; Yes;   M; Yes; F; F; F; Yes

White Magpie, Frank; 1931-7-14; Yes; M; Yes; F; F; F; Yes

White Whirlwind, Jennie Victoria; 1931-5-25; Yes; F; Yes; F; 7/8; 15/16; Yes

Williams, John; 1931-6-13; Yes; M; Yes; W; 1/8; 1/16; Yes

Wilson, James John; 1931-10-23; Yes; M; Yes; 1/8; 1/2; 5/16; Yes

Wilson, Zona Clara; 1931-9-23; Yes; F; Yes; 1/8; W; 1/16; Yes

Wolf, Myrtle; 1932-3-14; Yes; F; Yes W; 1/2; 1/4; Yes

Wounded, Ruby Daisy; 1931-10-17; Yes; F; Yes; F; F; F; Yes

Wounded Arrows, Harry James; 1931-8-2; Yes; M; Yes; F; 5/8; 13/16; Yes

Wounded Horse, Deloris; 1931-10-18; Yes; F; Yes; F; F; F; Yes

Wounded Horse, Mary Jane; 1931-11-29; Yes; F; Yes; F; F; F; Yes

Yellow Bird, Chester Wilbur; 1931-6-25; Yes; M; Yes; 3/4; 1/2; 5/8; Yes

Yellow Boy, Dorothy; 1931-10-25; Yes; F; Yes; 7/8; F; 15/16; Yes

Yellow Boy, Theodore; 1931-10-5; Yes; M; Cheyenne and Oglala Sioux; Yes; 7/8; F; 15/16; Yes

Yellow Horse, Elmer; 1931-11-20; Yes; M; Yes; 7/8; 7/8; 7/8; Yes

Yellow Horse, Wilson; 1931-5-6; Yes; M; Yes; 7/8; F; 15/16; Yes

Yellow Shirt, Vien Jefferson; 1931-7-10; Yes; M; Yes; F; 7/8; 15/16; Yes

Yellow Thunder, Winfred; 1931-11-10; Yes; M; Yes; F; F; F; Yes

Young Bear, Kenneth; 1931-9-13; Yes; M; Yes; F; F; F; Yes

MISCELLANEOUS DELINQUENT [BIRTHS] REPORTED

DURING YEAR 1932

PINE RIDGE RESERVATION
PINE RIDGE SOUTH DAKOTA

Key: Surname, Given; Date of Birth (Year-Month-Day); Live Births (Yes/No); Still Births (blank unless otherwise given); Sex; Tribe (Oglala Sioux unless given otherwise); Ward (Yes/No); Degree of Blood (Father; Mother; Child); At Jurisdiction Where Enrolled (Yes/No); (If no – Where)

Miscellaneous Delinquent [Births] Reported During Year 1932
~~Births Occurring Between April 1, 1931 and March 31, 1932 to Parents Enrolled at Jurisdiction~~

~~Bowman, Loran; 1927-11-4; Yes; M; Yes; ?; 3/16; ?; Yes~~
Trans to 1928

~~Cottier, William Jr; 1931-3-30; Yes; M; Yes; 1/2; 9/16; 17/16; Yes~~
Trans to 1931
~~Crane, Kenneth; 1929-12-6; Yes; M; Yes; W; 1/8; 1/16; Yes~~
Trans to 1930
~~Crane, Neil A; 1929-12-6; Yes; M; Yes; W; 1/8; 1/16; Yes~~
Trans to 1930
~~Crow, Rachel, 1927-2-27; Yes; F; Yes; F; ?; ?; Yes~~
Trans to 1927

~~DeWolf, Alice Marie; 1931-3-2; Yes; F; Yes; W; 1/4; 1/8; Yes~~
Trans to 1931
~~DeWolf, Frances Elva; 1931-3-2; Yes; F; Yes; W; 1/4; 1/8; Yes~~
Trans to 1931
~~Dixon, Frederick Edw; 1930-5-28; Yes; M; Yes; 1/4; 5/8; 7/16; Yes~~
Trans to 1931
~~Dixon, Raymond Leroy; 1926-10-20; Yes; M; Yes; 1/4; 5/8; 7/16; Yes~~
Trans to 1927

~~Fog, Henry; 1930-3-12; Yes; Crow Creek and Oglala Sioux; Yes; 5/8; F;13/16; Yes~~
Trans to 1930

~~Hawkins, Rene Bertha; 1930-4-9; Yes; F; Rosebud and Oglala Sioux; Yes; 13/16; F;~~
~~29/32; Yes~~ Trans to 1930

~~Janis, Mildred Grace; 1931-2-1; Yes; F; Rosebud and Oglala Sioux; Yes; ?; 7/8; ?;~~
~~Yes~~ Trans to 1931

Kills Small, Mary Alice; 1931-1-23; Yes; F; Yes; F; F; F; Yes

La Clair, Letoy; 1930-12-28; Yes; F; Pottawatomie & Oglala Sioux; Yes; 1/8; 7/16;
9/32; Yes
Left Hand, Orpha Jean; 1931-2-24; Yes; F; Rosebud and Oglala Sioux; Yes; F; F; F;
Yes
Little Bull, Rebecca; 1931-1-27; Yes; F; Yes; F; F; F; Yes
Loafer Joe, Mollie; 1931-2-23; Yes; F; Yes; F; F; F; Yes

Makes Shine, Oletha Magdaline; 1931-3-17; Yes; F; Yes; F; 3/4; 7/8; Yes

Key: Surname, Given; Date of Birth (Year-Month-Day); Live Births (Yes/No); Still Births (blank unless otherwise given); Sex; Tribe (Oglala Sioux unless given otherwise); Ward (Yes/No); Degree of Blood (Father; Mother; Child); At Jurisdiction Where Enrolled (Yes/No); (If no – Where)

Miscellaneous Delinquent [Births] Reported During Year 1932
Births Occurring Between April 1, 1931 and March 31, 1932 to Parents Enrolled at Jurisdiction

Peck, Mary Ann; 1930-3-28; Yes; F; 1/4; 3/16; 7/32; Yes
Trans to 1930
Peterson, Berdine Alys J; 1931-3-5; Yes; F; Yes; W; 5/16; 5/32; Yes

Randall, Julia May; 1929-4-27; Yes; F; Rosebud and Oglala Sioux; Yes; 3/4; 3/4; 3/4; Yes
Trans to 1929
Red Paint, Grace; 1931-3-6; Yes; F; Yes; F; F; F; Yes
Running Bear, Vernice; 1931-3-15; Yes; F; Yes; F; F; F; Yes

Six Feathers, Emma; 1931-3-17; Yes; F; Yes; 5/8; 7/8; 3/4; Yes
Sleeps, Robert; 1931-2-5; Yes; M; Yes; F; F; F; Yes
Stands, Hannah; 1931-3-21; Yes; F; Yes; F; 7/8; 15/16; Yes
Strikes Plenty, Theresa; 1930-11-7; Yes; F; Yes; F; F; F; Yes
Swallow, Joseph; 1930-8-6; Yes; M; Rosebud and Oglala Sioux; Yes; F; F; F; Yes
Swimmer, Wallace; 1931-3-25; Yes; M; Rosebud and Oglala Sioux; Yes; F; 3/4; 7/8; Yes

Tapia, Beatrice; 1928-2-14; Yes; F; Yes; 1/2; Mex; 1/4; Yes
Trans to 1928
Twiss, Lawrence; 1931-1-23; Yes; M; Yes; 1/2; 5/8; 9/16; Yes

Wellborn, Frances Aileen; 1923-7-27; Yes; F; Yes; W; 1/8; 1/16; Yes
White, Florine; 1920-1-23; Yes; F; Oneida and Oglala Sioux; Yes; 1/2; 1/2; 1/2; Yes
White Eyes, Jeanette Isabelle; 1931-3-13; Yes; F; Rosebud and Oglala Sioux; Yes; F; F; F; Yes
Wilson, Morgan; 1931-2-23; Yes; M; Cheyenne and Oglala Sioux; Yes; 1/2; F; 3/4; Yes
Woodley, Beverly Jean; 1930-6-4; Yes; F; Yes; W; 1/2; 1/4; Yes
Trans to 1930

Yellow Horse, Annie I; 1931-3-25; Yes; F; Yes; F; F; F; Yes

DEATH ROLL

EXCLUSIVE OF STILLBIRTHS

1925
(July 1, 1924 - June 30, 1925)

PINE RIDGE RESERVATION
PINE RIDGE SOUTH DAKOTA

State **South Dakota** Reservation **Pine Ridge** Agency or jurisdiction
Pine Ridge Office of Indian Affairs

Key: Year and Number On Last Census Roll; Surname, Given; Date of Death (Year-Month-Day); Age At Death; Sex; Tribe (Oglala Sioux unless given otherwise); Ward (Yes/No); Degree of Blood; Cause Of Death (if given); At Jurisdiction Where Enrolled (Yes/No); (If no – Where)

Deaths Occurring Between July 1, 1924 and June 30, 1925 of Indians Enrolled at Jurisdiction

1923   788;   Black Whistler, (none); 1924-July 5; 69; M; Yes; F; 10 days, Found dead after; Yes

----   none;   Blind Man, Dennis Wilbert; 1925-June 29; 1 yr; M; Yes; Yes F; No data; Yes

----   none;   Blue Legs, Theresa; 1925-March 26; 2 mo; F; Yes; F; LaGrippe; Yes

not listed   Brave; 1925-June 24; 71; M; Yes; F; No data; Yes

1923   890;   Brave, Thomas; 1925-May 11; 5; M; Yes; F; Operation; Yes

----   none;   Brewer, Charles; 1925-Apr 8; 9 da; M; Yes; plus 1/4; pneumonia; Yes

----   none;   Brown Bull, Chester; 1925-Jan 4; 1 mo; M; Yes; F; pneumonia; Yes

1924   3557;   Brown Bull-Left Hand, Mollie; 1925-Mch 25; 62; F; Yes; F; pneumonia; Yes

1924   1071;   Brown Thunder, Louisa; 1925-June 6; 34; F; plus 1/4; [blank]; Heart trouble; Yes

1924   1203;   Cedar Woman; 1925-May 18; 72; F; Yes; F; No data; Yes

1924   1213;   Charges Enemy, Martin; 1925-Apr 1; 14; M; Yes; F; Tuberculosis; Yes

----   none;   Chips, Adam; 1924-Aug 26; 9 mo; M; Yes; F; No data; Yes

1924   1364;   Clifford, Nathan; 1924-Aug 21; 8 yr; M; Yes; plus 1/4; no data; Yes

1924   1411;   Clincher, Beulah Mary; 1924-Oct 9; 1 yr; F; Yes; F; Dysentery; Yes

1924   1407;   Clincher, Julia; 1924-July 2; 17; F; Yes; F; Consumption; Yes

1924   1395;   Clincher, Laura; 1925-Jan 17; 51; F; Yes; F; Scrofula & boils; Yes

----   none;   Clown Horse, Ellen; 1925-Jan 22; 1 mo; F; Yes; plus 1/4; tuberculosis; Yes

1924   1469;   Condelario, Clara; 1925-Mch 16; 17; F; Yes; plus 1/4; tuberculosis; Yes

1924   1492;   Conquering Bear, William; 1925-Feb 21; 44; M; Yes; F; consumption; Yes

1924   1517;   Cook, Harley; 1925-Feb 19; 15; M; Yes; plus 1/4; tuberculosis; Yes

----   none;   Cottier, Ellen Rose; 1924-Sept 23; 7 mo; F; Yes; plus 1/4; Dysentery; Yes

----   none;   Cottier, Leonard Wm; 1924-Dec 30; 7 mo; M; Yes; plus 1/4; pneumonia; Yes

1923   1609;   Crazy Ghost; 1924-July 2; 74; M; Yes; F; No data; Yes

1924   5440;   Crow, John Raymond; 1915-May 9; 3 yr; M; Yes; 13/16; Pneumonia; Yes

1924   1644;   Crow Likes Water, Charles; 1924-Aug 8; 27 yr; M; Yes; F.B.; Tuberculosis; Yes

1924   7013;   Crow Woman, Ellen; 1924-Sept 2; 22 yr; F; Yes; F.B; Tuberculosis; Yes

1924   1706;   Cut, Abraham; 1925-March 29; 3 yr; M; Yes; FB; Pneumonia; Yes

1924   1719;   Davidson, John; 1924-Sept 22; 46 yr; M; Yes; 1/4; Heart trouble; Yes

1924   1817;   Dreams Jealous; 1925-Feb 17; 85 yr; F; Yes; FB; Old Age; Yes

1923   4652;   Days Going; 1924-July 8; 93 yr; F; Yes; FB; Old Age; Yes

1924   1868;   Eagle Bird, Simon; 1925-April 13; 4 yr; M; Yes; FB; No data; Yes

1924   1910;   Eagle Heart, Jackson; 1925-Mar 31; 26 yr; M; Yes; FB; No data; Yes

1924   1919;   Eagle Louse, Rosa; 1924-Aug 21; 16 yr; F; Yes; FB; Tuberculosis; Yes

89

State **South Dakota** Reservation **Pine Ridge** Agency or jurisdiction **Pine Ridge** Office of Indian Affairs

Key: Year and Number On Last Census Roll; Surname, Given; Date of Death (Year-Month-Day); Age At Death; Sex; Tribe (Oglala Sioux unless given otherwise); Ward (Yes/No); Degree of Blood; Cause Of Death (if given); At Jurisdiction Where Enrolled (Yes/No); (If no – Where)

Deaths Occurring Between July 1, 1924 and June 30, 1925 of Indians Enrolled at Jurisdiction

1924 1923; Eagle Ring; 1925-May 10; 56 yr; M; Yes; FB; Tuberculosis; Yes
1924 3247; Eagle Shirt, Lydia; 1925-April 30; 14 yr; F; Yes; FB; Tuberculosis; Yes
1924 609; Elk Woman; 1925-Mar 3; 64 yr; F; Yes; FB; Pneumonia; Yes
1924 2026; Fast Wolf, Inez; 1924-Oct 4; 12 yr; F; Yes; 7/8; No data; Yes
1924 2023; Fast Wolf, Isabel; 1925-Mar 28; 12 yr; F; Yes; 7/8; Flu; Yes
1924 2037; Featherman, Emma; 1925-Jan 18; 16 yr; F; Yes; FB; Tuberculosis; Yes
1924 2521; Fights Little, Fannie; 1924-Sept 7; 69 yr; F; Yes; FB; Hemorrhage; Yes
1924 5381; Fool Head, Mary; 1924-August 30; 22 yr; F; Yes; FB; Tuberculosis; Yes
----- ----- Good Buffalo, Louis; 1924-Sept 5; 1 yr; M; Yes; FB; No data; Yes
----- ----- Good Lance, Emerson Jos; 1925-Dec 23; 3 mo; M; Yes; FB; No data; Yes
----- ------ Good Plume, Lizzie; 1925-Jan 15; 1 da; F; Yes; FB; No data; Yes
1924 2456; Good Weasel, Leo; 1925-May 10; 1 yr; M; Yes; FB; No data; Yes
1924 2513; Groaning Bear, Stephen; 1924-July 21; 1 yr; M; Yes; FB; No data; Yes
----- ----- Ground Spider, Noah; 1925-Feb 17; 16 da; M; Yes; FB; No data; Yes
1924 2345; Hand, Leroy Jas; 1924-Sept 14; 11 mo; M; Yes; FB; Cholera Infantum; Yes
1924 2563; Hat, Joseph; 1924-July 26; 15 yr; M; Yes; FB; Tuberculosis; Yes
1924 2615; Heart Man; 1924-Sept 1; 78 yr; M; Yes; FB; Old Age; Yes
1924 1987; Her Good Shawl; 1924-Aug 22; 86 yr; F; Yes; FB; Old Age; Yes
1924 2657; Her Many Horses; 1923-July 27; 69 yr; F; Yes; FB; Old Age; Yes
---- ----- Herman, Grace Marie; 1925-May 7; 8 mo; F; Yes; 7/16; No Data; Yes
1924 2691; High Bull, Gilbert; 1924-Jan 13; 1 yr; M; Yes; FB; No Data; Yes
----- ------ Hollow Head, Benjamin; 1925-Feb 16; 7 mo; M; Yes; FB; Whooping Caugh[sic]; Yes
---- ---- Hollow Head, Levi; 1924-Aug 26; 2 da; M; Yes; FB; No Data; Yes
1924 2757; Hollow Head, Samuel; 1925-Jan 20; 35 yr; M; Yes; FB; Tuberculosis; Yes
---- ----- Hollow Horn, Adeline; 1925-May 7; 1 mo; F; Yes; FB; No Data; Yes
1924 2774; Hollow Horn, Minnie; 1924-Aug 25; 2 yr; F; Yes; FB; No Data; Yes
---- ---- Hollow Horn, Pearl; 1924-Sept 19; 2 mo; F; Yes; FB; Fever; Yes
1924 2709; Holy Pipe, Polly; 1925-May 24; 69 yr; F; Yes; FB; Old Age; Yes
1924 2856; Horse, Earl; 1924-Nov 14; 1 yr; M; Yes; FB; No data; Yes
1924 2853; Horse, Charles; 1925-Mar 8; 12 yr; M; Yes; FB; Tuberculosis; Yes
1924 2962; Iron Cloud, Mary; 1924-Sept 24; 28 yr; F; Yes; FB; Consumption; Yes
1924 2976; Iron Crow, Nellie; 1925-Apr 1; 1 yr; F; Yes; FB; No data; Yes
1924 2967; Iron Crow, William; 1925-June 6; 75 yr; M; Yes; FB; No data; Yes
---- ---- Iron Heart, Viola; 1924-Aug 29; 4 mo; F; Yes; 7/8; No data; Yes
1924 3971; Janis, Francis; 1924-Dec 29; 1 yr; M; Yes; 1/4; No data; Yes
---- ---- Janis, Jerome; 1924-Nov 4; 1 da; M; Yes; 1/2; No data; Yes
1924 3078; Janis, Jesse; 1924-Sept 19; 10 mo; M; Yes; 9/16; No data; Yes
---- ---- Janis, Jos Francis; 1924-Oct 2; 4 mo; M; Yes; 3/4; No data; Yes

Key: Year and Number On Last Census Roll; Surname, Given; Date of Death (Year-Month-Day); Age At Death; Sex; Tribe (Oglala Sioux unless given otherwise); Ward (Yes/No); Degree of Blood; Cause Of Death (if given); At Jurisdiction Where Enrolled (Yes/No); (If no – Where)

Deaths Occurring Between July 1, 1924 and June 30, 1925 of Indians Enrolled at Jurisdiction

1924 3147; Jealous Of Him, William; 1924-Sept 11; 1 yr; M; Yes; FB; Cholera Marbus[sic]; Yes

1924 3232; Kicking Bear, Edmond; 1925-Feb 6; 2 yr; M; Yes; FB; No data; Yes

1924 3239; Kills Across, Clara; 1925-Mar 6; 10 yr; F; Yes; FB; Tuberculosis; Yes

1924 3317; Kills Small, Rudolph; 1924-Spet[sic] 23; 1 yr; M; Yes; FB; Cholera Marbus; Yes

1924 3513; Lays Bad, Edward; 1924-Nov 23; 50 yr; M; Yes; FB; No data; Yes

---- ---- Lays Hard, Dorothy; 1925-Feb 14; 2 da; F; Yes; 3/4; No data; Yes

1924 3609; Lip, Eva; 1925-Jan 19; 14 yr; F; Yes; FB; Tuberculosis; Yes

1924 3615; Lip, Rosa; 1925-May 1; 21 yr; F; Yes; FB; Pneumonia; Yes

1924 3705; Little Dog, Francis; 1925-Jan 17; 1 yr; M; Yes; FB; No data; Yes

1924 3745; Little Killer, George; 1925-Feb 3; 26 yr; M; Yes; FB; Tuberculosis; Yes

----- ----- Little War Bonnet, Charles; 1924-Nov 8; 1 da; M; Yes; FB; No data; Yes

1924 3794; Little War Bonnet, Ida; 1925-Mar 12; 83 yr; F; Yes; FB; Old Age; Yes

---- ---- Little War Bonnet, James; 1924-Nov 7; 1 da; M; Yes; FB; No data; Yes

1924 3760; Little Scout; 1925-May 23; 75 yr; M; Yes; FB; Old Age; Yes

1924 3868; Lives Alone; 1925-May 5; 70 yr; F; Yes; FB; Old Age; Yes

1924 3883; Loafer Joe; Mary; 1924-Oct 24; 1 yr; F; Yes; FB; Fever; Yes

---- ---- Loafer Joe, Paul; 1924-Nov 12; 1 mo; M; Yes; FB; Fever; Yes

---- ---- Lone Wolf, Evelyn; 1925-Jan 8; 26 da; F; Yes; FB; No data; Yes

1924 3979; Long Soldier, Sarah Julia; 1924-Oct 29; 81 yr; F; Yes; FB; Old Age; Yes

---- ----- Looks Twice, Adolph; 1925-Jan 6; 3 mo; M; Yes; FB; No data; Yes

1924 4404; McGaa, William; 1925-May 9; 65 yr; M; Yes; 1/2; Flu; Yes

1924 4226; Mesteth, David Jr; 1925-Jan 14; 1 yr; M; Yes; 3/4; Pneumonia; Yes

1924 4215; Mesteth, Eva; 1925-May 3; 30 yr; F; Yes; 3/8; Tuberculosis; Yes

1924 550; Monroe, Thomas; 1925-June 13; 10 yr; M; Yes; FB; No data; Yes

1924 4352; Morrison, Frank; 1925-Apr 17; 25 yr; M; Yes; 7/8; Tuberculosis; Yes

1924 4361; Morrison, Ruth P; 1925-May 19; 19 yr; F; Yes; 3/8; Influenza; Yes

1924 4365; Mountain Sheep, Levi; 1924-Aug 17; 23 yr; M; Yes; FB; Tuberculosis; Yes

---- ---- Nelson, Thomas Jr; 1924-Dec 20; 1 mo; M; Yes; 13/16; Pneumonia; Yes

1924 4504; No Water, Roger; 1924-Aug 7; 1 yr; M; Yes; FB; Whooping Caugh[sic]; Yes

1923 4650; Otter; 1924-July 22; 66 yr; F; Yes; Yes FB; Old Age; Yes

1926 4624; Old Horse, Angelina; 1924-Oct 9; 1 yr; F; Yes; FB; No data; Yes

----- ----- Packed, Bertha; 1925-May 21; 2 mo; F; Yes; FB; No data; Yes

1924 4573; Pablo, Felix; 1924-Sept 11; 1 yr; M; Yes; 11/16; No data; Yes

1924; 4569; Pablo, Mary; 1924-Dec 6; 16 yr; F; Yes; 11/16; Tuberculosis; Yes

1924 4625; Parts His Hairs, Lucy; 1925-May 19; 2 yr; F; Yes; FB; No data; Yes

1924 4651; Peck, Julia B; 1925-Jan 1; 10 yr; F; Yes; 1/2; Diphtheria; Yes

1924 4691; Plenty Arrows, Rebecca; 1924-Sep-t 16; 1 yr; F; Yes; FB; No Data; Yes

State **South Dakota** Reservation **Pine Ridge** Agency or jurisdiction
Pine Ridge Office of Indian Affairs

Key: Year and Number On Last Census Roll; Surname, Given; Date of Death (Year-Month-Day); Age At Death; Sex; Tribe (Oglala Sioux unless given otherwise); Ward (Yes/No); Degree of Blood; Cause Of Death (if given); At Jurisdiction Where Enrolled (Yes/No); (If no – Where)

Deaths Occurring Between July 1, 1924 and June 30, 1925 of Indians Enrolled at Jurisdiction

1924 4689; Plenty Arrows, Roly; 1924-July 30; 4 yr; F; Yes; FB; Struck by lightning; Yes

1924 4823; Prays To Her; 1925-May 19; 82 yr; F; Yes; FB; Old Age; Yes

---- ---- Pretty Back, Amos; 1924-Aug 19; 1 mo; M; Yes; FB; No data; Yes

1924 4843; Pretty Boy, Joseph; 1925-Feb 20; 69 yr; M; Yes; FB; Pneumonia; Yes

1924 4851; Pretty Bull, George; 1924-Aug 14; 23 yr; M; Yes; Tuberculosis; Yes

1924 4907; Pumpkin Seed, Nancy; 1925-May 31; 17 yr; F; Yes; FB; Tuberculosis; Yes

1924 5038; Red Breath Bear, Floyd; 1924-Oct 10; 9 mo; M; Yes; FB; No data; Yes

---- ---- Red Cloud, Lavina; 1924-Dec 28; 2 da; F; Yes; FB; No data; Yes

1924 6432; Red Crow, Rosa; 1925-Apr 9; 25 yr; F; Yes; FB; Tuberculosis; Yes

1924 5667; Red Ear Horse, Emil; 1925-Apr 6; 15 yr; M; Yes; FB; Tuberculosis; Yes

1924 5143; Red Feather, Julia; 1924-Dec 16; 10 yr; F; Yes; FB; Tuberculosis; Yes

1924 4058; Red Hair; 1925-Jan 10; 81 yr; F; Yes; FB; Old Age; Yes

1924 5211; Red Shirt, Joseph; 1925-Jan 4; 77 yr; M; Yes; 1/2; Old Age; Yes

1924 5234; Red Shirt, William; 1924-Dec 11; 44 yr; M; Yes; 3/4; Heart disease; Yes

1924 5419; Romero, James; 1925-Mar 15; 26 yr; M; Yes; 3/4; No data; Yes

1924 5490; Ruff, Mary; 1925-Jan 20; 69 yr; F; Yes; Yes 1/2; Old Age; Yes

1924 5523; Running Bear; 1925-Mar 29; 65 yr; M; Yes; FB; Old Age; Yes

1924 5537; Running Eagle, Josephine; 1925-Mar 24; 10 mo; F; Yes; FB; Tuberculosis; Yes

1924 5562; Running Horse, Eva; 1925-Feb 8; 1 yr; F; Yes; FB; No data; Yes

1924 5588; Runs Close To Lodge, Joseph; 1925-Mar 21; 59 yr; M; Yes; FB; Drowned; Yes

1924 4579; Runs On, Sophia; 1925-Mar 25; 29 yr; F; Yes; FB; Childbirth; Yes

---- ----- Scabby Face, Albert; 1925-May 21; 6 mo; M; Yes; FB; No data; Yes

1924 1702; Scabby Legs; 1925-May 9; 66 yr; F; Yes; FB; Old Age; Yes

1924 5759; Shell Woman No.; 1924-Nov 27; 88 yr; F; Yes; FB; Old Age; Yes

----- ---- Short Bear, Orville; 1925-Mar 29; 1 da; M; Yes; 13/16; No data; Yes

1924 5808; Short Bull, Matilda; 1925-May 20; 69 yr; F; Yes; FB; Old Age; Yes

1924 6647; Shouts For, Henry; 1925-Mar 12; 25 yr; M; Yes; FB; Tuberculosis; Yes

1924 5826; Shot In The Eye, Susie; 1925-Mar 29; 88 yr; F; Yes; FB; Old Age; Yes

1924 5948; Slow Bear, Martha; 1925-May 10; 43 yr; F; Yes; FB; Tuberculosis; Yes

1924 6011; Spotted Bear, Cecelia; 1924-Nov 27; 46 yr; F; Yes; 1/2; Cancer; Yes

1924 6071; Stahl, R. Albert; 1924-Nov 13; 14 yr; M; Yes; 1/4; Gastric Enteritus[sic]; Yes

1924 1750; Stover, Gertrude; 1925-May 12; 24 yr; F; Yes; 5/8; Consumption; Yes

1924 6233; Struck By Crow, Henry; 1924-July 1; 47 yr; M; Yes; FB; No data; Yes

1924 6315; Tail, Nelly; 1925-May 30; 20 yr; F; Yes; FB; Tuberculosis; Yes

---- ----- Tail, Rosella; 1925-Feb 17; 2 mo; F; Yes; 7/8; No data; Yes

1924 6324; Takes Away From Them; 1925-Jan 7; 87 yr; F; Yes; FB; Old Age; Yes

1923 6456; Ten Fingers, Millard; 1924-July 23; 11 yr; M; Yes; FB; Tuberculosis; Yes

State **South Dakota** Reservation **Pine Ridge** Agency or jurisdiction
Pine Ridge Office of Indian Affairs

Key: Year and Number On Last Census Roll; Surname, Given; Date of Death (Year-Month-Day); Age At
Death; Sex; Tribe (Oglala Sioux unless given otherwise); Ward (Yes/No); Degree of Blood; Cause Of Death
(if given); At Jurisdiction Where Enrolled (Yes/No); (If no – Where)

Deaths Occurring Between July 1, 1924 and June 30, 1925 of Indians Enrolled at Jurisdiction

1924 6498; Troublesome Hawk, Adam; 1925-Mar 18; 10 mo; M; Yes; FB; No data;
Yes

1924 6506; Turning Bear, Mary; 1925-Jan 25; 80 yr; F; FB; Old Age; Yes

1924 6508; Turning Bear, Michael; 1925-Apr 19; 45 yr; M; Yes; FB; Pneumonia;
Yes

1924 6497; Troublesome Hawk, Alice; 1925-Dec 2; 13 yr; F; Yes; FB;
Tuberculosis; Yes

1924 6581; Twiss, Ethelbert; 1924-Aug 27; 1 yr; F; Yes; 7/8; No data; Yes

---- ---- Two Eagle, Rollan; 1925-Feb 14; 19 da; M; Yes; 7/8; No data; Yes

---- ----- Two Lance, Angelina; 1924-Aug 1; 6 mo; F; Yes; FB; No data; Yes

---- ----- Two Two, Spencer; 1925-May 18; 1 mo; M; Yes; 7/8; No data; Yes

---- ----- Under The Baggage, Jessie; 1925-May 10; 1 mo; F; Yes; FB; No data;
Yes

1924 6786; Walks Under Ground, Eliza; 1925-June 9; 45 yr; F; Yes; FB; No data;
Yes

1924 6873; Weston, Andrew R; 1924-Sept 17; 2 yr; M; Yes; 7/9; No data; Yes

1924 6880; Whalen, Lavina; 1924-Aug 25; 7 yr; F; Yes; 5/8; Tuberculosis; Yes

1924 6899; Whirlwind Bear, Alice; 1924-Nov 1; 21 yr; F; Yes; FB; Tuberculosis;
Yes

1924 6972; White Bull, George; 1925-Apr 9; 20 yr; M; Yes; FB; Tuberculosis; Yes

1924 6998; White Cow River; 1925-May 11; 85 yr; F; Yes; FB; Old Age; Yes

1924 7065; White Horse, George; 1925-May 30; 27 yr; M; Yes; FB; No data; Yes

1924 7262; Yellow Bear; 1925-Jan 30; 71 yr; M; Yes; FB; No data; Yes

DEATH ROLL

EXCLUSIVE OF STILLBIRTHS

1926
(July 1, 1925 - June 30, 1926)

PINE RIDGE RESERVATION
PINE RIDGE SOUTH DAKOTA

Key: Year and Number On Last Census Roll; Surname, Given; Date of Death (Year-Month-Day); Age At Death; Sex; Tribe (Oglala Sioux unless given otherwise); Ward (Yes/No); Degree of Blood; Cause Of Death; At Jurisdiction Where Enrolled (Yes/No); (If no – Where)

Deaths Occurring Between July 1, 1925 and June 30, 1926 of Indians Enrolled at Jurisdiction

1925	43;	Afraid Of His Horses, Chester; 1925-Sept 12; 4 yr; M; Yes; FB; Convulsions; Yes
1925	125;	American Horse, Denver; 1925-Aug 16; 1 yr; M; Yes; FB; No data; Yes
----	----	Apple, Sterling; 1926-Jan 1; 3 mo; M; Yes; FB; No data; Yes
----	----	Backward. Russell; 1926-Feb 18; 4 yr; M; Yes; FB; No data; Yes
1925	287;	Bad Yellow Hair; 1926-Jan 9; 92 yr; M; Yes; FB; Old Age; Yes
1925	299;	Bald Eagle; 1925-July 14; 63 yr; M; Yes; FB; R.R. accident; No; Albany, N. York
----	----	Bear Saves Life, Bessie; 1925-Feb 15; 7 mo; F; Yes; FB; Pneumonia; Yes
1925	389;	Bear Saves Life, Jos. Antoine; 1926-Apr 20; 13 yr; M; Yes; FB; Tuberculosis; Yes
1925	392;	Bear Saves Life, Luke; 1926-Apr 24; 34 yr; M; Yes; FB; Tuberculosis; Yes
1925	429;	Belt, Levi; 1926-Jan 15; 40 yr; F[sic]; Yes; FB; No data; Yes
1925	442;	Bettelyoun, Harry W; 1935-Au[sic] 21; 47 yr; M; Yes; 3/8; Rheumatism; Yes
1925	644;	Big Boy, Gertie; 1925-Aug 23; 13 yr; F; Yes; FB; Tuberculosis; Yes
1925	487;	Big Boy, Julia; 1926-Jan 23; 44 yr; F; Yes; FB; No data; Yes
1925	517;	Big Turnip, Leonard; 1926-Mar 27; 13 yr; M; Yes; FB; Tuberculosis; Yes
1925	559;	Bissonette, Peter; 1925-July 11; 78 yr; M; Yes; 1/2; Old Age; Yes
1925	629;	Black Bear, Vivian; 1926-Mar 6; 6 mo; F; Yes; FB; Pneumonia; Yes
1925	645;	Black Bird, Frank; 1926-June 14; 53 yr; M; Yes; FB; No data; Yes
1925	685;	Black Crow, Ethel; 1925-Oct 25; 3 yr; F; Yes; FB; No data; Yes
1925	722;	Black Feather, George; 1926-May 31; 15 yr; M; Yes; 7/8; Tuberculosis; Yes
1926	719;	Black Feather, Lema; 1925-Dec 7; 1 yr; F; Yes; 7/8; Tuberculosis; Yes
----	----	Black Horse, David; 1925-Oct 28; 2 mo; M; Yes; 3/4; No data; Yes
1925	768;	Black Wolf, Joshua; 1926-June 6; 24 yr; M; Yes; FB; Tuberculosis; Yes
1925	772;	Blind, Fannie; 1925-Aug 30; 55 yr; F; Yes; FB; Diarrhea; Yes
1925	784;	Blonde; 1925-Nov 3; 75 yr; F; Yes; FB; Old Age; Yes
----	-----	Blue Legs, Alvina; 1926-May 10; 8 da; F; Yes; FB; Pneumonia; Yes
1925	814;	Blue Legs, Armenia; 1926-June 12; 13 yr; F; Yes; FB; Tuberculosis; Yes
1925	853;	Boyer, Hazel; 1926-Jan 6; 3 yr; F; Yes; 3/4; Pneumonia; Yes
----	----	Brafford, Earl Patrick; 1926-June 14; 3 mo; M; Yes; 3/8; Heart Failure; Yes
----	----	Brave, Oris; 1925-Aug 24; [blank]; M; Yes; FB; Premature birth; Yes
1925	904;	Brave Heart, Sally; 1925-July 23; 4 yr; F, Yes; 7/8; Cholera Marbus[sic]; Yes
1925	959;	Broken Leg, Peter; 1925-Sept 7; 9 mo; M; Yes; FB; No data; Yes

State **South Dakota** Reservation **Pine Ridge** Agency or jurisdiction
Pine Ridge Office of Indian Affairs

Deaths Occurring Between July 1, 1925 and June 30, 1926 of Indians Enrolled at Jurisdiction

1925 980; Broken Rope, Homer; 1926-Apr 15; 25 yr; M; Yes; FB; Tuberculosis; 1 Yes

---- ---- Broken Rope, Sylvester; 1926-Jan 28; 6 mo; M; Yes; FB; No data; Yes

1925 1038; Brown, King; 1925-Sept 23; 1 yr; M; Yes; FB; Summer complaint; Yes

1925 1047; Brown Ears, James; 1925-Nov 26; 22 yr; M; Yes; FB; Drowned; Yes

---- ---- Brown Ears, Margaret; 1926-May 30; 4 mo; F; Yes; FB; No data; Yes

1925 1127; Bull Bear, Mabel; 1926-Feb 6; 2 yr; F; Yes; FB; Small Pox; Yes

1925 1150; Bull Tail, Pugh; 1925-Nov 26; 15 yr; M; Yes; FB; Tuberculosis; Yes

1925 1208; Catches, Allurreta; 1926-Feb 9; 3 yr; F; Yes; FB; Infantile paralysis; Yes

1925 1226; Center, DeWitte; 1925-Dec 30; 1 yr; M; Yes; FB; No data; Yes

1925 7095; Charging Thunder, Fannie; 1925-Dec 9; 3 yr; F; Yes; FB; Pneumonia; Yes

1925 1272; Chase In Winter, Louisa; 1925-Sept 15; 76 yr; F; Yes; FB; Old Age; Yes

1925 1279; Chase In Winter, Victoria; 1926-Mar 31; 9 yr; F; Yes; FB; Tuberculosis; Yes

1925 1291; Chasing Bear; 1925-Sept 4; 80 yr; M; Yes; FB; Old Age; Yes

1925 1293; Chasing Hawk, Henry; 1925-Aug 13; 75 yr; M; Yes; FB; Dropsy; Yes

1925 1245; Clement, Margaret M; 1926-Apr 12; 2 yr; F; Yes; FB; No data; Yes

---- ---- Clifford, Helena; 1925-Dec 14; 1 mo; F; Yes; 3/8; No data; Yes

1925 1419; Clincher, Ida; 1925-Aug 11; 43 yr; ; Yes; FB; Child birth; Yes

---- ---- Clincher, Mathew; 1925-Nov 22; 3 mo; M; Yes; FB; Pneumonia; Yes

1925 1451; Colhoff, Fannie; 1926-Apr 10; 50 yr; F; Yes; 1/8; Tuberculosis; Yes

1925 5018; Cottier, Grace; 1925-June 30; 26 yr; F; Yes; 3/16; Nervous breakdown; No; Merriman, Nebr.

1925 1609; Crazy Ghost, Daisy; 1925-July 20; 22 yr; F; Yes; FB; Tuberculosis; Yes

---- ----- Crazy Ghost, Zack; 1926-Feb 24; 10 da; M; Yes; FB; No data; Yes

---- ----- Crooked Eyes, Ethel; 1925-Sept 5; 6 mo; F; Yes; FB; Cholera Marbus[sic]; Yes

---- ----- Cuny, Paul; 1925-Sept 29; 1 yr; M; Yes; 7/16; No data; Yes

---- ---- Cuny, Peter; 1925-Sept 15; 1 yr; M; Yes; 7/16; No data; Yes

---- ---- Dismounts Thrice, Normal; 1926-Apr 4; 8 mo; M; Yes; FB; Mumps and complications; Yes

1925 1836; Door; 1926-May 3; 77 yr; F; Yes; FB; Old Age; Yes

1925 1859; Dubray, Lillian; 1926-June 21; 24 yr; F; Yes; 13/16; No data; Yes

---- ---- Dubray, Margaret E; 1925-Oct 14; 4 mo; F; Yes; 11/32; No data; Yes

---- ---- Eagle Bull, Leo; 1926-May 22; 6 mo; M; Yes; FB; No data; Yes

1925 1904; Eagle Feather; 1926-Jan 2; 81 yr; F; Yes; FB; Old Age; Yes

1925 1907; Eagle Feather; 1925-Dec 18; 65 yr; F; Yes; FB; No data; Yes

1925 1940; Eagle Shield, Mary; 1926-Mar 27; 74 yr; F; Yes; FB; Old Age; Yes

1925 1967; Elbow Shield, Daisy; 1925-Oct 4; 46 yr; F; Yes; FB; Tuberculosis; Yes

1925 2050; Featherman, Douglas; 1926-June 4; 4 yr; M; Yes; FB; No data; Yes

1925 6119; Featherman, Eva; 1926-Feb 23; 25 yr; F; Yes; FB; Tuberculosis; Yes

State **South Dakota** Reservation **Pine Ridge** Agency or jurisdiction
Pine Ridge Office of Indian Affairs

Key: Year and Number On Last Census Roll; Surname, Given; Date of Death (Year-Month-Day); Age At Death; Sex; Tribe (Oglala Sioux unless given otherwise); Ward (Yes/No); Degree of Blood; Cause Of Death; At Jurisdiction Where Enrolled (Yes/No); (If no – Where)

Deaths Occurring Between July 1, 1925 and June 30, 1926 of Indians Enrolled at Jurisdiction

1925 2182; Foolish Woman, Nancy; 1926-Feb 27; 37 yr; F; Yes; FB; Tuberculosis; Yes

---- ---- Gay, Lawrence; 1926-Jan 26; 1 mo; M; Yes; 3/4; No data; Yes

1925 2282; Gerry, Benjamin; 1925-Sept 19; 53 yr; M; Yes; 1/2; FB; Appendicitis; Yes

1925 2422; Good Buffalo, Alice; 1925-July 15; 34 yr; F Yes; FB; Tuberculosis; Yes

1925 1182; Good Day; 1926-Jan 15; 84 yr; F; Yes; FB; No data; Yes

1925 2441; Good Horse; 1925-Sept 4; 57 yr; M; Yes; FB; No data; Yes

1925 2478; Good Voice Flute; 1926-June 25; 83 yr; M; Yes; FB; Old Age; Yes

---- ---- Grabbing Bear. Bell; 1026-Mar 24; 6 mo; F; Yes; 7/8; No data; Yes

1924 6150; Gray Cow; 1926-Jan 29; 67 yr; F; Yes; FB; No data; Yes

1925 2686; Her Horse; 1926-Mar 15; 76 yr; F; Yes; FB; Old Age; Yes

1925 2728; Her Red Blanket; 1926-June 18; 70 yr; F; Yes; FB; No data; Yes

1925 2732; High Bull, Edward; 1926-Apr 21; 21 yr; M; Yes; FB; Tuberculosis; Yes

1925 2797; Hollow Head, Minnie; 1926-Apr 22; 10 yr; F; Yes; FB; No data; Yes

1925 2823; Holy Bear No. 2; 1925-Aug 6; 78 yr; M; Yes; FB; No data; Yes

1925 4570; Holy Cloud, Myra or Nellie; 1925-Aug 28; 25 yr; F; Yes; FB; Tuberculosis; Yes

1925 2847; Holy Lake; 1926-June 1; 71 yr; F; Yes; FB; Old Age; Yes

1925 2926; Hunter, Julia; 1926-May 16; 17 yr; F; Yes; 1/2; Tuberculosis; Yes

1925 2926; Hunts Horses, Nancy; 1926-Jan 19; 76 yr; F; Yes; FB; No data; Yes

1925 2974; Iron Bull; 1926-Feb 26; 70 yr; M; Yes; FB; Pneumonia; Yes

1925 2978; Iron Bull, James; 1925-Nov 15; 44 yr; M; Yes; FB; Pneumonia; Yes

1925 3011; Iron Deer, Noah; 1925-July 1; 1 yr; M; Yes; FB; No data; Yes

1925 3033; Iron Rope, Anna; 1926-Mar 27; 1 yr; F; Yes; FB; Constipation; Yes

1925 3048; Iron Shield; 1925-Aug 8; 71 yr; M; Yes; FB; Accident; Yes

1925 3049; Iron Shield, Ida; 1925-Dec 9; 63 yr; F; Yes; FB; No data; Yes

1925 3295; Kills At Night, Annie; 1925-July 28; 66 yr; F; Yes; FB; Sun Stroke; Yes

1925 3434; LaBuff, Alice; 1926-May 25; 55 yr; F; Yes; 1/2; No data; Yes

1925 3563; Late Warrior, (Annie); 1926-May 8; 78 yr; F; Yes; FB; Old Age; Yes

---- ---- Little Boy, Chauncey; 1926-Feb 2; 3 mo; M; Yes; FB; Pneumonia; Yes

1925 3697; Little Bird, Philip; 1926-Mar 19; 45 yr; M; Yes; FB; Tuberculosis; Yes

1925 3721; Little Chief, Peter; 1925-July 28; 23 yr; M; Yes; FB; Tuberculosis; Yes

1925 3728, Little Cloud, Norman; 1926-Feb 21; 1 yr; M; Yes; FB; No data; Yes

1925 3765; Little Hawk, Moses; 1926-Jan 4; 21 yr; M; Yes; FB; Tuberculosis; Yes

1925 3791; Little Leader, Susie; 1925-Aug 21; 57 yr; F; Yes; FB; Tuberculosis; Yes

1925 3792; Little Moon, Bessie; 1925-Aug 20; 74 yr; F; Yes; FB; Blood Poison; Yes

1925 3810; Little Soldier, Rudolph; 1925-Aug 18; 29 yr; M; Yes; FB; Tuberculosis; Yes

1925 3845; Little White Man, Hattie; 1926-Apr 24; 11 yr; F; Yes; FB; Tuberculosis; Yes

1925 3935; Lone Elk, Fannie; 1925-Dec 28; 65 yr; F; Yes; FB; Tuberculosis; Yes

State **South Dakota** Reservation **Pine Ridge** Agency or jurisdiction
Pine Ridge Office of Indian Affairs

Key: Year and Number On Last Census Roll; Surname, Given; Date of Death (Year-Month-Day); Age At Death; Sex; Tribe (Oglala Sioux unless given otherwise); Ward (Yes/No); Degree of Blood; Cause Of Death; At Jurisdiction Where Enrolled (Yes/No); (If no – Where)

Deaths Occurring Between July 1, 1925 and June 30, 1926 of Indians Enrolled at Jurisdiction

1925   382;   Long Knife; 1925-Dec 14; 61 yr; F; Yes; FB; No data; Yes

1925 4018;   Long Soldier, Oscar; 1926-Feb 16; 45 yr; M; Yes; FB; No data; Yes

1925 4193;   Meat, Violet; 1925-July 31; 13 yr; F; Yes; FB; Tuberculosis; Yes

1925 4075;   Makes Good, Julia; 1925-Sept 26; 9 yr; F; Yes; FB; Tuberculosis; Yes

1925 4198;   Meat, Joseph; 1926-May 30; 43 yr; M; Yes; FB; Tuberculosis; Yes

1925 4449;   McGaa, Ethel Doris; 1926-Apr 28; 17 yr; F; Yes; 1/4; Tuberculosis; Yes

1925 4197;   Meat, Nelson Jos; 1925-Aug 30; 6 mo; M; Yes; FB; Summer complaint; Yes

1925 5188;   Medicine Horse; 1925-Mar 11; 80 yr; F; Yes; FB; Heart Trouble; Yes

1925 4281;   Medicine Woman; 1926-Mar 7; 67 yr; F; Yes; FB; No data; Yes

----   ----   Mesteth, Roy; 1925-Dec 25; 1 day; M; Yes; FB; No data; Yes

1925 4312;   Mills, Arthur; 1925-Sept 11; 3 yr; M; Yes; 5/8; Convulsions; Yes

1925 4296;   Mills, Thomas Sr; 1926-Feb 11; 62 yr; M; Yes; 1/2; No data; Yes

----   ----   Three Stars, Emily Mildred; 1926-Mar 29; 7 mo; F; Yes; 13/16; No data; Yes

1925 6533;   Thunder Club, Mary; 1926-May 7; 44 yr; F; Yes; FB; Tuberculosis; Yes

1925 6542;   Thunder Hawk, Berdena; 1925-Aug 28; 7 mo; F; Yes; 7/8; Cholera Marbus[sic]; Yes

1925 6557;   Thunder Tail, Emily; 1925-Mar 1; 9 mo; F; Yes; FB; No data; Yes

1925 6551;   Thunder Horse, Ethel E; 1925-July 30; 5 yr; F; Yes; FB; No data; Yes

1925 6587;   Top Bear. Rosa; 1926-Feb 24; 14 yr; F; Yes; FB; Tuberculosis; Yes

1925 6703;   Twist, Henry; 1925-Sept 23; 73 yr; M; Yes; F; Old Age; Yes

1925 6821;   Two Two, Aloysius; 1925-Nov 27; 2 yr; M; Yes; 7/8; Tuberculosis; Yes

1925 6847;   Understanding Crow, Alex Thomas; 1926-May 23; 19 yr; M; Yes; FB; No data; Yes

1925 1252;   Walks Fast, Arthur; 1925-Nov 12; 16 yr; M; Yes; FB; Tuberculosis; Yes

1925 6931;   Warrior Woman; 1926-May 19; 56 yr; F; Yes; FB; No data; Yes

1925 7014;   Weston, Rachel Lavina; 1925-Oct 25; 1 yr; F; Yes; FB; Dysentery; Yes

1925 7039;   Whirlwind Horse, Josie; 1926-Feb 1; 61 yr; F; Yes; FB; No data; Yes

1925 7073;   White Arrow, Leaf; 1926-Apr 28; 80 yr; F; Yes; FB; No data; Yes

1925; 7059;   White, Mamie; 1925-Dec 16; 45 yr; F; Yes; FB; No data; Yes

1925 7084;   White Bear Claws, Oliver; 1925-Sept 30; 18 yr; M; Yes; FB; No data; Yes

----   ----   White Bull, Ivan;; 1926-Apr 9; 4 mo; M; Yes; FB; Pneumonia; Yes

1925 7106;   White Bull, Vergel; 1925-Nov 26; 1 yr; M; Yes; FB; Tuberculosis; Yes

1925 7182;   White Face; 1925-Aug 24; 78 yr; F; Yes; FB; Old Age; Yes

1925 7212;   White Hawk, Lawrence; 1926-Mar 26; 1 yr; M; Yes; FB; No data; Yes

1925 7243;   White Mouse, Rachel; 1925-July 18; 60 yr; F Yes; FB; Dropsy; Yes

1925 7262;   White Shield, Lizzie; 1925-Nov 10; 61 yr; F; Yes; FB; Uremia weakness; Yes

----   ----   White Wash, Albert; 1924-May 3; 2 da; M; Yes; FB; No data; Yes

1925 7358;   Woman Dress, Lenora Mary; 1926-Feb 27; 1 ye; F; Yes; FB; Tuberculosis; Yes

State **South Dakota** Reservation **Pine Ridge** Agency or jurisdiction
Pine Ridge Office of Indian Affairs

Key: Year and Number On Last Census Roll; Surname, Given; Date of Death (Year-Month-Day); Age At Death; Sex; Tribe (Oglala Sioux unless given otherwise); Ward (Yes/No); Degree of Blood; Cause Of Death; At Jurisdiction Where Enrolled (Yes/No); (If no – Where)

Deaths Occurring Between July 1, 1925 and June 30, 1926 of Indians Enrolled at Jurisdiction

---- ---- Wounded Arrow, Jene F; 1925-Oct 24; 3 mo; F; Yes; FB; Pneumonia; Yes

1925 7158; White Dress, Richard; 1926-Mar 16; 2 yr; M; Yes; FB; No data; Yes

1925 7439; Yellow Bear, Francis; 1925-Sept 6; 6 mo; M; Yes; FB; Diarrhea; Yes

1925 7533; Yellow Shirt, Titus; 1926-June 25; 17 yr; M; Yes; FB; Tuberculosis; Yes

DEATH ROLL

EXCLUSIVE OF STILLBIRTHS

1927
(July 1, 1926 - June 30, 1927)

PINE RIDGE RESERVATION
PINE RIDGE SOUTH DAKOTA

State __South Dakota__ Reservation __Pine Ridge__ Agency or jurisdiction __Pine Ridge__ Office of Indian Affairs

Key: Year and Number On Last Census Roll; Surname, Given; Date of Death (Year-Month-Day); Age At Death; Sex; Tribe (Oglala Sioux unless given otherwise); Ward (Yes/No); Degree of Blood; Cause Of Death; At Jurisdiction Where Enrolled (Yes/No); (If no – Where)

Deaths Occurring Between July 1, 1926 and June 30, 1927 of Indians Enrolled at Jurisdiction

1926 21a; Addison, Martha; 1927-Jan 10; 6 mo; F; Yes; FB; Pneumonia; Yes
1926 190; Apple, Kenneth; 1927-Jan 21; 3 yr; M; Yes; 7/8; No data; Yes
---- ---- Ant, Hobart; 1927-May 4; 1/2 hr; M; Yes; 13/16; No data; Yes
1926 165; Apple, Christina; 1927-Feb 26; 10 yr; F; Yes; 3/4; Tuberculosis; Yes
1926 209; Arrow Wound, Jessie; 1927-Apr 9; 16 yr; F; Yes; FB; Tuberculosis; Yes
1926 283; Bad Wound, Leroy S; 1926-Oct 12; 6 mo; M; Yes; 5/8; No data; Yes
1926 313; Bald Head, Paul; 1927-Mar 30; 9 yr; M; Yes; FB; Pneumonia; Yes
1926 335; Bear Eagle; 1927-June 29; 71 yr; M; Yes; FB; Tuberculosis; Yes
1926 357; Bear Nose, Elwin; 1927-Mar 19; 2 yr; M; Yes; FB; Measles; Yes
1926 369; Bear Robe, Antoine K; 1927-Feb 27; 4 yr; M; Yes; 7/8; Measles; Yes
1926 376; Bear Robe, Ida; 1927-Mar 18; 45 yr; F; Yes; FB; Tuberculosis; Yes
1926 354; Bear Nose, Rosa; 1927-June 13; 25 yr; F; Yes; FB; No data; Yes
1926 384; Bear Robe, Margaret; 1926-Oct 7; 8 mo; F; Yes; FB; No data; Yes
1926 398; Bear Saves Life, Todd; 1927-May 1; 3 yr; M; Yes; 7/8; Measles and pneumonia; Yes
1926 429; Belt, Philip; 1927-Mar 28; 7 yr; M; Yes; FB; Tuberculosis; Yes
1926 5948; Between Lodges, Kate; 1927-Apr 14; 17 yr; F; Yes; FB; Tuberculosis; Yes
1926 524; Big Wolf, Fannie; 1927-May 5; 63 yr F; Yes; FB; Fell from wagon; Yes
1926 548; Bird Head, Lorinda; 1926-July 16; 3 mo; F; Yes; FB; Tuberculosis; Yes
1926 556; Bird Head, William; 1926-Sept 6; 68 yr; M; Yes; FB; Tuberculosis; Yes
---- ---- Bissonette, Lawrence F; 1927-Jan 9; 5 mo; M; Yes; 3/4; Pneumonia; Yes
1926 592; Bissonette, Rosa; 1926-Dec 27; 46 yr; F; Yes; 3/4; Hemorrhage; Yes
1926 643; Black Bear, Duffy; 1927-Mar 9; 6 yr; M; Yes; FB; Measles; Yes
---- ---- Black Bear, Simon; 1927-June 24; 3 mo; M; Yes; FB; Pneumonia; Yes
1926 647; Black Beard, Ella; 1927-June 26; 49 ye; F; Yes; FB; Flu; Yes
1926 654; Black Bird, Maggie; 1927-Jan 9; 26 yr; F; Yes; 1/2; Tuberculosis; Yes
1926 667; Black Bull, Mathew; 1927-Apr 5; 4 yr; M; Yes; FB; No data; Yes
1926 672; Black Cat, Sadie; 1926-Oct 13; 19 yr; F; Yes; FB; Tuberculosis; Yes
---- ---- Black Crow, Leona; 1927-Mar 2; 2 da; F; Yes; FB; Measles; Yes
1926 711; Black Eyes, Abe; 1926-Sept 29; 16 yr; M; Yes; FB; No data; Yes
---- ---- Black Elk, Charlotte R; 1926-Oct 30; 3 mo; F; Yes; 3/4; No data; Yes
1926 727; Bleack[sic] Feather, Sylvester; 1926-Sept 2; 3 yr; M; Yes; 7/8; Tuberculosis; Yes
1926 742; Black Horse, William; 1927-May 28; 44 yr; M; Yes; FB; Lightning; Yes
---- ---- Blind Man, Amelia; 1927-May 7; 8 mo; F; Yes; FB; Whooping Cough; Yes
---- ----- Blacksmith, Mathew; 1927-June 5; 6 da; M; Yes; FB; Premature birth; Yes
---- ---- Blue Bird, Dorothy; 1927-Jan 8; 5 mo; F; Yes; 15/16; No data; Yes
1926 795; Blue Bird, James Theo; 1927-Jan 16; 2 yr; M; Yes; 15/16; Pneumonia; Yes

State **South Dakota** Reservation **Pine Ridge** Agency or jurisdiction
Pine Ridge Office of Indian Affairs

Key: Year and Number On Last Census Roll; Surname, Given; Date of Death (Year-Month-Day); Age At Death; Sex; Tribe (Oglala Sioux unless given otherwise); Ward (Yes/No); Degree of Blood; Cause Of Death; At Jurisdiction Where Enrolled (Yes/No); (If no – Where)

Deaths Occurring Between July 1, 1926 and June 30, 1927 of Indians Enrolled at Jurisdiction

1926 794; Blue Bird, Olive B; 1917-Feb 18; 4 yr; F; Yes; 15/16; Tuberculosis; Yes

1926 856; Brafford, Robert L; 1926-Oct 3; 5 yr; M; Yes; 3/8; No data; Yes

1926 865; Brave, Anna; 1926-Oct 5; 40 yr; F; Yes; FB; Miscarriage; Yes

---- --- Brave, Mary; 1927-June 21; 2 mo; F; Yes; FB; No data; Yes

1926 884; Brave Dog; 1926-Nov 13; 84 yr; M; Yes; FB; No data; Yes

1926 890; Brave Heart; 1926-Dec 15; 84 yr; M; Yes; FB; Old Age; Yes

1926 911; Breast, Ida; 1927-May 18; 10 yr; F; Yes; 3/4; Tuberculosis; Yes

---- --- Brewer, William L; 1927-Feb 13; 5 mo; M; Yes; 3/8; No data; Yes

---- --- Brings Yellow, Vernon; 1926-Oct 22; 1 yr; M; Yes; FB; Convulsions; Yes

---- --- Brown, Ephraim N; 1927-Feb 1; 25 da; M; Yes; FB; Pneumonia; Yes

1926 982; Broken Rope, Laura E; 1927-Mar 7; 3 yr; F; Yes; 13/16; Measles; Yes

1926 1063; Brown Eyes, John; 1927-Mar 15; 30 yr; M; Yes; 3/4; Tuberculosis; Yes

1926 1067; Brown Eyes, Lome; 1927-Feb 5; 10 yr; F; Yes; 7/8; Tuberculosis; Yes

1926 1076; Brown Wolf; 1926-Nov 27; 83 yr; M; Yes; FB; Old Age; Yes

1926 1088; Buckskin Strings; 1926-Aug 11; 69 yr; F; Yes; FB; Gonorrhea; Yes

1926 1115; Bull Bear, Jesse; 1927-May 18; 39 yr; M; Yes; FB; Heart Trouble; Yes

1926 1133; Bull Bear, Lorain S; 1927-Jan 23; 8 mo; F; Yes; FB; No data; Yes

---- ---- Bull Bear, Lucy; 1927-Feb 9; 10 mo; F; Yes; FB; No data; Yes

1926 1149; Bull Man, Everett; 1927- Jan 31; 2 yr; M; Yes; FB; No data; Yes

1926 1150; Bull Man, Laura; 1927-Feb 7; 11 mo; F; Yes; FB; No data; Yes

---- ---- Burns Prairie, Clement; 1927-Jan 1; 8 mo; M; Yes; FB; Pneumonia; Yes

1926 1166; Bush, Louis; 1927-Mar 26; 11 mo; M; Yes; 7/8; Pneumonia; Yes

1926 1184; Calico; 1926-July 30; 86 yr; M; Yes; FB; Old Age; Yes

---- ---- Cedar Face, Lucy; 1926-Sept 24; 1 yr; F; Yes; FB; No data; Yes

1926 1228; Center, Wm Jr; 1926-Nov 15; 4 yr; M; Yes; FB; No data; Yes

1926 1264; Charging Thunder, Sophie; 1927-Jan 24; 1 yr; F; Yes; FB; Pneumonia; Yes

1926 1272; Chase Close To Lodge, Adelia; 1926-July 31; 68 yr; F; Yes; FB; Tuberculosis; Yes

1926 1326; Chief Eagle, Peter; 1926-July 28; 49 yr; M; Yes; FB; Tuberculosis; Yes

1926 1334; Chips, Charles; 1927-Mar 24; 3 yr; M; Yes; FB; Pneumonia; Yes

---- ---- Chips, Ethel May; 1927-Mar 30; 8 mo; F; Yes; FB; Measles; Yes

1926 1357; Clifford, Belva; 1927-Apr 7; 11 yr; F; Yes; 5/16[sic]; No data; Yes

1926 1426; Clincher, John (Jas); 1927-Apr 15; 23 yr; M; Yes; FB; Tuberculosis; Yes

1926 1423; Clincher, Kiva Tina; 1926-Oct 30; 15 yr; F; Yes; FB; Tuberculosis; Yes

---- ---- Clincher, Mathew; 1926-Nov 4; 1 mo; M; Yes; FB; No data; Yes

1926 1665; Cross, Curtis; 1927-Mar 2; 10 mo; M; Yes; 15/16; No data; Yes

---- ---- Crow, Dorothy; 1927-Mar 9; 5 mo; F; Yes; FB; Pneumonia; Yes

1926 7226; Dancing Bear; 1926-July 2; 63 yr; F; Yes; FB; No data; Yes

1926 1077; Day; 1926-Sept 20; 80 yr; F; Yes; FB; Summer Complaint; Yes

1926 1797; Dirt Kettle; 1926-Aug 30; 78 yr; M; Yes; FB; Old Age; Yes

Key: Year and Number On Last Census Roll; Surname, Given; Date of Death (Year-Month-Day); Age At Death; Sex; Tribe (Oglala Sioux unless given otherwise); Ward (Yes/No); Degree of Blood; Cause Of Death; At Jurisdiction Where Enrolled (Yes/No); (If no – Where)

Deaths Occurring Between July 1, 1926 and June 30, 1927 of Indians Enrolled at Jurisdiction

1926 1803; Dismounts Thrice, Delia; 1927-June 27; 29 yr; F; Yes; FB; Strangulation; Yes

---- ---- Dismounts Thrice, Martha; 1926-Nov 21; 1 yr; F; Yes; FB; No data; Yes

1926 1840; Don't Think, Charles; 1927-Apr 21; 55 yr; M; Yes; FB; Rheumatism; Yes

1926 1839; Dog On Hill; 1927-June 17; 88 yr; M; Yes; FB; No data; Yes

1926 1874; Dubray, Henry A; 1926-Sept 22; 10 mo; M; Yes; 21/32; No data; Yes

---- ---- Eagle Fox, Pearl; 1926-July 18; 4 da; F; Yes; FB; Convulsions; Yes

---- ---- Eagle Bull, Henry; 1927-Mar 4; 10 da; M; Yes; FB; Measles; Yes

---- ---- Eagle Elk, Robert E; 1927-Apr 28; 8 mo; M; Yes; FB; Pneumonia; Yes

1926 1924; Eagle Feather, William; 1927-Feb 5; 66 yr; M; Yes; FB; Disease of esophagus; Yes

1926 1946; Eagle Hill; 1927-Feb 17; 81 yr; F; Yes; FB; No data; Yes

1926 1989; Elk Boy, Huron; 1927-Feb 16; 78 yr; M; Yes; FB; Old Age; Yes

1926 2009; Fast Eagle; 1926-July 19; 67 yr; M; Yes; FB; No data; Yes

---- ---- Feather, Leo; 1926-Oct 11; 2 mo; M; Yes; FB; No data; Yes

1926 2066; Featherman, Josephine; 1927-Jan 18; 3 yr; F; Yes; FB; No data; Yes

1926 2087; Feather On Head, Emma; 1927-Jan 14; 2 yr; F; Yes; 7/8; Pneumonia; Yes

1926 2085; Feather On Head, Silas; 1926-Sept 12; 1 yr; M; Yes; 7/8; Pneumonia; Yes

1926 2086; Feather On Head, Susie; 1927-Jan 4; 1 yr; F; Yes; 7/8; Pneumonia; Yes

1926 2096; Fights Bear, Adam; 1927-May 15; 14 yr; M; Yes; FB; Tuberculosis; Yes

---- ----- Fire Thunder, Annie; 1927-Feb 27; 2 hr; F; Yes; FB; No data; Yes

1926 2180; Flying Hawk, Lucy; 1927-May 15; 19 yr; F; Yes; FB; Tuberculosis; Yes

1926 2205; Fool Head, Ella; 1927-Mar 12; 11 yr; F; Yes; FB; Tuberculosis; Yes

1926 2210; Fool Head, Mabel Ruth; 1927-Jan 18; 1 yr; F; Yes; FB; No data; Yes

1926 2215; Foot, Jennie; 1926-Dec 6; 74 yr; F; Yes; FB; Old Age; Yes

1926 2280; Garcia, Cornelia; 1927-Jan 24; 1 yr; F; Yes; 3/8; No data; Yes

1926 2279; Garcia, Peter; 1927-June 11; 2 1/2 yr; M; Yes; 8/8; Tuberculosis; Yes

1926 2289; Garnett, Evelyn; 1927-Apr 1; 4 yr; F; Yes; 1/2; No data; Yes

1926 2287; Garnett, Lucille; 1917-Apr 2; 10 yr; F; Yes; 1/2; No data; Yes

1926 2296a; Garnier, Wesley; 1927-June 5; 1 yr; M; Yes; 9/16; Whooping Cough; Yes

1926 2347; Ghost Bear, Hobert; 1927-Apr 7; 6 yr; M; Yes; FB; Pneumonia; Yes

1926 2339; Ghost Bear, Sarah; 1926-Sept 24; 57 yr; F; Yes; FB; Burned; Yes

1926 2413; Goes In Center, Beulah; 1927-Mar 9; 8 yr; F; Yes; FB; Pneumonia; Yes

1926 2414; Goes In Center, Joseph; 1927-Apr 6; 4 yr; M; Yes; FB; Measles & pneumonia; Yes

1926 2415; Goes In Center, May; 1927-Apr 6; 2 yr; F; Yes; FB; Measles & pneumonia; Yes

1926 2467; Good Cloud; 1927-Mar 10; 88 yr; F; Yes; FB; Old Age; Yes

State **South Dakota** Reservation **Pine Ridge** Agency or jurisdiction
Pine Ridge Office of Indian Affairs

Key: Year and Number On Last Census Roll; Surname, Given; Date of Death (Year-Month-Day); Age At
Death; Sex; Tribe (Oglala Sioux unless given otherwise); Ward (Yes/No); Degree of Blood; Cause Of Death;
At Jurisdiction Where Enrolled (Yes/No); (If no – Where)

Deaths Occurring Between July 1, 1926 and June 30, 1927 of Indians Enrolled at Jurisdiction

1926 2468; Good Crow, Abraham; 1927-Jan 28; 43 yr; M; Yes; FB; Pneumonia;
Yes

---- ---- Good Crow, Zona; 1927-Jan 11; 1 mo; F; Yes; FB; No data; Yes

1926 2516 Good Voice Elk, May; 1927-May 28; 3 yr; F; Yes; FB; Whooping
Cough; Yes

---- ---- Good Voice Elk, Sterman; 1927-May 18; 2 mo; M; Yes; FB; Whooping
Cough; Yes

1926 2519; Good Voice Elk, Victoria; 1927-Jan 9; 11 mo; F; Yes; FB; No data; Yes

1926 2535; Good Voice Flute, Louis; 1927-Jan 16; 1 yr; M; Yes; FB; Fever; Yes

1926 2534; Good Voice Flute, Stewart; 1927-Apr 17; 3 yr; M; Yes; FB; Fever; Yes

---- ---- Grass, May Greda; 1927-Apr 11; 2 yr; F; Yes; FB; No data; Yes

1926 2575; Grass, Victor R; 1927-Apr 7; 2 yr; M; Yes; FB; Pneumonia; Yes

1926 415; Gray Cow, Sadie; 1926-Nov 22; 26 yr; F; Yes; FB; No data; Yes

1926 2585; Gray Grass; 1926-Aug 8; 65 yr; F; Yes; FB; Tuberculosis; Yes

1926 2583; Gray Grass, Kiva Jane; 1927-Feb 9; 6 yr; F; Yes; FB; Scarlet fever; Yes

1926 2584; Gray Grass, Mercy E; 1926-Aug 30; 11 yr; F; Yes; FB; No data; Yes

1926 2587; Green, Lloyd; 1926-Aug 11; 29 Yr; M; Yes; 3/16; Gastric Ulcer; Yes

1926 2605; Groaning Bear, Elsie; 1927-Feb 3; 9 yr; F; Yes; FB; No data; Yes

---- ---- Hauff, Vernon Dale; 1927-Feb 18; 6 da; M; Yes; 3/16; No data; Yes

---- ---- Helm, Julias Jean; 1926-Aug 8; 1 yr; M; Yes; 1/8; Gastro intestinal
taxemia[sic]; Yes

1926 2717; Helper, Noah; 1926-July 3; 27 yr; M; Yes; FB; Intoxication; Yes

1926 2725; Henry, Eunice; 1927-Jan 28; 6 yr; F; Yes; FB; No data; Yes

1926 2786; High Cat, Leonard; 1926-Dec 9; 7 yr; M; Yes; FB; Tuberculosis; Yes

1926 2791; High Crane, Cordelia R; 1927-Feb 3; 8 mo; F; Yes; 15/16; Measles; Yes

---- ---- High Wolf, Clarence; 1927-June 16; 1 yr; M; Yes; 11/16; Whooping
Cough; Yes

1926 2877; Holy Breath, Kate; 1927-Jan 2; 58 yr; F; Yes; FB; Bowl[sic] trouble; Yes

1926 2878; Holy Cloud; 1927-Jan 9; 76 yr; M; Yes; FB; Old Age; Yes

1926 2883; Holy Day; 1927-June 3; 83 yr; F; Yes; FB; Old Age; Yes

1926 2896; Holy Elk, Jos; 1927-June 9; 2 yr; M; Yes; 7/8; Tuberculosis; Yes

1926 2850; Hollow Head, George; 1927-Apr 17; 48 yr; SM; Yes; FB; Tuberculosis;
Yes

1926 2871; Hollow Horn, Gilbert; 1927-Feb 17; 1 yr; M; Yes; FB; High Fever; Yes

1926 2870; Hollow Horn, Norbert; 1927-Mar 24; 4 yr; M; Yes; FB; High Fever; Yes

1926 2917; Hopkins, Lillian E; 1927-Feb 26; 1 yr; F; Yes; FB; No data; Yes

---- ---- Horse, Oliver; 1927-Apr 8; 5 mo; M; Yes; FB; Measles; Yes

---- ---- Ice, Vernie; 1927-June 4;

1926 3064; Iron Crow, Noah; 1927-Jan 16; 11 mo; M; Yes; FB; No data; Yes

1926 3059; Iron Crow, Morris; 1927-Jan 18; 1 yr; M; Yes; FB; No data; Yes

1926 3086; Iron Horse, Leo; 1927-Mar 25; 4 yr; M; Yes; FB; Measles; Yes

1926 3092; Iron Rope, Joseph; 1927-Mar 27; 7 yr; M; Yes; FB; Pneumonia; Yes

State **South Dakota** Reservation **Pine Ridge** Agency or jurisdiction **Pine Ridge** Office of Indian Affairs

Key: Year and Number On Last Census Roll; Surname, Given; Date of Death (Year-Month-Day); Age At Death; Sex; Tribe (Oglala Sioux unless given otherwise); Ward (Yes/No); Degree of Blood; Cause Of Death; At Jurisdiction Where Enrolled (Yes/No); (If no – Where)

Deaths Occurring Between July 1, 1926 and June 30, 1927 of Indians Enrolled at Jurisdiction

---- ---- Iron Rope, Joseph; 1927-June 21; 3 mo; M; Yes; FB; Whooping Cough; Yes

1926 3102; Iron Teeth, Mary; 1927-June 9; 52 yr; F; Yes; FB; Cancer of Stomach; Yes

1926 3133; Jack, Christina; 1927-Apr 12; 2 yr; F; Yes; FB; Measles & pneumonia; Yes

1926 3151; Janis, Antoine; 1926-Nov 28; 68 yr; M; Yes; 1/2; Cystitis; Yes

1926 3190; Janis, Edsel; 1927-Feb 5; 3 yr; M; Yes; 1/2; Pneumonia; Yes

1926 3147; Janis, Louie; 1927-Jan 23; 5 yr; M; Yes; 7/8; No data; Yes

1926 3177; Janis, Benjamin; 1927-Apr 27; 62 yr; F[sic]; Yes; 1/2; No data; Yes

---- ---- Jealous Of Him, Edith; 1927-Jan 28; 2 mo; F; Yes; 15/16; Pneumonia; Yes

1926 3322; Jumping Eagle, Alpha Amelia; 1927-Mar 6; 3 yr; F; Yes; 3/4; Pertussis; Yes

1926 3342; Kicking Bear, Adolph; 1927-Feb 19; 10 mo; M; Yes; FB; No data; Yes

1926 3341; Kicking Bear, Lema; 1927-Apr 5; 7 yr; F; Yes; FB; Pneumonia; Yes

1926 3368; Kills And Comes Back, Claude; 1927-June 22; 27 yr; M; Yes; FB; Tuberculosis; Yes

1926 3392; Kills Enemy, Ambrose; 1927-Jan 18; 3 yr; M; Yes; FB; No data; Yes

---- ---- Kills Game; 1926-Oct 12; 69 yr; F; Yes; FB; No data; Yes

1926 3430; Kills Right, Emma; 1927-Jan 3; 1 yr; F; Yes; FB; Pneumonia; Yes

1926 3461; Kindle, Amy; 1927-Jan 22; 11 yr; F; Yes; FB; Tuberculosis; Yes

1926 3473; King, Moses B; 1927-Jan 25; 10 mo; M; Yes; 7/8; No data; Yes

1926 3635; Lays Bad, Ramsey; 1927-Apr 27; 4 yr; M; Yes; FB; Hemorrhage; Yes

1926 3644; Lays Hard, Amos; 1927-Jan 19; 6 yr; M; Yes; 3/4; Tuberculosis; Yes

1926 3651 Lays Hard, Verine; 1927-Apr 6; 2 yr; F; Yes; FB; Pneumonia; Yes

1926 3735; Little, Mary; 1927-May 3; 51 yr; F; Yes; FB; Tuberculosis; Yes

1926 3754; Little Bear, Mamie; 1927-Mar 25; 10 mo; F; Yes; 5/8; Measles; Yes

1926 3760; Little Bird, Daniel; 1926-July 23; 1 yr; M; Yes; FB; Fever; Yes

1926 3774; Little Bull, Alice; 1927-May 28; 62 yr; F Yes; FB; No data; Yes

1926 3805; Little Crow, Grace; 1927-Mar 5; 3 yr; F; Yes; FB; Pneumonia; Yes

1926 3806; Little Crow, Laura; 1927-Apr 7; 1 yr; F; Yes; FB; Pneumonia; Yes

1926 3815; Little Elk, Maggie; 1927-Apr 16; 46 yr; F; Yes; FB; Tuberculosis; Yes

1926 3819; Little Elk, Thomas; 1927-Mar 25; 25 yr; M; Yes; FB; Tuberculosis; Yes

1926 3857; Little Moon, Raymond; 1927-Jan 21; 1 yr; M; Yes; 7/8; Pneumonia; Yes

1926 6558; Lives Above; 1927-Apr 28; 80 yr; F; Yes; FB; No data; Yes

1926 3972; Living Outside, Elmore; 1927-Mar 20; 42 yr; M; Yes; FB; Tuberculosis; Yes

1926 3983; Loafer Joe, Leo; 1927-Feb 27; 1 yr; M; Yes; FB; Fever; Yes

1926 3985; Loafer Joe, Lucy; 1927-Apr 17; 3 yr; F; Yes; FB; Tuberculosis; Yes

---- ---- Locke, Titus Philomen; 1927-May 30; 3 mo; M; Yes; FB; No data; Yes

1926 4022; Lone Hill, Bryan; 1927-Mar 17; 2 yr; M; Yes; 7/8; Pneumonia; Yes

1926 4016; Lone Hill, Eva; 1927-Feb 20; 1 yr; F; Yes; 7/8; Pneumonia; Yes

Key: Year and Number On Last Census Roll; Surname, Given; Date of Death (Year-Month-Day); Age At Death; Sex; Tribe (Oglala Sioux unless given otherwise); Ward (Yes/No); Degree of Blood; Cause Of Death; At Jurisdiction Where Enrolled (Yes/No); (If no – Where)

Deaths Occurring Between July 1, 1926 and June 30, 1927 of Indians Enrolled at Jurisdiction

1926 4023; Lone Hill, Mildred P; 1927-Mar 18; 10 mo; F; Yes; 7/8; Measles; Yes

1926 4012; Lone Hill, Rebecca; 1927-Mar 14; 15 yr; F; Yes; 7/8; Tuberculosis; Yes

1926 4026; Lone Wolf, Leo; 1927-Jan 4; 17 yr; M; Yes; FB; Tuberculosis; Yes

1926 4036; Lone Wolf, Sylvia; 1927-Apr 2; 1 yr; F; Yes; FB; Fever; Yes

1926 4045; Long Bear, Howard; 1926-Oct 19; 57 yr; M; Yes; FB; No data; Yes

1926 4058; Long Dog, Joseph; 1926-Dec 14; 38 yr; M; Yes; FB; No data; Yes

1926 4064; Long Horn, Aaron; 1927-Apr 23; 68 yr; M; Yes; FB; Kidney nephritis; Yes

---- ---- Long Woman, Chas; 1927-Feb 12; 3 mo; M; Yes; FB; No data; Yes

---- ---- Long Woman, Eugene; 1927-Feb 15; 2 mo; M; Yes; FB; No data; Yes

1926 4137; Makes Good, Susie; 1927-Apr 4; 7 yr; F; Yes; FB; Tuberculosis; Yes

1926 4152; Makes Shine, William; 1927-Feb 16; 2 yr; M; Yes; FB; Whooping Cough; Yes

1926 4155; Man Above, Mary; 1926-Nov 21; 60 yr; F; Yes; FB; Tuberculosis; Yes

---- ---- Marrow Bone, Ephraim; 1927-Jan 15; 19 da; M; Yes; FB; No data; Yes

---- ---- Marrow Bone, Joseph; 1926-July 12; 7 yr; M; Yes; FB; Typhoid Fever; Yes

1926 4516; McGaa, Lawrence; 1927-June 15; 19 yr; M; Yes; 3/16; Tuberculosis; Yes

1926 4231; Means, Woodrow G; 1927-Mar 9; 14 yr; M; Yes; 3/4; Tuberculosis; Yes

1926 4269; Menard, Rufus; 1927-Feb 18; 27 yr; M; Yes; 3/4; Tuberculosis; Yes

1926 4332; Mesteth, Ambrose; 1927-June 12; 1 yr; M; Yes; FB; No data; Yes

1926 4307; Mesteth, Rita Geneva; 1927-May 13; 2 yr; F; Yes; 1/2; No data; Yes

1926 4325; Mesteth, Theodore C; 1927-Mar 9; 3 yr; M; Yes; 7/16; Measles & pneumonia; Yes

1926 4379; Mills, Kenneth J; 1927-Apr 19; 2 yr; M; Yes; 3/4; No data; Yes

1926 4383; Mills, Naomi; 1927-Apr 28; 29 yr; F; Yes; 5/16; Child birth; Yes

1926 4365; Mills, Richard; 1927-Mar 14; 31 yr; M; Yes; 3/4; Auto accident skull & thorax crushed; No; Downey, California

1926 4416; Moore, Henry; 1926-Oct 4; 52 yr; M; Yes; 1/2; No data; Yes

---- ---- Morrison, Christensen; 1927-Feb 20; 2 mo; M; Yes; 7/8; Pneumonia; Yes

---- ---- Morrison, Clyde; 1927-Feb 9; 6 mo; M; Yes; 7/8; No data; Yes

1926 4457; Morrison, Wilbert; 1927-Feb 28; 11 yr; M; Yes; 7/8; Tuberculosis; Yes

1926 4506; Moves Camp, Albert; 1927-Apr 17; 5 yr; M; Yes; FB; Tuberculosis; Yes

1926 4559; Nelson, James; 1926-Aug 25; 32 yr; M; Yes; FB; Inflammatory rheumatism; Yes

1926 4572; New Holy, Levi; 1927-Feb 12; 3 yr; M; Yes; FB; No data; Yes

1926 4616; Old Hair, Bernice; 1927-Jan 29; 2 yr; F; Yes; FB; No data; Yes

---- ---- Old Hair, Catherine; 1927-May 6; 16 da; F; Yes; FB; Measles & pneumonia; Yes

1926 4614; Old Hair, Thomas; 1926-Dec 4; 29 yr; M; Yes; FB; No data; Yes

---- ---- Old Horse, Mary; 1927-Feb 14; 6 mo; F; Yes; FB; No data; Yes

110

State **South Dakota** Reservation **Pine Ridge** Agency or jurisdiction
Pine Ridge Office of Indian Affairs

Key: Year and Number On Last Census Roll; Surname, Given; Date of Death (Year-Month-Day); Age At Death; Sex; Tribe (Oglala Sioux unless given otherwise); Ward (Yes/No); Degree of Blood; Cause Of Death; At Jurisdiction Where Enrolled (Yes/No); (If no – Where)

Deaths Occurring Between July 1, 1926 and June 30, 1927 of Indians Enrolled at Jurisdiction

1926 4638; One Feather, Mary; 1926-Oct 30; 70 yr; F; Yes; FB; No data; Yes
---- ---- Owen, Mervin B; 1927-Mar 16; 8 mo; M; Yes; 7/32; No data; Yes
---- ---- Pacer, Christine; 1927-Apr 27; 4 mo; F; Yes; FB; No data; Yes
1926 4680; Pablo, Lilly; 1927-Jan 2; 7 yr; F; Yes; 11/16; Tuberculosis; Yes
1926 4695; Pain On Hip, Cecelia; 1927-Mar 16; 3 yr; F; Yes; FB; No data; Yes
---- ---- Pain On Hip, Louisa; 1917-Apr 17; 4 mo; F; Yes; FB; Whooping
Cough; Yes
1926 4703; Palmier, Charles; 1926-Aug 6; 46 yr; M; Yes; 1/4; Bright's disease; Yes
1926 4756; Pawnee Leggins, Mary; 1927-Jan 18; 1 yr; F; Yes; FB; No data; Yes
1926 4779; Pine Bird, Charles; 1927-June 28; 39 yr; M; Yes; 7/8; Tuberculosis; Yes
1926 4783; Pine Bird, Dorothy; 1927-Mar 22; 1 yr; F; Yes; FB; Measles; Yes
1926 4793; Pipe On Head, Virginia; 1927-Jan 21; 2 yr; F; Yes; FB; Whooping
Cough; Yes
1926 4798; Plenty Arrows, Irene; 1927-Mar 7; 2 yr; F; Yes; FB; Pneumonia; Yes
---- ---- Plenty Wolf, Zack T; 1927-Mar 27; 4 mo; M; Yes; FB; Pneumonia; Yes
1926 4931; Pouting; 1927-Jan 2; 83 yr; F; Yes; FB; Old Age; Yes
---- ---- Pumpkin Seed, Francis; 1927-Mar 3; 3 da; M; Yes; FB; Measles; Yes
1926 5039; Pumpkin Seed, Grace; 1927-Mar 17; 3 yr; F; Yes; FB; Measles; Yes
1926 5040; Pumpkin Seed, Jefferson; 1927-Feb 26; 1 yr; M; Yes; FB; Measles; Yes
1926 7695; Pumpkin Seed, Sophia; 1926-Oct 29; 22 yr; F; Yes; FB; Tuberculosis;
Yes
1926 4975; Pretty Weasel; 1927-Jan 8; 69 yr; M; Yes; FB; Old Age; Yes
1926 5060; Quick Bear, Sarah; 1927-June 21; 23 yr; F; Yes; 3/4; No data; Yes
1926 5089; Randall, Alvina E; 1927-Jan 17; 4 yr; F; Yes; 5/8; Pneumonia; Yes
1926 5107; Randall, Helen; 1926-July 11; 13 yr; F; Yes; FB; Tuberculosis; Yes
---- ---- Randall, Noah; 1927-Apr 1; 5 da; M; Yes; FB; Pneumonia; Yes
1926 5139; Red Bow, Katherine; 1927-Feb 21; 2 yr; F; Yes; FB; Fever; Yes
1926 5179; Red Cloud, Alice; 1927-Apr 6; 3 yr; F; Yes; FB; Measles; Yes
1926 5191; Red Cloud, Evelyn J; 1927-Mar 22; 2 yr; F; Yes; FB; Pneumonia; Yes
1926 5217; Red Eagle, Lee; 1927-Feb 6; 4 yr; M; Yes; FB; No data; Yes
1926 5218; Red Eagle, Nora; 1927-Feb 2; 11 mo; F; Yes; FB; No data; Yes
1926 5225; Red Ear Horse, Susan; 1926-Nov 16; 13 yr; Yes; FB; Tuberculosis; Yes
1926 6409; Red Elk, Marguerite; 1926-Dec 25; 10 yr; F; Yes; FB; Tuberculosis; Yes
1926 5234; Red Elk, Ole; 1927-May 9; 10 yr; M; Yes; FB; Tuberculosis; Yes
1926 5257; Red Eyes, Julia; 1927-May 13; 44 yr; F; Yes; FB; Gallstones; Yes
---- ---- Red Feather, Bertha E; 1926-Sept 17; 2 mo; F; FB; Diarrhea; Yes
1926 5277; Red Feather, Jessie; 1927; Mar; 25; 19 yr; F; Yes; FB; Tuberculosis;
Yes
1926 5273; Red Feather, Robert; 1927-Feb 27; 2 yr; M; Yes; FB; Measles; Yes
1926 5320; Red Owl, Dorothy; 1927-Mar 11; 6 yr; F; Yes; FB; Pneumonia; Yes
1926 5325; Red Paint, Sarah; 1927-May 17; 17 yr; F; Yes; FB; Epilepsy; Yes
1926 5370; Red Shirt, Joseph; 1927-Feb 15; 2 yr; M; Yes; 7/8; Pneumonia and
whooping cough; Yes

State **South Dakota** Reservation **Pine Ridge** Agency or jurisdiction
Pine Ridge Office of Indian Affairs

Key: Year and Number On Last Census Roll; Surname, Given; Date of Death (Year-Month-Day); Age At Death; Sex; Tribe (Oglala Sioux unless given otherwise); Ward (Yes/No); Degree of Blood; Cause Of Death; At Jurisdiction Where Enrolled (Yes/No); (If no – Where)

Deaths Occurring Between July 1, 1926 and June 30, 1927 of Indians Enrolled at Jurisdiction

1926 5374; Red Star, Goldie; 1927-Mar 20; 7 yr; F; Yes; FB; Tuberculosis; Yes

1926 5375; Red Star, Lydia; 1927-Ap-r 2; 1 yr; F; Yes; FB; Pneumonia; Yes

---- ---- Red Star, Samuel; 1926-Oct 30; 1 yr; M; Yes; FB; No data; Yes

1926 5414; Returns From Scout, Agnes; 1926-Aug 18; 85 yr; F; Yes; FB; Old Age; Yes

1926 5423; Returns From Scout, Stephen; 1927-Apr 3; 3 yr; M; Yes; FB; Measles and pneumonia; yes

1926 5459; Richard, Albert V; 1927-Mar 23; 3 yr; M; Yes; 9/16; No data; Yes

---- ---- Richard, Alfred; 1927-Jan 7; 1 yr; M; Yes; 11/16; No data; Yes

1926 5488; Richard, Louis; 1927-Mar 24; 9 yr; M; Yes; 7/8; Tuberculosis; Yes

1926 5522a; Ringing Shield, Zelma; 1926-Nov 8; 7 mo; F; Yes; FB; Pneumonia; Yes

1926 5559; Romero, Florence; 1927-June 8; 53 yr; F; Yes; FB; Tuberculosis; Yes

1926 5708; Running Shield, Grace; 1927-June 6; 47 yr; F; Yes; FB; Tuberculosis; Yes

1926 5716; Runs Above, George; 1926-July 2; 26 yr; M; Yes; FB; Lightning; Yes

---- ---- Runs Along The Edge, Lydia; 1927-Feb 14; 1 yr; F; Yes; 15/16; No data; Yes

1926 5337; Red Road; 1927-Mar 19; 66 yr; F; Yes; FB; No data; Yes

1926 5767; Salway, Hermis C; 1927-Mar 14; 1 yr; M; Yes; 9/32; Measles; Yes

1926 5855; Shakes Hard; 1926-Dec 6; 99 yr; F; Yes; FB; No data; Yes

1926 5883; Shangreau, Vera; 1927-May 13; 5 yr; F; Yes; 3/8; No data; Yes

---- ---- Shangreau, Theodore; 1927-May 19; 9 mo; M; Yes; 3/9; No data; Yes

1926 5912; Sharp Pointed, Fred; 1927-May 24; 43 yr; M; Yes; FB; Tuberculosis; Yes

1926 5913; She Elk Voice Walking, Edward; 1927-May 16; 43 yr; M; Yes; FB; Tuberculosis; Yes

1926 5917; She Elk Voice Walking, Margery; 1927-May 16; 1 yr; F; Yes; FB; Whooping Cough; Yes

1926 5952; Short Bear, Stanley; 1927-Mar 1; 1 yr; M; Yes; 15/16; Pneumonia; Yes

1926 5981; Shot, Anthony; 1927-Mar 26; 4 yr; M; Yes; FB; Pneumonia; Yes

1926 5982; Shot, Robert; 1927-Mar 30; 2 yr; M; Yes; FB; Measles and Pneumonia; Yes

1926 5993; Shot With Arrow; 1926-Sept 28; 57 yr; M; Yes; FB; Heart trouble; Yes

1926 6008; Shoulder, Stewart; 1927-May 11; 1 yr; M; Yes; FB; Pneumonia; Yes

1926 6021; Sierro, Aloysius H; 1927-May 10; 5 yr; M; Yes; 3/4; Tuberculosis; Yes

---- ---- Sierro, Loretta K; 1927-May 1; 4 mo; F; Yes; 3/4; Pneumonia; Yes

1926 6020; Sierro, Virginia E; 1927-May 10; 9 yr; F; Yes; 3/4; Tuberculosis; Yes

1926 6077; Sits Poor, Vincent; 1927-Feb 16; 1 yr; M; Yes; FB; No data; Yes

1926 6084; Skalander, Mary A; 1927-May 29; 56 yr; F; Yes; 1/4; No data; Yes

---- ---- Slow Bear, Annie; 1926-July 27; 1 mo; F; Yes; FB; Fever; Yes

1926 6112; Slow Bear, Francis; 1926-June 15; 9 mo; M; Yes; FB; Pneumonia; Yes

1926 6123; Slow Woman; 1927-Jan 23; 84 yr; F; Yes; FB; Old Age; Yes

State __South Dakota__ Reservation __Pine Ridge__ Agency or jurisdiction __Pine Ridge__ Office of Indian Affairs

Key: Year and Number On Last Census Roll; Surname, Given; Date of Death (Year-Month-Day); Age At Death; Sex; Tribe (Oglala Sioux unless given otherwise); Ward (Yes/No); Degree of Blood; Cause Of Death; At Jurisdiction Where Enrolled (Yes/No); (If no – Where)

Deaths Occurring Between July 1, 1926 and June 30, 1927 of Indians Enrolled at Jurisdiction

1926 6137; Smooth Quiver, Jessie; 1927-Mar 1; 21 yr; F; Yes; FB; Tuberculosis; Yes

1926 6170; Spider, Blanche; 1927-Mar 14; 2 yr; F; Yes; FB; Measles; Yes

1926 7379; Spotted Bear, Thomas; 1926-Oct 15; 5 yr; M; Yes; 1/2; No data; Yes

1926 6197; Spotted Eagle, Felix; 1926-Oct 19; 9 mo; M; Yes; FB; No data; Yes

1926 6209; Spotted Elk, Philip; 1927-May 31; 1 yr; M; Yes; FB; Diarrhea; Yes

1926 6251; Standing Bear, Lawrence; 1927-May 9; 21 yr; M; Yes; 3/4; Tuberculosis; Yes

---- ----; Standing Bear, Lee; 1927-Apr 3; 1 yr; M; Yes; 7/8; Measles; Yes

1926 6250; Standing Bear, Lizzie; 1927-Jan 27; 53 yr; F; Yes; 3/4; Pneumonia; Yes

1926 6272; Standing Elk; 1927-June 14; 73 yr; M; Yes; FB; Gangrene; Yes

1926 6288; Standing Soldier, Martha; 1926-July 8; 5 yr; F; Yes; 13/16; T.B. of brain; Yes

---- ----; Standing Soldier, Rhoda; 1927-Feb 11; 6 mo; F; Yes; FB; No data; Yes

1926 6296; Standing Soldier, William Jr; 1927-Apr 19; 12 yr; M; Yes; 5/8; Appendicitis; Yes

1926 6378; Strikes Enemy, Eugene; 1926-Aug 26; 3 yr; M; Yes; 7/8; No data; Yes

1926 6390; Struck By Crow; 1927-Apr 25; 79 yr; M; Yes; FB; Old Age; Yes

1926 6405; Sun Bear, Randolph; 1927-Mar 17; 1 yr; M; Yes; FB; Measles; Yes

---- ----; Swallow, Thompson; 1926-Oct 6; 2 mo; M; Yes; FB; Pneumonia; Yes

1926 6471; Swick, Joseph; 1927-Mar 22; 1 yr; M; Yes; 3/8; Measles; Yes

---- ----; Tail, Hermis N; 1927-June 24; 1 yr; M; Yes; 3/8; Pneumonia; Yes

1926 6493; Tail, John; 1927-May 2; 5 yr; M; Yes; FB; Tuberculosis; Yes

1926 6502; Takes Away From Them, Joseph; 1927-Apr 22; 26 yr; M; Yes; FB; Tuberculosis; Yes

1926 6509; Takes War Bonnet, Adam; 1927-Feb 14; 5 yr; M; Yes; FB; No data; Yes

1926 6510; Takes War Bonnet, Rena; 1927-Jan 19; 1 yr; F; Yes; FB; Pneumonia; Yes

---- ----; Ten Fingers, Effie; 1926-Oct 12; 1 mo; F; Yes; FB; No data; Yes

1926 6549; Ten Fingers, Sarah; 1926-Oct 7; 30 yr; F; Yes; FB; Tuberculosis; Yes

1926 6611; Thunder Hawk, Johnson; 1927-Apr 16; 4 yr; M; Yes; 7/8; Pneumonia; Yes

1926 6639; Tobacco, Adam; 1926-Sept 15; 51 yr; M; Yes; FB; Necrosis of pelvic bone; Yes

1926 6668; Trimble, Ralph V; 1927-Mar 29; 11 mo; M; Yes; 3/8; Pneumonia; Yes

1926 6693; Turning Hawk, Asa; 1927-Jan 9; 7 yr; M; Yes; FB; No data; Yes

1926 6703; Turning Holy, Abel; 1927-May 19; 6 yr; M; Yes; FB; Tuberculosis; Yes

1926 6726; Twiss, Rose; 1926-Sept 9; 40 yr; F; Yes; FB; Tuberculosis; Yes

1926 6762; Twiss, Willis Paul; 1927-Mar 11; 2 yr; M; Yes; 7/8; Measles; Yes

1926 2938; Two Dogs, Mary; 1927-May 13; 7 yr; F; Yes; FB; Tuberculosis; Yes

1926 6888; Two Two, Peter; 1927-Feb 9; 1 yr; M; Yes; 7/8; Measles and whooping cough; Yes

1926 6880; Two Two, Veronica; 1927-Feb 12; 1 yr; F; Yes; 7/8; Measles; Yes

State **South Dakota**   Reservation   **Pine Ridge**   Agency or jurisdiction
      Pine Ridge   Office of Indian Affairs

Key: Year and Number On Last Census Roll; Surname, Given; Date of Death (Year-Month-Day); Age At Death; Sex; Tribe (Oglala Sioux unless given otherwise); Ward (Yes/No); Degree of Blood; Cause Of Death; At Jurisdiction Where Enrolled (Yes/No); (If no – Where)

Deaths Occurring Between July 1, 1926 and June 30, 1927 of Indians Enrolled at Jurisdiction

1926 6878; Two Two, Vina; 1927-Feb 25; 5 yr; F; Yes; 7/8; Measles; Yes
---- ----   Vlandry, Augusta Clara; 1926-Sept 26; 3 mo; F; Yes; 13/16; No data; Yes
1926 6965; Walking, Nellie; 1927-Apr 23; 4 yr; F; Yes; FB; No data; Yes
1926 6996; War Bonnet, Anne; 1926-Nov 7; 10 yr; F; Yes; FB; Tuberculosis; Yes
1926 6998; War Bonnet, Lizzie; 1926-Sept 5; 24 yr; F; Yes; FB; Tuberculosis; Yes
1926 6995; War Bonnet, Moses; 1927-May 26; 19 yr; M; Yes; FB; Tuberculosis; Yes
1926 7026; Water, Louis; 1926-Aug 18; 4 yr; M; Yes; 7/8; Diarrhea; Yes
1926 7091; Whetstone, Cecelia; 1926-Nov 4; 6 yr; F; Yes; FB; No data; Yes
1926 7192; White Calf, Richard; 1927-Jan 4; 47 yr; M; Yes; FB; Accident; Yes
1926 7139; White Arrow; 1927-Jan 18; 94 yr; F; Yes; FB; Old Age; Yes
1926 7223; White Dress, Rosa; 1927-Feb 27; 1 yr; F; Yes; FB; Measles; Yes
1926 7240; White Eyes, Myrtle J; 1927-Jan 26; 1 yr; F; Yes; FB; No data; Yes
1926 7354; White Woman, Agnes; 1927-Mar 4; 13 yr; F; Yes; FB; Tuberculosis; Yes
---- ----   White Woman, Baptiste; 1927-Mar 4; 1 yr; M; Yes; FB; Measles; Yes
---- ----   White Woman, Catherine; 1926-Oct 2; 2 mo; F; Yes; FB; No data; Yes
1926 7384; Wilson, John E; 1926-Nov 22; 3 yr; M; Yes; 1/16; Pneumonia; Yes
1926 7439; Wounded, Mary; 1927-Mar 29; 2 yr; F; Yes; FB; Measles; Yes
---- ----   Wounded, Stephen; 1927-Jan 25; 4 mo; M; Yes; FB; No data; Yes
1926 7452; Wounded Head, Lizzie; 1927-Jan 9; 10 yr; F; Yes; 7/8; No data; Yes
1926 7287; White Iron; 1927-Apr 9; 68 yr; F; Yes; FB; Pneumonia; Yes
1926 7474; Yankton, Alice; 1927-Apr 19; 6 yr; F; Yes; FB; Tuberculosis; Yes
1926 7476; Yankton, Emil; 1927-Apr 19; 1 yr; M; Yes; FB; No data; Yes
1926 7484; Yankton, Grace; 1927-June 25; 8 yr; F; Yes; 13/16; Spinal Meninghitis[sic]; Yes
1926 7487; Yankton, Vina; 1927-Feb 11; 10 mo; F; Yes; 13/16; Pneumonia; Yes
1926 7481; Yankton, Vina; 1927-May 16; 20 yr; F; Yes; 3/4; Dropsy; Yes
---- ----   Yellow Bear, Johnson; 1927-June 22; 1 da; M; Yes; FB; Premature birth; Yes
1926 7492; Yellow Bear, Luke; 1927-Apr 18; 80 yr; M; Yes; FB; Old Age; Yes
1926 7503; Yellow Bear, Anna; 1927-June 14; 69 yr; F; Yes; FB; Gallstones; Yes
1926 7528; Yellow Boy, Charles; 1927-Sept 19; 31 yr; M; Yes; FB; No data; Yes
1926 7530; Yellow Boy, Chrispin; 1927-Feb 23; 8 yr; M; Yes; FB; No data; Yes
1926 7544; Yellow Boy, Ethel; 1927-Mar 1; 2 yr; F; Yes; 15/16; Measles; Yes
---- ----   Yellow Boy, Winona; 1927-May 26; 9 yr; F; Yes; 15/16; Infantile paralysis; Yes
1926 7500; Yellow Bear, Jenny; 1927-June 22; 27 yr; F; Yes; FB; Tuberculosis; Yes
---- ----   Yellow Bull, Chester; 1927-May 30; 2 mo; M; Yes; FB; Pneumonia; Yes
1926 7568; Yellow Hair, Emma; 1927-Mar 1; 3 yr; F; Yes; FB; Measles; Yes

State **South Dakota** Reservation **Pine Ridge** Agency or jurisdiction
Pine Ridge Office of Indian Affairs

Key: Year and Number On Last Census Roll; Surname, Given; Date of Death (Year-Month-Day); Age At Death; Sex; Tribe (Oglala Sioux unless given otherwise); Ward (Yes/No); Degree of Blood; Cause Of Death; At Jurisdiction Where Enrolled (Yes/No); (If no – Where)

Deaths Occurring Between July 1, 1926 and June 30, 1927 of Indians Enrolled at Jurisdiction

1926 7591; Yellow Horse, Delbert; 1927-Mar 26; 2 yr; M; Yes; 15/16; Pneumonia; Yes

1926 7693; Young Bear, Howard; 1926-Aug 16; 32 yr; M; Yes; FB; Gonorrhea; Yes

DEATH ROLL

EXCLUSIVE OF STILLBIRTHS

1928
(July 1, 1927 - June 30, 1928)

PINE RIDGE RESERVATION
PINE RIDGE SOUTH DAKOTA

State **South Dakota** Reservation **Pine Ridge** Agency or jurisdiction
Pine Ridge Office of Indian Affairs

Key: Year and Number On Last Census Roll; Surname, Given; Date of Death (Year-Month-Day); Age At
Death; Sex; Tribe (Oglala Sioux unless given otherwise); Ward (Yes/No); Degree of Blood; Cause Of Death;
At Jurisdiction Where Enrolled (Yes/No); (If no – Where)

Deaths Occurring Between July 1, 1927 and June 30, 1928 of Indians Enrolled at Jurisdiction

1927	205;	Around Him, Julia; 1928-Jan 19; 11 mo; F; Yes; FB; Tuberculosis; Yes
1927	228;	Back, Marion; 1928-Mar 2; 52 yr; F; Yes; FB; Gallstones; Yes
1927	231;	Backward, Rosa; 1928-June 5; 23 yr; F; Yes; FB; Tuberculosis; Yes
----	---	Badger, Mathew; 1928-Feb 1; 1 mo; M; Yes; 3/4; Pneumonia; Yes
1927	252;	Badger, Myrtle; 1928-Mar 30; 3 yr; F; Yes; 3/4; Pneumonia; Yes
1927	246;	Bad Cob, Christina; 1927-July 16; 1 yr; F; Yes; FB; Pneumonia; Yes
1927	244;	Bad Cob, Louisa; 1927-July 14; 25 yr; F; Yes; FB; Tuberculosis; Yes
1927	268;	Bad Wound, Alice; 1928-Feb 3; 20 yr; F; Yes; FB; Hemorrhage; Yes
1927	274;	Bad Wound, Leroy; 1927-July 6; 20 yr; M; Yes; 3/4; Tuberculosis; Yes
1927	311;	Bald Eagle Bear, Jerome; 1928-Mar 30; 1 yr; M; Yes; FB; Tubercular meninghitis[sic]; Yes
1927	327;	Bates, Katherine R; 1927-Nov 29; 42 yr; F; Yes; 1/4; Cancer; Yes
1927	873;	Bear Bone, Blanche; 1927-Nov 21; 78 yr; F; Yes; FB; Old Age; Yes
----	---	Beard, Cecelia; 1927-Dec 6; 4 da; F; Yes; FB; Cardiovascular insufficiency; Yes
1927	345;	Bear Eagle, Elmer; 1927-Oct 17; 11 mo; M; Yes; FB; Pneumonia; Yes
1927	354;	Bear Nose, Frank; 1928-Mar 12; 72 yr; M; Yes; FB; Angina pectoris; Yes
----	---	Bear Nose, Phoebe; 1927-Dec 23; 7 da; F; Yes; FB; Cold; Yes
1927	390;	Bear Runs In The Woods; 1928-Jan 21; 72 yr; M; Yes; FB; Cancer; Yes
1927	403;	Bear Shield, Mathew; 1928-Mar 26; 1 yr; M; Yes; FB; Intestinal flu; Yes
1927	417;	Bear Tail, Elmer; 1928-May 15; 5 yr; M; Yes; FB; No data; Yes
1927	415;	Bear Tail, Mabel; 1928-May 5; 10 yr; F; Yes; FB; Tuberculosis; Yes
1927	434;	Belt, Irene; 1927-Aug 4; 15 yr; F; Yes; FB; Phthisis florida[sic]; Yes
1927	508;	Big Hawk, Mary; 1927-Sept 23; 65 yr; F; Yes; FB; Old Age; Yes
1927	521;	Big Turnip, Clara; 1928-Feb 25; 15 yr; F; Yes; FB; Tuberculosis; Yes
1927	522;	Big Wolf; 1928-May 19; 71 yr; M; Yes; FB; Myocarditis; Yes
1927	552;	Bird Head, Emma; 1927-July 5; 37 yr; F; Yes; FB; Heart Failure; Yes
1927	538;	Bird Head, John Sr; 1927-Aug 12; 71 yr; M; Yes; FB; Old Age; Yes
1927	560;	Bissonette, Clement; 1928-Jan 22; 27 yr; M; Yes; 3/4; Tuberculosis; Yes
----	---	Bissonette, Ester May; 1928-Mar 15; 1 mo; F; Yes; 11/16; No data; Yes
1927	733;	Black Horse, Mildred L; 1928-Feb 9; 9 mo; F; Yes; 3/4; Pneumonia; Yes
1927	741;	Black Sheep, Ella; 1927-Nov 2; 76 yr; F; Yes; FB; Old Age; Yes
1927	758;	Black Whirlwind, Joseph; 1927-July 17; 31 yr; M; Yes; FB; Tuberculosis; Yes
1927	760;	Black Wolf, Teresa R; 1927-Oct 12; 3 yr; F; Yes; FB; Intestinal obstruction; Yes
1927	777;	Blue Bird, Annie; 1928-Feb 3; 57 yr; F; Yes; FB; Cancer; Yes
1927	791;	Blue Bird, Curtis; 1927-July 24; 1 yr; M; Yes; 7/8; Pneumonia; Yes
1927	785;	Blue Bird, Lucy; 1927-Aug 30; 26 yr; F; Yes; 7/8; Tuberculosis; Yes

State **South Dakota** Reservation **Pine Ridge** Agency or jurisdiction
Pine Ridge Office of Indian Affairs

Key: Year and Number On Last Census Roll; Surname, Given; Date of Death (Year-Month-Day); Age At Death; Sex; Tribe (Oglala Sioux unless given otherwise); Ward (Yes/No); Degree of Blood; Cause Of Death; At Jurisdiction Where Enrolled (Yes/No); (If no – Where)

Deaths Occurring Between July 1, 1927 and June 30, 1928 of Indians Enrolled at Jurisdiction

1927 827; Bores A Hole, Alvina; 1927-July 8; 5 yr; F; Yes; FB; Whooping Cough; Yes

1927 881; Brave Heart, Rosa Gladys; 1927-Sept 24; 11 yr; F; Yes; FB; Tuberculosis; Yes

1927 929; Brings, Joseph; 1927-Aug 31; 55 yr; M; Yes; FB; Tuberculosis; Yes

1927 940; Brings Plenty, Joseph; 1927-July 1; 54 yr; M; Yes; 1/2; Cancer; Yes

1927 950; Broken Leg, Rosa; 1928-Mar 23; 26 yr; F; Yes; FB; Tuberculosis; Yes

1927 963; Broken Rope, Sarah; 1927-Oct 6; 90 yr; F; Yes; FB; No data; Yes

1927 1022; Brown, Norman; 1927-Aug 26; 13 yr; M; Yes; FB; Tuberculosis; Yes

1927 1030; Brown Bull, Thompson Jr; 1927-July 28; 1 yr; M; Yes; 3/4; Entero Colitis; Yes

1927 1034; Brown Ear Horse, Alice; 1927-Aug 26; 52 yr; F; Yes; FB; Cancer of Stomach; Yes

1927 1106; Bull Bear, Ida May; 1927-Aug 30; 1 yr; F; Yes; 7/8; Pneumonia; Yes

---- ---- Bullman; 1928-Feb 29; 2 da; M; Yes; FB; Premature birth; Yes

1927 1142; Bush, Sally; 1927-Oct 30; 80 yr; F; Yes; FB; Old Age; Yes

1927 1265; Chase In Morning, Charles; 1927-Nov 28; 7 yr; M; Yes; FB; No data; Yes

1927 1266; Chase In Morning, Grace; 1928-Feb 29; 2 yr; F; Yes; FB; Flu; Yes

---- ---- Chase In Mroning[sic], Laura; 1928-Feb 16; 1 mo; F; Yes; FB; Flu; Yes

1927 1320; Clear, Thomas Sr; 1928-Apr 21; 71 yr; M; Yes; FB; Senility; Yes

1927 1409; Close, Alice; 1928-Feb 8; 25 yr; F; Yes; FB; Tuberculosis; Yes

1927 4156; Crazy Ghost, Julia; 1928-May 6; 23 yr; F; Yes; FB; Puerperal septicemia; Yes

1927 1613; Crazy Horse; 1927-Nov 26; 76 yr; M; Yes; FB; No data; Yes

1927 1622; Crazy Thunder; 1928-Jan 29; 74 yr; M; Yes; FB; Myocarditis; Yes

---- ---- Crier, Dorothy; 1927-Oct 13; 12 mo; F; Yes; FB; Pneumonia; Yes

1927 1744; Cut, Ada; 1928-Feb 16; 53 yr; F; Yes; FB; No data; Yes

1927 1831; Dog, Lucy; 1928-May 20; 32 yr; F; Yes; FB; No data; Yes

1927 1942; Eagle Louse, Lydia; 1928-Apr 12; 11 yr; F; Yes; FB; Tuberculosis; Yes

1927 1948; Eagle Ring, Bessie; 1927-Sept 6; 58 yr; F; Yes; FB; Heart Trouble; Yes

1927 3658; Eagle Track; 1927-July 15; 75 ye; F; Yes; FB; No data; Yes

1927 2007; Fast Horse, Eva; 1928-May 7; 25 yr; F; Yes; FB; Tuberculosis; Yes

---- ---- Fast Horse, Harry; 1927-Oct 22; 2 mo; M; Yes; 3/4; Croup; Yes

1927 2040; Fast Wolf, Isabelle; 1927-Aug 11; 1 yr; F; Yes; FB; Whooping Cough; Yes

1927 2049; Feather, Frank; 1927-Aug 29; 68 yr; M; Yes; FB; Tuberculosis; Yes

1927 2055; Featherman, Delia; 1927-Sept 7; 48 yr; F; Yes; FB; Tuberculosis; Yes

1927 2058; Featherman, Douglas; 1928-Mar 31; 1 1/2 yr; M; Yes; FB; Leptomaninghitis[sic]; Yes

1927 2066; Featherman, Gertie; 1927-July 26; 2 yr; F; Yes; FB; Pneumonia; Yes

1927 2067; Featherman, Tresa; 1927-Aug 26; 4 mo; F; Yes; FB; No data; Yes

1927 2089; Fights Bear, Lizzie; 1928-May 6; 1 yr; F; Yes; FB; Pneumonia; Yes

Key: Year and Number On Last Census Roll; Surname, Given; Date of Death (Year-Month-Day); Age At Death; Sex; Tribe (Oglala Sioux unless given otherwise); Ward (Yes/No); Degree of Blood; Cause Of Death; At Jurisdiction Where Enrolled (Yes/No); (If no – Where)

Deaths Occurring Between July 1, 1927 and June 30, 1928 of Indians Enrolled at Jurisdiction

1927 2188; Fool Crow, Mattie; 1928-Mar 12; 2 yr; F; Yes; FB; Intestinal flu; Yes

1927 2199; Forward; 1928-Apr 12; 98 yr; F; Yr; FB; No data; Yes

---- ---- Ghost Bear, Gilbert; 1928-Mar 14; 5 da; M; Yes; FB; No data; Yes

1927 2321; Ghost Bear, Laura; 1927-July 14; 20 yr; F; Yes; FB; Tuberculosis; Yes

1927 2357; Gibbons, Emelda; 1928-May 1; 7 mo; F; Yes; 3/4; Pneumonia; Yes

1927 1108; Good Crow, Minnie; 1927-Oct 24; 37 yr; F; Yes; FB; Abdominal ptosis; Yes

1927 2462; Good Lance, Frank; 1928-Mar 5; 22 yr; M; Yes; FB; Tuberculosis; Yes

1927 2496; Good Voice Dog, Frank; 1927-Sept 21; 29 yr; M; Yes; FB; Tuberculosis; Yes

1927 2498; Good Voice Elk, Minnie; 1927-Aug 22; 27 yr; F; Yes; FB; Tuberculosis; Yes

1927 2587; Ground Spider, Noah; 1927-Aug 1; 1 yr; M; Yes; 7/8; Pneumonia; Yes

1927 2760; High Bull, Nellie; 1927-Oct 17; 29 yr; F; Yes; FB; Tuberculosis; Yes

1927 2839; Hollow Horn, Louis; 1927-Aug 11; 35 yr; M; Yes; FB; Tuberculosis; Yes

1927 2912; Horse, Levi; 1927-July 12; 22 yr; M; Yes; FB; Tuberculosis; Yes

1927 2962; Hunts Enemy; 1927-Sept 29; 77 yr; M; Yes; FB; Old Age; Yes

1927 2963; Hunts Enemy, Amy; 1928-Feb 23; 67 yr; F; Yes; FB; Dyspepsia; Yes

1927 2964; Hunts Enemy, Clarence; 1928-Jan 31; 46 yr; M; Yes; FB; Tuberculosis; Yes

1927 2997; Iron Boy, Stella; 1928-Jan 10; 15 yr; F; Yes; FB; Tuberculosis; Yes

1927 3006; Iron Bull, Abraham; 1927-Dec 12; 8 yr; M; yes; FB; Pneumonia; Yes

1927 3035; Iron Crow, James; 1927-Oct 30; 11 da; M; Yes; FB; Spina bifida non-hydrocephalac[sic]; Yes

1927 3036; Iron Deer, Dolly; 1927-July 13; 46 yr; F; Yes; FB; No data; Yes

---- ---- Janis, Catherine E; 1928-Jan 29; 1 yr; F; Yes; 7/8; Pneumonia; Yes

1927 3213; Janis, Virgil; 1927-Nov 2; 1 yr; M; Yes; 3/4; Pneumonia; Yes;

1927 3286; Jumping Bull, Jacob; 1928-Feb 6; 21 yr; M; Yes; FB; Tuberculosis; Yes

1927 3290; Jumping Eagle, Laurene; 1927-Aug 9; 16 yr; F; Yes; 3/4; Tuberculosis; Yes

---- ---- Kicking Bear, Bertha; 1928-Mar 6; 17 da; F; Yes; FB; Pneumonia; Yes

1927 3316; Kills Acros[sic]; 1928-Feb 27; 56 yr; M; Yes; FB; Cardiovascular insufficiency; Yes

1927 3328; Kills And Comes Back, Joseph; 1928-Mar 3; 26 yr; M; Yes; FB; Tuberculosis; Yes

1927 3350 Kills Crow Indian, Andrew; 1928-Apr 12; 7 yr; M; Yes; FB; Tuberculosis; Yes

1927 6392; Kills In Water; 1928-Feb 18; 48 yr; F; Yes; FB; Tuberculosis; Yes

1927 3374; Kills In Water; 1927-Nov 26; 72 yr; F; Yes; FB; Rheumatism; Yes

1927 3386; Kills On Horseback, Martha; 1928-Jan 21; 7 yr; F; Yes; 7/8; No data; Yes

---- ---- Kills Warrior, Leroy; 1928-June 5; 1 mo; M; Yes; FB; Acute cold; Yes

121

State **South Dakota** Reservation **Pine Ridge** Agency or jurisdiction
Pine Ridge Office of Indian Affairs

Key: Year and Number On Last Census Roll; Surname, Given; Date of Death (Year-Month-Day); Age At Death; Sex; Tribe (Oglala Sioux unless given otherwise); Ward (Yes/No); Degree of Blood; Cause Of Death; At Jurisdiction Where Enrolled (Yes/No); (If no – Where)

Deaths Occurring Between July 1, 1927 and June 30, 1928 of Indians Enrolled at Jurisdiction

1927 3474; LaBuff, Thomas; 1928-May 23; 29 yr; M; Yes; 1/2; Heart Failure; Yes

1927 3485; Ladeaux, Baptiste; 1927-Aug 4; 54 yr; M; Yes; 3/4; Cancer of stomach; Yes

1927 3574; LaPointe, Adele; 1928-Mar 29; 21 yr; F; Yes; 1/2; Pthysis pichmonalis[sic]; Yes

1927 3591; Larvie, Lizzie; 1928-June 10; 24 yr; F; Yes; FB; Tuberculosis; Yes

1927 1215; Lays Bad, Theresa; 1928-Jan 26; 8 mo; F; Yes; 3/4; Pneumonia; Yes

1927 3622; Lays On The Ground; 1928-Feb 29; 80 yr; F; Yes; FB; Senility; Yes

1927 3650; Left Hand, George; 1928-Jan 30; 54 yr; M; Yes; FB; Tuberculosis; Yes

1927 2156; Little Boy, Abraham; 1927-July 8; 11 yr; M; Yes; FB; Tuberculosis; Yes

1927 3740; Little Bull, Rosa; 1927-Aug 21; 19 yr; F; Yes; FB; Tuberculosis; Yes

---- ----; Little Crow, Florence; 1928-Feb 6; 9 da; F; Yes; FB; Pneumonia; Yes

---- ----; Little Hoop, Nancy; 1928-Feb 29; 3 da; F; Yes; 15/16; Premature birth; Yes

1927 3803; Little Horse, Lucy; 1927-Nov 23; 19 yr; F; Yes; FB; Tuberculosis; Yes

1927 3811; Little Killer, Fanny; 1928-Feb 20; 53 yr; F; Yes; FB; Tuberculosis of kidneys; Yes

1927 3858; Little War Bonnet, Silas; 1927-Dec 2; 15 yr; M; Yes; FB; Tuberculosis; Yes

1927 3914; Livermont, Leroy D; 1928-Apr 18; 15 yr; M; Yes; 3/16; Influenza; Yes

1927 3999; Long Bull, Esther; 1928-Apr 30; 78 yr; F; Yes; FB; Myocarditis; Yes

1927 4027; Long Soldier; 1927-July 9; 80 yr; M; Yes; FB; Old Age; Yes

1927 4072; Looking Horse, Geneva; 1928-Apr 25; 11 yr; F; Yes; 15/16; Tuberculosis; Yes

1927 4089; Loves War, Edna; 1928-Apr 24; 34 yr; F; Yes; FB; Tuberculosis; Yes

1927 4098; Makes Enemy, Henry; 1928-June 20; 78 yr; M; Yes; FB; Senility; Yes

1927 4128; Many Spotted Horses; 1928-June 4; 64 yr; F; Yes; FB; Myocarditis; Yes

1927 4137; Marrow Bone, Therese; 1928-Mar 5; 9 mo; F; Yes; FB; Pneumonia; Yes

1927 4146; Marshall, Frank; 1928-May 1; 65 yr; M; Yes; 1/2; No data; Yes

1927 4219; Meat, Frank; 1928-Feb 18; 73 yr; M; Yes; FB; Cardiovascular insufficiency; Yes

---- ----; Mesteth, Leo Thomas; 1927-Oct 21; 18 da; M; Yes; 5/8; No data; Yes

1927 4248; Mesteth, Mary; 1927-Dec 6; 58 yr; F; Yes; FB; Tuberculosis; Yes

---- ----; Mills, Catherine E; 1928-June 5; 1 yr; F; Yes; 3/4; Auto Intoxication; Yes

1927 6261; Moves Camp, Bethel; 1927-Dec 5; 9 yr; F; Yes; 7/8; Tuberculosis; Yes

---- ----; New Holy, Mary; 1928-Feb 28; 6 mo; F; Yes; FB; Pneumonia; Yes

---- ----; Pacer, Veronica; 1928-May 29; 2 mo; F; Yes; FB; Acute cold; Yes

1927 4658; Packed, Nellie; 1928-May 4; 32 yr; F; Yes; FB; Appendicitis; Yes

1927 4716; Pawnee Leggins, Paul; 1928-Mar 16; 17 yr; M; Yes; FB; Serofibrinous pleurisy; Yes

1927 4746; Pine Bird, Samuel; 1928-June 5; 46 yr; M; Yes; FB; Accident; No; Elizabeth, N.J.

State **South Dakota** Reservation **Pine Ridge** Agency or jurisdiction
Pine Ridge Office of Indian Affairs

Key: Year and Number On Last Census Roll; Surname, Given; Date of Death (Year-Month-Day); Age At Death; Sex; Tribe (Oglala Sioux unless given otherwise); Ward (Yes/No); Degree of Blood; Cause Of Death; At Jurisdiction Where Enrolled (Yes/No); (If no – Where)

Deaths Occurring Between July 1, 1927 and June 30, 1928 of Indians Enrolled at Jurisdiction

1927 4190; Pipe On Head, Ada; 1928-Feb 20; 17 yr; F; Yes; 3/4; Kidney trouble; Yes

---- ---- Plenty Arrow, Leroyal; 1928-Apr 12; 2 da; M; Yes; FB; Premature; Yes

1927 4797; Plenty Wounds, Hazel; 1928-Apr 21; 12 yr; F; Yes; FB; Tuberculosis; Yes

1927 4812; Poor Bear, Rebecca; 1927-Oct 24; 4 yr; F; Yes; 15/16; Tuberculosis; Yes

1927 4932; Poor Thunder, Kate; 1927-Aug 25; 33 yr; F; Yes; FB; Hernia operation; Yes

1927 4922; Pretty Back, Oscar; 1927-Dec 8; 1 yr; M; Yes; FB; Pneumonia; Yes

1927 5056; Randall, Jessie; 1927-Sept 8; 63 yr; F; Yes; FB; No data; Yes

---- ---- Red Cloud, Albert; 1928-Jan 3; 1 mo; M; Yes; FB; Pneumonia; Yes

1927 5175; Red Dog; 1927-Dec 15; 85 yr; M; Yes; FB; Old Age; Yes

1927 5176; Red Dog Track; 1927-Dec 31; 73 yr; F; Yes; FB; No data; Yes

1927 5249; Red Hawk, Austin; 1928-Mar 29; 71 yr; M; Yes; FB; Myocarditis; Yes

---- ---- Red Owl, Robert Lewis; 1928-Apr 1; 7 mo; M; Yes; 3/4; Congenital hepatitis; Yes

1927 5292; Red Paint, Rachel; 1928-Jan 22; 76 yr; F; Yes; FB; Old Age; Yes

1927 5302; Red Rock, George; 1927-July 26; 71 yr; F; Yes; FB; Myocarditis; Yes

1927 5309; Red Shirt, Emma; 1927-Dec 31; 68 yr; F; Yes; 1/2; Rheumatism; Yes

1927 5462; Richard, Isabel; 1927-Nov 25; 20 yr; F; Yes; 9/16; Tuberculosis; Yes

1927 5421; Richard, Julia; 1928-Jan 15; 70 yr; F; Yes; FB; No data; Yes

1927 5513; Rocky Mountain, Harold; 1928-Feb 23; 45 yr; M; Yes; FB; Tuberculosis; Yes

---- ---- Running Eagle, Samuel; 1928-Feb 19; 8 mo; M; Yes; FB; Intestinal Flu; Yes

1927 5658; Running Hawk, Daisy; 1928-Feb 5; 17 yr; F; Yes; 7/8; Tuberculosis; Yes

1927 5685; Running Shield, Mabel; 1927-July 15; 21 yr; F; Yes; FB; Tuberculosis; Yes

---- ---- Shangreau, Gertrude Rose; 1927-Dec 5; 21 da; F; Yes; 11/16; Pneumonia; Yes

---- ---- Shangreau, Helena Pearl; 1928-Jan 29; 9 mo; F; Yes; 11/16; Pneumonia; Yes

1927 5821; Shangreau, Louise; 1927-Dec 8; 73 yr; F; Yes; 1/2; Cerebral hemorrhage; Yes

1927 5857; Shangreau, Mabel Gussie; 1927-Sept 19; 25 yr; F; Yes; 1/2; Tuberculosis; Yes

1927 5834; Shangreau, Vera Emma; 1928-Feb 3; 28 yr; F; Yes; 1/4; Auto Accident; Yes

1927 5887; Shell Woman #3: 1927-Oct 16; 84 yr; F; Yes; F; No data; Yes

---- ---- Sherman, Caroline; 1928-June 8; 3 da; F; Yes; 9/16; Cardiovascular insufficiency; Yes

__Pine Ridge__ Office of Indian Affairs

Key: Year and Number On Last Census Roll; Surname, Given; Date of Death (Year-Month-Day); Age At Death; Sex; Tribe (Oglala Sioux unless given otherwise); Ward (Yes/No); Degree of Blood; Cause Of Death; At Jurisdiction Where Enrolled (Yes/No); (If no – Where)

Deaths Occurring Between July 1, 1927 and June 30, 1928 of Indians Enrolled at Jurisdiction

---- ---- Short Bear; 1927-Sept 10; 4 mo; M; Yes; 15/16; No data; Yes

1927 5940; Short Man; 1928-Jan 9; 68 yr; M; Yes; FB; Dropsy; Yes

1927 5961; Shot To Pieces, Joseph; 1928-Apr 13; 24 yr; M; Yes; FB; Tuberculosis; Yes

1927 5964; Shot With Arrows, Jessie; 1928-May 2; 26 yr; F; Yes; FB; Tuberculosis; Yes

1927 5969; Shoulder, Pugh; 1928-Jan 6; 17 yr; M; Yes; FB; Tuberculosis; Yes

1927 5982; Shouts At; 1827[sic]-Feb 16; 85 yr; F; Yes; FB; Nephritis; Yes

1927 6044; Sits Poor, Alice; 1928-June 1; 16 yr; F; Yes; FB; Tuberculosis; Yes

1927 6147; Spider Back Bone, Cyrus; 1928-Feb 28; 17 yr; M; Yes; FB; Tuberculosis; Yes

1927 6300; Stand Up, Julia; 1928-June 10; 65 yr; F; Yes; FB; Nephritis chronic; Yes

1927 6299; Stands Up; 1928-Mar 9; 57 yr; M; Yes; FB; Endocarditis; Yes

---- ---- Standing Soldier, Joseph; 1927-Oct 19; 18 da; M; Yes; 5/8; No data; Yes

1927 6308; Star, Annie; 1927-Sept 6; 55 yr; F; Yes; FB; Tuberculosis; Yes

1927 6378; Struck By Crow, Susie; 1927-Spet[sic] 20; 58 yr; F; Yes; FB; Tuberculosis; Yes

1927 6469; Swollen Face; 1928-Mar 5; 70 yr; F; Yes; FB; Tuberculosis; Yes

1927 6544; Thick Bread; 1928-Apr 23; 88 yr; M; Yes; FB; Myocarditis; Yes

1927 6570; Thunder Beard, Chas J; 1927-Sept 14; 74 yr; M; Yes; FB; Tuberculosis; Yes

1927 6668; Troublesome Hawk, James; 1927-Sept 17; 5 mo; M; Yes; FB; Stomach trouble; Yes

1927 6715; Twiss, Rosella; 1927-Dec 5; 71 yr; F; Yes; 1/2; Old Age; Yes

1927 4592; Two Sticks, Rose; 1928-Jan 26; 23 yr; F; Yes; Pneumonia; Yes

1927 6864; Two Two, David; 1928-Feb 25; 10 mo; M; Yes; FB; Tuberculosis; Yes

1927 6869; Two Two, Frances; 1927-July 3; 4 yr; F; Yes; 7/8; Tuberculosis; Yes

1927 6863; Two Two, Jacob; 1928-Apr 23; 2 da; M; Yes; FB; No data; Yes

1927 6861; Two Two, Michael; 1928-Sept 12; 13 yr; M; Yes; FB; Accident with horse; Yes

1927 6976; Walks Under Ground, Martha; 1928-Jan 8; 14 yr; F; Yes; FB; Tuberculosis; Yes

---- ---- Wellborn, Clauda; 1928-Apr 25; 15 da; F; Yes; 1/16; No data; No; Noland, Arkansas

---- ---- Wellborn, Clays 1928-Apr 25; 15 da; F; Yes; 1/16; No data; No; Noland, Arkansas

1927 7080; Whetstone, Esther; 1927-July 15; 5 yr; F; Yes; FB; No data; No; No data as to town, Somewhere in Colo.

1927 7085; Whirlwind, Ernest; 1928-Jan 6; 9 yr; M; Yes; FB; Heart Trouble; Yes

1927 7085; Whirlwind, Jonas; 1927-Dec 28; 4 yr; M; Yes; FB; Pneumonia; Yes

1927 7090; Whirlwind, Lizzie; 1928-Mar 16; 67 yr; F; Yes; FB; No data; Yes

State **South Dakota** Reservation **Pine Ridge** Agency or jurisdiction
  Pine Ridge Office of Indian Affairs

Key: Year and Number On Last Census Roll; Surname, Given; Date of Death (Year-Month-Day); Age At Death; Sex; Tribe (Oglala Sioux unless given otherwise); Ward (Yes/No); Degree of Blood; Cause Of Death; At Jurisdiction Where Enrolled (Yes/No); (If no – Where)

Deaths Occurring Between July 1, 1927 and June 30, 1928 of Indians Enrolled at Jurisdiction

1927 2171; Whirlwind Horse, Etta; 1928-June 1; 10 yr; F; Yes; FB; Tuberculosis; Yes

1927 7162; White Bull, Charles; 1927-Nov 24; 8 yr; M; Yes; FB; Tuberculosis; Yes

---- ---- White Bull, Isabelle; 1928-Feb 2; 2 hr; F; Yes; FB; Premature birth; Yes

---- ---- White Calf, Francis; 1927-Oct 7; 13 da; M; Yes; FB; No data; Yes

1927 7311; White Rabbit, James; 1928-Apr 7; 6 1/2 yr; M; Yes; FB; Tuberculosis; Yes

1927 7320; White Thunder, Eliza; 1928-Mar 21; 11 yr; F; Yes; FB; Tuberculosis; Yes

1927 7325; White Turtle, Emma; 1927-Aug 28; 43 yr; F; Yes; FB; No data; Yes

1927 7406; Woman Dress, Edward Jr; 1927-Sept 3; 26 yr; M; Yes; FB; Fractured skull; No; Hot Springs, S.D.

---- ---- Woman Dress, Eldon; 1927-Oct 10; 4 da; M; Yes; FB; Premature birth; Yes

1927 7462; Yankton, Saulmon; 1928-May 28; 5 yr; M; Yes; FB; Acute indigestion; Yes

1927 7519; Yellow Boy, Antoine; 1928-Jan 31; 30 yr; M; Yes; 7/8; Tuberculosis; Yes

1927 7527; Yellow Boy, Raymond; 1928-Mar 23; 1 yr; M; Yes; 15/16; Pneumonia; Yes

1927 7595; Yellow Wolf, Mary; 1928-Feb 6; 57 yr; F; Yes; FB; Childbirth; Yes

DEATH ROLL

EXCLUSIVE OF STILLBIRTHS

1929
(July 1, 1928 - June 30, 1929)

PINE RIDGE RESERVATION
PINE RIDGE SOUTH DAKOTA

Key: Year and Number On Last Census Roll; Surname, Given; Date of Death (Year-Month-Day); Age At Death; Sex; Tribe (Oglala Sioux unless given otherwise); Ward (Yes/No); Degree of Blood; Cause Of Death; At Jurisdiction Where Enrolled (Yes/No); (If no – Where)

Deaths Occurring Between July 1, 1928 and June 30, 1929 of Indians Enrolled at Jurisdiction

1928   8; Adams, Bruce V; 1928-Aug 13; 18 yr; M; Yes; 7/8; Appendicitis; Yes

1928   50; Afraid Of His Horses, Sadie; 1928-Dec 18; 18 yr; F; Yes; 15/16; Tuberculosis; Yes

1928   165; Ant, Thomas; 1928-Oct 1; 4 da; M; Yes; 7/8; Cardio vascular insufficiency; Yes

1928   210; Around Him, Emily; 1929-Mar 16; 37 yr; F; Yes; FB; Tuberculosis; Yes

1928   275; Bad Wound, Stanley; 1929-Feb 14; 26 yr; M; Yes; 3/4; Suicide; Yes

1928   294; Bad Wound, Susie; 1929-Feb 3; 1 yr; F; Yes; 3/4; No data; Yes

1928   311; Bald Eagle, Raymond; 1928-Dec 29; 15 yr; M; Yes; FB; Tuberculosis; Yes

1928   319; Bald Head, Cecelia; 1929-Apr 22; 51 yr; F; Yes; FB; Spinal meningitis; Yes

1928   353; Bear Eagle, Isabelle; 1929-Apr 5; 1 yr; F; Yes; FB; Infantile paralysis; Yes

1928   356; Bear Horse, Maggie; 1929-May 21; 38 yr; F; Yes; FB; Dropsy; Yes

----   --- Bear Saves Life, Charles; 1928-Dec 3; 11 da; M; Yes; FB; No data; Yes

1928 2632; Big Charger, Susie; 1929-Mar 16; 29 yr; F; Yes; FB; Pelvic abcess[sic]; Yes

1928   515; Big Head, Callie; 1928-Aug 14; 82 yr; F; Yes; FB; No data; Yes

1928   520; Big Mouth, Mrs. (Proud Woman); 1928-Nov 21; 67 yr; F; Yes; FB; Tuberculosis; Yes

1928   543; Bird Head, Susie; 1929-Apr 17; 28 yr; F; Yes; FB; Tuberculosis; Yes

----   --- Black Bear, Lorna; 1928-Nov 26; 43 da; F; Yes; FB; Pneumonia; Yes

1928   672; Black Cat, Christina; 1929-June 4; 7 yr; F; Yes; FB; Tuberculosis; Yes

1928   670; Black Cat, John; 1929-May 6; 53 yr; M; Yes; FB; Tuberculosis; Yes

1928   669; Black Cat, Sallie; 1928-Dec 23; 25 yr; F; Yes; FB; Tuberculosis; Yes

1928   674; Black Chicken; 1928-Dec 29; 73 yr; M; Yes; FB; Cardio vascular insufficiency; Yes

1928   694; Black Elk, Minnie; 1929-Mar 13; 31 yr; F; Yes; FB; Tuberculosis; Yes

1928 7477; Black Mule; 1929-June 21; 71 yr; F; Yes; FB; Senility; Yes

1928   750; Black Road, Catherine R; 1928-Aug 3; 1 mo; F; Yes; FB; Cholera infantum; Yes

1928   746; Black Road, Silas; 1929-May 20; 36 yr; M; Yes; FB; Tuberculosis; Yes

1928   354; Black Whirlwind, Richard; 1928-Sept 19; 19 ye; M; Yes; FB; Tuberculosis; Yes

1928   858; Brafford, Marion L; 1928-Nov 7; 4 mo; F; Yes; 3/8; Pneumonia; Yes

----   --- Blue Legs, Edith; 1929-Apr 4; 28 da; F; Yes; FB; No data; Yes

1928   832; Bores A Hole, Nancy; 1929-Jan 15; 70 yr; F; Yes; FB; No data; Yes

1928   874; Brave, Robert; 1929-Feb 5; 4 yr; M; Yes; FB; Influenza; Yes

1928   873; Brave, Allie; 1929-May 26; 28 yr; F; Yes; FB; No data; Yes

1928   877; Brave, Sarah; 1928-Dec 28; 43 yr; F; Yes; FB; Pneumonia; Yes

1928   905; Brave Heart, Christopher; 1928-Dec 1; 1 yr; M; Yes; 7/8; No data; Yes

1928   918; Breast, Joseph F; 1929-May 13; 14 yr; M; Yes; FB; Typhoid fever; Yes

Key: Year and Number On Last Census Roll; Surname, Given; Date of Death (Year-Month-Day); Age At Death; Sex; Tribe (Oglala Sioux unless given otherwise); Ward (Yes/No); Degree of Blood; Cause Of Death; At Jurisdiction Where Enrolled (Yes/No); (If no – Where)

Deaths Occurring Between July 1, 1928 and June 30, 1929 of Indians Enrolled at Jurisdiction

1928　915;　Breast, James; 1929-Jan 21; 17 yr; M; Yes; FB; Spinal meningitis; Yes

1928　948;　Brings Plenty; 1928-Dec 15; 80 yr; F; Yes; FB; No data; Yes

1928　972;　Broken Nose, Rebecca; 1929-Jan 24; 28 yr; F; Yes; FB; Influenza; Yes

----　---　Broken Nose, Vivian Jane; 1929-Mar 11; 1 yr; F; Yes; FB; Influenza; Yes

1928　1054;　Brown Ears; 1919-Mar 2; 73 yr; F; Yes; FB; Taxaemia[sic]; Yes

1928　1068;　Brown Eyes, Lena; 1928-Oct 13; 1 yr; F; Yes; FB; Pneumonia; Yes

1928　1127;　Bull Bear, Edward; 1929-Mar 18; 4 yr; M; Yes; 3/4; Lepte[sic] meningitis; Yes

1928　1133;　Bull Bear, Lewis; 1929-May 13; 7 yr; M; Yes; FB; Taenia solium; Yes

----　----　Bullman, Raymond; 1929-June 24; 1 mo; M; Yes; FB; No data; Yes

----　----　Bush, Theresa; 1929-Mar 4; 9 da; F; Yes; 3/4; Acute cold; Yes

1928　2872;　Charges Enemy; 1928-Aug 21; 86 yr; F; Yes; FB; No data; Yes

1928　1251;　Charging Bear, Annie; 1929-Jan 29; 76 yr; F; Yes; 1/2; No data; Yes

1928　1250;　Charging Bear, Eli; 1928-July 26; 84 yr; M; Yes; FB; Pneumonia; Yes

----　----　Chief, William; 1928-Mar 3; 2 da; M; Yes; 5/8; No data; Yes

1928　1323;　Chief Eagle, (Thomas); 1929-Feb 5; 60 yr; M; Yes; FB; Senility; Yes

1928　1396;　Clifford, Lloyd; 1927-Sept 13; 1 yr; M; Yes; 7/32; No data; Yes

1928　1420;　Clincher, James; 1929-Apr 4; 72 yr; M; Yes; FB; Acute indigestion; Yes

1928　1444;　Cloud Shield, Hair; 1929-May 21; 73 yr; F; Yes; FB; Pneumonia; Yes

---　----　Comes From Among Them, Hermus; 1929-May 13; 6 da; M; Yes; 31/32; No data; Yes

1928　1551;　Conroy, Dorothy A; 1929-Feb 18; 1 yr; F; Yes; 5/8; Pneumonia; Yes

1928　1545;　Conroy, Lola Lucille; 1928-Nov 10; 1 yr; F; Yes; 1/2; Infantile paralysis; Yes

1928　4270;　Cottier, Nellie; 1929-Jan 13; 28 yr; F; Yes; 1/2; No data; Yes

1928　1644;　Crazy Horse, Ellen; 1928-July 8; 76 yr; F; Yes; 1/2; Chronic hepatitis; Yes

----　----　Crooked Eyes, Terry; 1928-Aug 12; 2 mo; M; Yes; F; Intestinal flu; Yes

----　----　Cross, Rosa Anna; 1929-Jan 29; 11 mo; F; Yes; 15/16; No data; Yes

1928　1761;　Cuny, Leroy; 1928-Oct 23; 20 yr; M; Yes; 5/8; Pneumonia; Yes

1929[sic]1775;Curtis, Harry Walter; 1928-Nov 27; 1 yr; M; Yes; 3/16; No data; Yes

1928　1779;　Cut, Adam; 1928-July 14; 5 yr; M; Yes; FB; Tuberculosis; Yes

1928　1781;　Cut, Irene; 1928-Dec 30; 1 yr; F; Yes; FB; Pneumonia; Yes

----　----　Cut Grass, Asay; 1929-Mar 7; 1 mo; M; Yes; FB; Cardio vascular insufficiency; Yes

----　----　Dixon, Stanley R; 1928-Aug 24; 1 yr; M; Yes; 3/8; No data; Yes

1928　1927;　Eagle Bear, Louis; 1929-May 9; 34 yr; M; Yes; FB; No data; Yes

1928　1958;　Eagle Elk, Rosanna N; 1929-Mar 8; 1 yr; F; Yes; FB; Influenza; Yes

1928　1977;　Eagle Hawk, Robert; 1929-Mar 11; 3 yr; M; Yes; FB; Influenza; Yes

1928　2000;　Eagle Tail Feather; 1929-May 24; 75 yr; M; Yes; FB; No data; Yes

1928　2048;　Fast Eagle, Oscar; 1928-Dec 5; 36 yr; M; Yes; FB; Transever[sic] myelitis; Yes

State **South Dakota** Reservation **Pine Ridge** Agency or jurisdiction
Pine Ridge Office of Indian Affairs

Key: Year and Number On Last Census Roll; Surname, Given; Date of Death (Year-Month-Day); Age At Death; Sex; Tribe (Oglala Sioux unless given otherwise); Ward (Yes/No); Degree of Blood; Cause Of Death; At Jurisdiction Where Enrolled (Yes/No); (If no – Where)

Deaths Occurring Between July 1, 1928 and June 30, 1929 of Indians Enrolled at Jurisdiction

1928 2057; Fast Horse, Avelina; 1928-Oct 16; 5 yr; F; Yes; 7/8; No data; Yes

1928 2078; Fast Whirlwind, Mary; 1929-Feb 24; 77 yr; F; Yes; FB; Influenza; Yes

1928 2097; Feather, Sarah; 1928-Feb 24; 23 yr; F; Yes; FB; Tuberculosis; Yes

1928 2122; Fights, Samuel; 1929-Feb 26; 8 yr; M; Yes; FB; No data; Yes

---- ---- Fights Over, Rosaline; 1929-Feb 10; 3 mo; F; Yes; FB; No data; Yes

1928 2202; Flies Over Her; 1929-Mar 25; 81 yr; F; Yes; FB; Pneumonia; Yes

1928 2244; Four Blankets; 1929-Apr 15; 82 yr; M; Yes; FB; Tuberculosis; Yes

1928 2262; Friday Scares, Oliver; 1929-June 30; 16 yr; M; Yes; FB; Acute cold; Yes

1928 2281; Frog, Jessie; 1928-Oct 8; 4 mo; F; Yes; FB; Acute cold; Yes

1928 2308; Garnett, William; 1928-Oct 12; 73 yr; M; Yes; 1/2; Asthma; Yes

---- ---- Garnier, Margery T; 1929-Feb 3; 8 da; F; Yes; 9/16; Acute cold; Yes

1928 2342; Gerry, William; 1928-July 30; 64 yr; M; Yes; 1/2; Arteriosclerosis; Yes

1928 2395; Gibbons, Alphonso H; 1928-July 22; 7 yr; M; Yes; 1/2; Variola; Yes

1928 2391; Gibbons, Kate; 1928-July 11; 69 yr; F; Yes; FB; Nephritis; Yes

1928 2406; Gillespie, Sarah; 1929-May 22; 76 yr; F; Yes; FB; No data; Yes

---- ---- Goes In Center, Elizabeth; 1928-Dec 27; 1 mo; F; Yes; 3/4; Althrepsia[sic]; Yes

---- ----- Good Lance, Elaine; 1929-Apr 22; 11 mo; F; Yes; FB; Pneumonia; Yes

---- ---- Good Plume, Theressa; 1020-Jan 13; 9 da; F; Yes; FB; Cardiovascular insufficiency; Yes

---- ---- Good Voice Flute, Claude; 1928-Dec 29; 1 mo; M; Yes; FB; Acute cold; Yes

---- ---- Good Weasel, Art Cleveland; 1929-Jan 5; 6 mo; N; Yes; FB; Pneumonia; Yes

1928 2665; Hard To Hit, Nellie; 1929-Jan 1; 52 yr; F; Yes; FB; Pneumonia; Yes

1928 2667; Harvey, George; 1928-July 11; 66 yr; M; Yes; 1/2; Cancer; Yes

1928 2694; Hawk, Charles; 1929-Jan 19; 25 yr; M; Yes; FB; Suicide; Yes

1928 2733; Head Of Creek; 1928-Aug 18; 93 yr; F; Yes; FB; No data; Yes

1928 2765; Her Good Horses; 1929-Apr 12; 80 yr; F; Yes; FB; No data; Yes

---- ---- Hernandez, Marie M; 1929-May 22; 16 da; F; Yes; 5/8; No data; Yes

1928 2815; High Bull, Thomas; 1928-Sept 26; 2 yr; M; Yes; FB; No data; Yes

---- ----- High Pine, Lucille; 1928-Aug 26; 1 mo; F; Yes; FB; No data; Yes

1928 2832; High Pine, Mary; 1928-Aug 3; 19 yr; F; Yes; FB; Tuberculosis; Yes

1928 2830; High Pine, Oliver; 1928-Sept 5; 24 yr; M; Yes; FB; Suicide; No; Ft. Meade, S. Dak.

1928 2933; Holy In Center; 1929-Mar 25; 86 yr; F; Yes; FB; No data; Yes

1928 2968; Horse, Eva; 2939-June 7; 4 yr; F; Yes; FB; Tuberculosis; Yes

1928 3021; Hunts Horses, Henry; 1929-Mar 21; 79 yr; M; Yes; FB; No data; Yes

1928 3074; Iron Cloud, Leo; 1929-Feb 23; 3 yr; M; Yes; FB; Tuberculosis; Yes

1928 3072; Iron Cloud, Vincent; 1929-Jan 2; 6 yr; M; Yes; FB; Polis encephalitis; Yes

1928 3-79; Iron Crow, Wallace; 1928-Aug 15; 68 yr; M; Yes; FB; Myocarditis; Yes

Key: Year and Number On Last Census Roll; Surname, Given; Date of Death (Year-Month-Day); Age At Death; Sex; Tribe (Oglala Sioux unless given otherwise); Ward (Yes/No); Degree of Blood; Cause Of Death; At Jurisdiction Where Enrolled (Yes/No); (If no – Where)

Deaths Occurring Between July 1, 1928 and June 30, 1929 of Indians Enrolled at Jurisdiction

1928 3112;   Iron Rope; 1928-Nov 20; 70 yr; M; Yes; FB; No data; Yes

1928 3115;   Iron Rope, Mary; 1929-Mar 25; 47 yr; M; Yes; 3/8; Tuberculosis; Yes

1928 3144;   Irving, William; 1929-Mar 23; 47 yr; M; Yes; 3/8; Tuberculosis; Yes

1928 3268;   Janis, Kenneth M; 1928-Oct 30; 2 yr; M; Yes; 3/4; Pneumonia; Yes

1928 3314;   Jones, Henry; 1928-July 20; 67 yr; M; Yes; FB; Nephritis; Yes

---- ----   Jumping Bull, William H; 1929-Feb 23; 5 mo; M; Yes; 3/4; No data; Yes

1928 3412;   Kills Crow Indian, Irene; 1928-Dec 23; 1 yr; F; Yes; FB; No data; Yes

1928 3466;   Kills Small, Henry; 1928-Aug 30; 8 mo; M; Yes; FB; Summer complaint; Yes

1928 3127;   Kiss Me; 1929-Feb 15; 82 yr; F; Yes; FB; Pneumonia; Yes

1928 3506;   Knife, Jackson; 1929-Feb 3; 26 yr; M; Yes; FB; Cerebral hemorrhage; Yes

---- ----   Ladeaux, Sam'l Edw; 1928-Oct 1; 4 da; M; Yes; 7/8; Premature birth; Yes

1928 3668;   Last Horse, Ellis; 1928-Aug 13; 6 yr; M; Yes; FB; Phthisis florida[sic]; Yes

1928 3666;   Last Horse, Lottie; 1928-Oct 16; 14 yr; F; Yes; FB; Phthisis florida; Yes

1928 3683;   Lays Hard, Mathew; 1929-Jan 18; 14 yr; M; Yes; 3/4; Tuberculosis; Yes

1928 3693;   Lee, John; 1929-Apr 11; 64 yr; M; Yes; 1/2; Pneumonia; Yes

1928 3729;   Left Heron, Sallie; 1929-Apr 7; 32 yr; F; Yes; F; Appendicitis; Yes

1928 3748;   Lessert, Benjamin H; 1928-Sept 31; 2 yr; M; Yes; 1/4; Enteritis; Yes

1928 3781;   Little, James; 1929-Jan 29; 7 mo; M; Yes; 17/32; Acute cold; Yes

1928 3770;   Little, Oliver; 1928-Aug 17; 24 yr; M; Yes; FB; Intestinal obstruction; Yes

1928 3812;   Little Bull, Thomas; 1929-June 18; 64 yr; M; Yes; FB; Tuberculosis; Yes

1928 3853;   Little Dog, Emma; 1929-Apr 23; 1 yr; F; Yes; 15/16; Pneumonia; Yes

1928 3907;   Little Soldier, Pacific; 1929-May 21; 5 yr; M; Yes; FB; Diarrhea; Yes

---- ----   Little Spotted Horse, Catherine; 1929-May 30; 1 mo; FB; Yes; Enteritis; Yes

1928 3942;   Little War Bonnet, Oliver; 1929-Feb 5; 9 mo; M; Yes; FB; No data; Yes

1928 3953;   Little Wolf, Ruth; 1929-Mar 5; 77 yr; F; Yes; FB; Influenza; Yes

1928 4042;   Lone Dog, Roy; 1928-Dec 5; 77 yr; M; Yes; FB; Senility; Yes

1928 4056;   Lone Hill, Bessie; 1928-Dec 19; 37 yr; F; Yes; FB; Double pneumonia; Yes

1928 4069;   Lone Wolf, Jennie; 1929-Mar 18; 71 yr; F; Yes; FB; Pneumonia; Yes

1928 4088;   Long Bull, Daniel; 1928-Sept 15; 86 yr; M; Yes; FB; Myocarditis; Yes

1928 4098;   Long Fish, Jenny; 1919-May 30; 30 yr; F; Yes; FB; Tuberculosis; Yes

1928 6784;   Long Horn, Mrs (Tribe); 1929-Feb 9; 70 yr; F; Yes; FB; Cerebral hemorrhage; Yes

1928 4136;   Long Woman, Stephen; 1929-Feb 17; 4 yr; M; Yes; FB; Pneumonia; Yes

State **South Dakota** Reservation **Pine Ridge** Agency or jurisdiction
Pine Ridge Office of Indian Affairs

Key: Year and Number On Last Census Roll; Surname, Given; Date of Death (Year-Month-Day); Age At Death; Sex; Tribe (Oglala Sioux unless given otherwise); Ward (Yes/No); Degree of Blood; Cause Of Death; At Jurisdiction Where Enrolled (Yes/No); (If no – Where)

Deaths Occurring Between July 1, 1928 and June 30, 1929 of Indians Enrolled at Jurisdiction

---- ---- Looks Twice, Dallas L; 1929-Mar 15; 2 mo; M; Yes; FB; Pneumonia; Yes

1928 4166; Loves War, Clara Ruth; 1928-Dec 25; 2 yr; F; Yes; FB; Influenza; Yes

1928 4163; Loves War, Nancy; 1929-Mar 2; 11 yr; F; Yes; FB; Influenza; Yes

1928 4198; Many Cartridges, Henry; 1928-Dec 16; 56 yr; M; Yes; FB; Pneumonia; Yes

1928 4215; Marshall, Harrison; 1929-Mar 27; 45 yr; M" Yes; 1/2; Apoplexy; Yes

1928 4250; Martinez, Geraldine M; 1929-June 21; 4 yr; F; Yes; 5/8; Influenza; Yes

---- ---- Martinez, James Jr; 1929-Jan 13; 1 mo; M; Yes; FB; No data; Yes

1928 4305; Medicine, Louisa; 1929-Mar 22; 14 yr; F; Yes; FB; Tuberculosis; Yes

1928 4307; Medicine, Thomas; 1929-May 26; 6 yr; M; Yes; FB; Tuberculosis; Yes

1928 4347; Mesteth, Louisa; 1929-May 8; 32 yr; F; Yes; 3/4; Tuberculosis; Yes

1928 4406; Mills, Thomas Jr; 1929-Feb 17; 31 yr; M; Yes; 3/4; Influenza; Yes

1928 4444; Montileaux, Joseph Sr; 1929-Feb 21; 50 yr; M; Yes; 3/4; Cancer of liver; Yes

1928 4627; New Holy, Joseph Jr; 1928-Dec 24; 1 yr; M; Yes; FB; Influenza; Yes

1928 3428; No Braid, Mathew; 1928-Nov 2; 8 yr; M; Yes; FB; Pneumonia; Yes

1928 4019; No Fat, Walter; 1929-Apr 4; 8 yr; M; Yes; FB; Influenza; Yes

1928 4667; Old Hair, Stephen; 1929-May 31; 66 yr; M; Yes; FB; Measles; Yes

1928 4676; Old Horse, Christina; 1929-Feb 8; 4 yr; F; Yes; FB; Pneumonia; Yes

1928 4740; Packed; 1928-Dec 8; 82 yr; M; Yes; FB; Cardio vascular insufficiency; Yes

1928 4748; Pain On Hip, Fannie; 1929-June 9; 31 yr; F; Yes; FB; Gallstones; Yes

1928 4838; Pine Bird, Gertie; 1929-Feb 11; 44 yr; F; Yes; FB; Pneumonia; Yes

---- ---- Plenty Wounds, Joseph; 1929-Jan 23; 2 mo; M; Yes; FB; Acute cold; Yes

---- ---- Plenty Wounds, Raymond; 1929-Mar 24; 2 da; M; Yes; FB; No data; Yes

1928 4929; Poor Thunder, Aaron; 1928-Aug 39; 16 yr; F; Yes; FB; Tuberculosis; Yes

1928 4941; Pourier, Baptiste; 1928-Sept 7; 86 yr; M; Yes; White; Myocarditis; Yes

1928 2721; Powder Woman; 1929-May 3; 65 yr; F; Yes; FB; No data; Yes

1928 5001; Powder Woman, David or Dewitt; 1929-Jan 8; 4 yr; M; Yes; FB; Pneumonia; Yes

1928 5019; Pretty Back, Lucy; 1928-Aug 17; 15 yr; F; Yes; FB; Tuberculosis; Yes

1928 5088; Pugh, William L; 1928-Aug 2; 9 yr; M; Yes; 3/16; Paleomyelitis[sic]; No; Hot Springs, S. Dak.

1928 5178; Randall, Frank; 1929-Feb 26; 59 yr; M; Yes; 1/2; Myocarditis; Yes

1928 5174; Randall, Lucy; 1929-Jan 6; 66 yr; F; Yes; FB; Taxaemia[sic]; Yes

1928 5235; Red Bow, John; 1929-May 23; 22 yr; M; Yes; FB; Suicide; Yes

1928 5249; Red Cloud, Lorene; 1928-Oct 3; 1 yr; F; Yes; FB; Pneumonia; Yes

1928 5272; Red Crow; 1928-Nov 13; 28 yr; M; Yes; FB; Tuberculosis; Yes

1928 7008; Red Deer, Mary; 1929-Jan 11; 37 yr; F; Yes; FB; Pneumonia; Yes

State **South Dakota** Reservation **Pine Ridge** Agency or jurisdiction
Pine Ridge Office of Indian Affairs

Key: Year and Number On Last Census Roll; Surname, Given; Date of Death (Year-Month-Day); Age At Death; Sex; Tribe (Oglala Sioux unless given otherwise); Ward (Yes/No); Degree of Blood; Cause Of Death; At Jurisdiction Where Enrolled (Yes/No); (If no – Where)

Deaths Occurring Between July 1, 1928 and June 30, 1929 of Indians Enrolled at Jurisdiction

1928 5298; Red Ear Horse, Levi; 1929-Feb 15; 25 yr; M; Yes; FB; Tuberculosis; Yes

1928 5319; Red Elk, George; 1929-Jan 24; 48 yr; M; Yes; FB; Tuberculosis; Yes

---- ---- Red Elk, Thelma E; 1929-May 1; 24 da; F; Yes; FB; Acute cold; Yes

1928 5320; Red Eyes; 1929-Jan 6; 81 yr; M; Yes; FB; Old Age; Yes

1928 5346; Red Feather, Terry; 1928-July 9; 21 yr; M; Yes; FB; Tuberculosis; Yes

1928 5379; Red Owl, Harry; 1929-Feb 28; 20 yr; M; Yes; FB; Tuberculosis; Yes

1928 5406; Red Rock, Benjamin; 1928-Oct 15; 51 yr; M; Yes; FB; Carcinoma of tongue and rectum; Yes

1928 5425; Red Shirt, Asay; 1929-Jan 13; 1 yr; M; Yes; 7/8; Tuberculosis; Yes

1928 5419; Red Shirt, Mary; 1928-Dec 22; 9 mo; F; Yes; 3/4; Pnaumonia[sic]; Yes

1928 5448; Red Star, Cinderella; 1929-Mar 10; 2 yr; F; Yes; FB; Pnaumonia; Yes

1928 5451; Red Star, David; 1929-Feb 7; 13 yr; M; Yes; FB; Pnaumonia; Yes

1928 5506; Ribs, (Louis); 1928-Sept 24; 70 yr; M; Yes; FB; Hemorrhage; Yes

1928 5629; Rock, Gloria G; 1928-Sept 19; 6 mo; F; Yes; FB; Intestinal flu; Yes

1928 5633; Rock, Rebecca; 1928-Aug 14; 3 mo; F; Yes; FB; Intestinal flu; Yes

1928 5664; Rooks, Joseph Jr; 1928-July 9; 57 yr; M; Yes; 1/2; Asthma; Yes

1928 5717; Ruff, Emma; 1928-July 29; 59 yr; F; Yes; 1/4; Carcinoma; Yes

1928 5759; Running Bear, Haston; 1928-Dec 4; 11 yr; M; Yes; FB; Pneumonia; Yes

1928 7174; Running Hawk, Daniel; 1928-Nov 27; 13 yr; M; Yes; FB; Tuberculosis; Yes

1928 5785; Running Horse, Freed; 1928-Sept 25; 68 yr; M; Yes; FB; Senility; Yes

1928 5813; Runs Against, Jacob; 1929-Apr 2; 56 yr M; Yes; FB; Infection rectal fistula; Yes

---- ---- Runs Against, Bernice J; 1928-Dec 21; 10 mo; F; Yes; FB; Pneumonia; Yes

1928 6055; Short Bull, Lizzie; 1928-Sept 27; 30 yr; F; Yes; FB; Tuberculosis; Yes

1928 6067; Short Tree, Francis; 1929-Feb 23; 31 yr; M; Yes; FB; Tuberculosis; Yes

1928 6093; Shoulder, Gladys; 1929-Apr 19; 7 yr; F; Yes; FB; Tuberculosis; Yes

1928 6142; Sitting Elk, Beth; 1928-Sept 23; 73 yr; F; Yes; FB; Senility; Yes

---- ---- Six Feathers, Henry; 1928-Oct 13; 2 mo; M; Yes; 21/32; No data; Yes

1928 6197; Sleeps, Adam; 1929-Jan 22; 8 mo; M; Yes; FB; Pneumonia; Yes

1928 6206; Slow Bear, John; 1929-June 29; 50 yr; M; Yes; FB; No data; Yes

1928 6233; Smooth Quiver; 1928-Aug 24; 56 yr; M; Yes; FB; No data; Yes

1928 6234; Smooth Quiver, Sophia; 1928-July 19; 54 yr; F; Yes; FB; Struck by auto; No; Dayton, Ohio

1928 6307; Spotted Eagle, Clara; 1928-Sept 2; 10 yr; F; Yes; FB; Pthysis[sic] pulmonatis[sic]; Yes

1928 6309; Spotted Eagle, Gladys; 1928-Aug 17; 5 mo; F; Yes; FB; Diarrhea; Yes

1928 6331; Spotted Horse, Robert; 1929-Mar 14; 23 yr; M; Yes; FB; Tuberculosis; Yes

1928 6338; Spotted Weasel; 1928-Sept 11; 77 yr; M; Yes; FB; Dysentery; Yes

1928 6342; Stabber, Bessie; 1929-May 19; 19 yr; F; Yes; FB; No data; Yes

State __South Dakota__ Reservation __Pine Ridge__ Agency or jurisdiction __Pine Ridge__ Office of Indian Affairs

Key: Year and Number On Last Census Roll; Surname, Given; Date of Death (Year-Month-Day); Age At Death; Sex; Tribe (Oglala Sioux unless given otherwise); Ward (Yes/No); Degree of Blood; Cause Of Death; At Jurisdiction Where Enrolled (Yes/No); (If no – Where)

Deaths Occurring Between July 1, 1928 and June 30, 1929 of Indians Enrolled at Jurisdiction

1928 6355; Standing Bear, Susie; 1929-Mar 2; 28 yr; F; Yes; FB; Pnaumonia[sic]; Yes

1928 6375; Standing Cloud, Twin; 1928-Nov 4; 73 yr; F; Yes; FB; No data; Yes

---- ---- Strikes Plenty, Raymond; 1929-Jan 22; 5 mo; M; Yes; FB; Influenza; Yes

1928 6510; Sugar; 1929-Jan 4; 84 yr; F; Yes; FB; Influenza; Yes

1928 6454; Stewart, Christie; 1929-June 8; 2 yr; M[sic]; Yes; FB; No data; Yes

1928 6619; Tail, Victoria; 1929-June 2; 4 yr; V; Yes; 7/8; Spinal Meningitis; Yes

1928 6627; Takes War Bonnet, Virginia; 1929-Jan 27; 1 yr; F; Yes; FB; Acute indigestion; Yes

1928 6672; Ten Fingers, Norman; 1928-Sept 2; 1 yr; M; Yes; FB; Accident with team; Yes

1928 6736; Thunder Horse, Lucille; 1928-Sept 12; F; Yes; FB; Pneumonia; Yes

1928 6738; Thunder Tail, Clara; 1929-May 9; 74 yr; F; Yes; FB; Senility; Yes

---- ---- Tobacco, Florence L; 1929-Jan 18; 16 da; F; Yes; 11/16; Acute cold; Yes

1928 6776; Top Bear, Louis; 1929-Feb 9; 12 yr; M; Yes; FB; Myocarditis; Yes

1928 6961; Two Elk, Emily; 1928-Nov 7; 19 yr; F; Yes; 1/4; No data; Yes

---- ---- Two Two, Louie; 1929-Jan 5; 9 mo; M; Yes; 7/8; Influenza; Yes

1928 7063; Van Wert, Mary; 1928-Sept 6; 53 yr; F; Yes; 1/8; Cancer of uterus; Yes

1928 7142; Water, Herman N; 1929-Mar 7; 9 mo; M; Yes; 7/8; Pneumonia; Yes

1928 7158; Wears Eagle, Julia; 1929-Mar 4; 56 yr; F; Yes; FB; No data; Yes

1928 7162; Weasel, Jessie; 1929-May 1; 50 yr; F; Yes; FB; No data; Yes

1928 7212; Weston, Earl R; 1928-Sept 6; 3 yr; M; Yes; FB; Hydrociphalus[sic]; Yes

1928 7244; Whirlwind Horse, Albert; 1928-Sept 2; 5 yr; M; Yes; FB; Pneumonia; Yes

1928 7243; Whirlwind Horse, Julia; 1929-Apr 26; 7 yr; F; Yes; 15/16; Pthysis[sic] pulmonalis[sic]; Yes

1928 7257; White, Philip; 1929-Feb 19; 64 yr; M; Yes; FB; Pneumonia; Yes

1928 7290; White Bird, Emma; 1928-Aug 30; 55 yr; F; Yes; FB; Goitre operation; Yes

1928 7289; White Bird, Leon; 1929-Apr 1; 56 yr; M; Yes; FB; Pneumonia; Yes

1928 7318; White Butterfly, Leo; 1929-Feb 13; 2 yr; M; Yes; FB; Pneumonia; Yes

1928 7399; White Face, Rena; 1928-Aug 19; 2 yr; F; Yes; FB; Cholera infantum; Yes

1928 7393; White Face, Salina M; 1928-Sept 7; 7 yr; F; Yes; FB; Intero colitis; Yes

1928 7476; White Wolf; 1929-Jan 9; 84 yr; M; Yes; FB; Senility; Yes

---- ---- Witt, Nelson; 1928-Nov 7; 7 da; M; Yes; 1/2; No data; Yes

1928 7619; Yankton, Bernard; 1929-Jan 16; 11 mo; M; Yes; 7/8; Pneumonia; Yes

---- ---- Yellow Bull, Lorene; 1929-Feb 4; 4 mo; F; Yes; FB; No data; Yes

1928 7698; Yellow Hair, Josie; 1929-June 16; 33 yr; F; Yes; FB; Sunstroke; Yes

1928 7709; Yellow Hawk, Minnie; 1929-July 29; 33 yr; F; Yes; F; Sunstroke; Yes

1929 2979; Yellow Wolf, Ella; 1929-Jan 21; 33 yr; F; Yes; 3/4; Tuberculosis; Yes

DEATH ROLL

EXCLUSIVE OF STILLBIRTHS

1930
(July 1, 1929 - June 30, 1930)

PINE RIDGE RESERVATION
PINE RIDGE SOUTH DAKOTA

Key: Year and Number On Last Census Roll; Surname, Given; Date of Death (Year-Month-Day); Age At Death; Sex; Tribe (Oglala Sioux unless given otherwise); Ward (Yes/No); Degree of Blood; Cause Of Death; At Jurisdiction Where Enrolled (Yes/No); (If no – Where)

Deaths Occurring Between July 1, 1929 and June 30, 1930 of Indians Enrolled at Jurisdiction

1929   36;   Afraid Of Hawk, Harold; 1929-Aug 8; 1 yr; M; Yes; FB; Summer complaint; Yes

1929   111;   American Bear, Philip; 1929-Oct 20; 58 yr; M; Yes; FB; Tuberculosis; Yes

1929   167;   Ant, Grace; 1929-June 15; 1 yr; F; Yes; 13/16; No data; Yes

----   ----   Bank, Homer; 1929-July 1; 1/2 hr; M; Yes; FB; Premature; Yes

1929   949;   Bend; 1929-July 27; 85 yr; F; Yes; FB; No data; Yes

----   ---   Black Bear, Dorothy; 1929-Dec 25; 1 yr; F; Yes; FB; No data; Yes

1929   613;   Black Bear, Paul; 1929-July 22; 37 yr; M; Yes; FB; Tuberculosis; Yes

----   ---   Black Bird, E. Thomas; 1929-Dec 1; 7 mo; M; Yes; 7/8; Acute cold; Yes

----   ---   Black Cat, Florence; 1929-Sept 5; 1 yr; F; Yes; FB; Diarrhea; Yes

1929   747;   Black Road, Lottie; 1930-Mar 26; 38 yr; F; Yes; FB; Tuberculosis; Yes

1929   769;   Black Wolf, Eugene; 1929-May 2; 2 yr; M; Yes; FB; erysipelas and diarrhea; Yes

1929   784;   Blue Bird, Jefferson; 1929-Sept 1; 61 yr; M; Yes; FB; cardio vascular insufficiency; Yes

1929   800;   Blue Horse Owner, Rufus; 1930-Mar 31; 62 yr; M; Yes; FB; Tuberculosis; Yes

----   ---   Blue Legs, Armine; 1929-Aug 5; 1 yr; F; Yes; FB; No data; Yes

1929   875;   Brave, Laverne; 1929-Nov 24; 2 yr; M; Yes; FB; Indigestion; Yes

1929   904;   Brave Heart, Angeline; 1929-Aug 18; 5 yr; F; Yes; 7/8; Tuberculosis; Yes

----   ---   Brings Yellow, Philip; 1929-Jluy[sic] 13; 21 da; M; Yes; FB; No data; Yes

1929   986;   Broken Rope, William; 1930-Jan 5; 18 yr; M; Yes; FB; Tuberculosis; Yes

1929   1101;   Bullard, Lizzie; 1929-Oct 7; 90 yr; F; Yes; 1/2; Arterial sclerosis; Yes

1929   1131;   Bull Bear, Abraham; 1930-Mar 12; 17 yr; M; Yes; FB; Tuberculosis; Yes

1929   1173;   Bush, Lorene A; 1929-Oct 29; 1 yr; F; Yes; FB; No data; Yes

1929   395;   Chief Eagle. Angeline; 1020-Spet[sic] 12; 75 yr; F; Yes; cardio vascular insufficiency; Yes

1929   1333;   Chief Eagle, Cecelia; 1929-Oct 28; 7 yr; F; Yes; FB; Chorea; Yes

----   ----   Chips, Elizabeth; 1930-Jan 7; 2 ,p; F; Yes; FB; No data; Yes

1929   3777;   Colhoff, Wilhemina[sic]; 1929-Oct 9; 28 yr; F; Yes; 5/16; Typhoid fever; Yes

1929   1514;   Conquering Bear, Edward; 1929-Nov 5; 16 yr; M; Yes; FB; Tuberculosis; Yes

1929   1628;   Craven, Thomas; 1929-Sept 3; 15 yr; M; Yes; 1/2; Myocarditis; No; Rapid City, S.D.

1929   1865;   Dixon, John H; 1930-Jan 22; 6 yr; M; Yes; 3/8; No data; Yes

1929   ----   Dixon, Robert C; 1929-Oct 15; 1 yr; M; Yes; 3/8; No data; Yes

State **South Dakota** Reservation **Pine Ridge** Agency or jurisdiction
Pine Ridge Office of Indian Affairs

Key: Year and Number On Last Census Roll; Surname, Given; Date of Death (Year-Month-Day); Age At Death; Sex; Tribe (Oglala Sioux unless given otherwise); Ward (Yes/No); Degree of Blood; Cause Of Death; At Jurisdiction Where Enrolled (Yes/No); (If no – Where)

Deaths Occurring Between July 1, 1929 and June 30, 1930 of Indians Enrolled at Jurisdiction

1929 1881; Dreamer, Lydia; 1929-Dec 27; 24 yr; F; Yes; FB; Pneumonia; Yes

1929 1883; Dreaming Bear, Smith; 1929-Oct 5; 62 yr; M; Yes; FB; Struck by train; No; Hemingford, Neb.

---- ---- Dubray, Pauline R; 1929-Oct 20; 1 yr; F; Yes; 9/16; No data; Yes

1929 1921; Dull Knife, Pearl; 1929-Oct 27; 19 yr; F; Yes; FB; Tuberculosis; Yes

1929 1919; Dull Knife, George Jr; 1929-Dec 24; 11 yr; M; Yes; FB; Pott's disease; Yes

---- ---- Fast, Phoebe; 1929-Aug 18; 1 yr; F; Yes; FB; No data; Yes

1929 2386; Ferguson, Anna; 1930-Mar 4; 21 yr; F; Yes; 1/4; Typhoid fever; No; Norfolk, Neb.

1929 2363; Ghost Bear, Edgar; 1929-July 15; 41 yr; M; Yes; FB; Tuberculosis; Yes

---- ---- Gibbons; 1929-Nov 11; 4 mo; F; Yes; 3/4; No data; Yes

1929 2450; Goes White Cow; 1929-Sept 5; 78 yr; F; Yes; FB; Mitral insufficiency; Yes

1929 2535; Good Soldier, Eliza; 1929-July 20; 36 yr; F; Yes; FB; Septiceamia[sic]; Yes

1929 2558; Good Voice Flute, Alice; 1929-Nov 2; 40 yr; F; Yes; FB; No data; Yes

---- ---- Grass, Raymond; 1929-Oct 31; 1 yr; M; Yes; FB; Cholera infantum; Yes

1929 2655; Hand, Marshall; 1929-Oct 25; 61 yr; M; Yes; FB; Doubl[sic] pneumonia; Yes

1929 2660; Hanging; 1929-Nov 29; 70 yr; F; Yes; FB; Senility; Yes

1929 3030; Imitates Dog, Wallace; 1929-July 30; 55 yr; M; Yes; FB; Tuberculosis; Yes

1929 3054; Iron Bull, Fannie; 1929-Sept 29; 61 yr; F; Yes; FB; Cerebral apoplexy; Yes

1929 3235; Janis, Elizabeth M; 1930-Mar 15; 11 yr; F; Yes; 7/8; Cerebral meningitis; Yes

1929 4836; Janis, Fannie; 1930-Feb 27; 34 yr; F; Yes; 1/2; Influenza; Yes

1929 3259; Janis, Glorita[sic] C; 1930-Mar 16; 3 yr; M; Yes; 1/2; Aedimaglottis[sic]; Yes

1929 3379; Kills Across, Luke; 1929-July 11; 19 yr; M; Yes; FB; Tuberculosis; Yes

1929 3386; Kills A Hundred, John; 1929-July 11; 78 yr; M; Yes; FB; Senility; Yes

1929 3457; Kills Right, George; 1929-Oct 25; 4 yr; M; Yes; FB; Hepatic distomiasis; Yes

1929 3455; Kills Small, Eugene; 1930-Feb 22; 4 yr; M; Yes; FB; T.b. of intestines; Yes

1929 3568; Lamb, Adolph; 1929-Sept 20; 34 yr; M; Yes; 1/8; Ruptured appendix; Yes

1929 3337; Left Hand Bull, Agnes; 1920-Dec 7; 31 yr; F; Yes; 3/4; Tuberculosis; No; Rosebud, S.D.

1929 3809; Little Boy; 1929-Nov 14; 64 yr; M; Yes; FB; Pneumonia; Yes

---- ---- Little Bull, Leo; 1929-Dec 25; 1 mo; M; Yes; FB; Acute cold; Yes

Key: Year and Number On Last Census Roll; Surname, Given; Date of Death (Year-Month-Day); Age At Death; Sex; Tribe (Oglala Sioux unless given otherwise); Ward (Yes/No); Degree of Blood; Cause Of Death; At Jurisdiction Where Enrolled (Yes/No); (If no – Where)

Deaths Occurring Between July 1, 1929 and June 30, 1930 of Indians Enrolled at Jurisdiction

1929 3905; Little Soldier, Darline[sic]; 1929-July 19; 8 yr; F; Yes; FB; Bronchictasis[sic]; Yes

1929 4026; Loafer, Eunice; 1929-Sept 21; 1 yr; F; Yes; FB; No data; Yes

---- ---- Long Soldier, Lucille; 1929-Sept 25; 3 mo; F; Yes; 3/4; cerebrospinal meningitis; Yes

1929 4158; Loud Voice Hawk, Levi; 1929-Dec 24; 60 yr; M; Yes; FB; Pneumonia; Yes

1929 4192; Makes Shine, Cecelia; 1930-Mar 16; 12 yr; F; Yes; FB; Tuberculosis; Yes

1929 4200; Many Cartridges, Levi; 1930-Feb 25; 16 yr; Yes; FB; Tuberculosis; No; Toledo Sans[sic] Ia.

1929 4557; McDaniels, Frederick J; 1929-Dec 11; 3 yr; M; Yes; 7/16; Diphtheria; Yes

1929 4330; Mesteth, George; 1929-Nov 22; 33 yr; M; Yes; 3/4; Tuberculosis; Yes

1929 4400; Mills, Frank; 1929-Aug 19; 26 yr; M; Yes; 3/4; Tuberculosis; Yes

1929 4486; Morrison, Alice; 1929-Aug 11; 13 yr; F; Yes; 7/8; Tuberculosis; Yes

1929 4503; Morrison, Serina; 1929-Sept 16; 5 yr; F; Yes; 7/8; Diarrhea; Yes

1929 4590; Nelson, Daniel; 1930-Feb 10; 19 yr; M; Yes; 5/8; Tuberculosis; Yes

1929 4605; Nelson, Truit L; 1929-Aug 21; 2 yr; M; Yes; 1/2; Diphtheria; Yes

---- ---- No Belt, Gertie; 1929-July 6; 9 mo; F; Yes; FB; Diarrhea; Yes

1929 4643; Noisy Walk, James; 1929-Dec 18; 24 yr; M; Yes; FB; Hodgekins[sic] disease; Yes

1929 4642; No Name; 1929-July 7; 77 yr; F; Yes; FB; Infected hand; Yes

1929 4655; Not Help Him, King; 1929-July 15; 28 yr; M; Yes; FB; Tuberculosis; Yes

1929 4658; Not Help Him, Victor; 1929-Aug 28; 1 yr; M; Yes; FB; No data; Yes

1929 4678; Old Shield, Joseph; 1929-Oct 19; 28 yr; M; Yes; FB; Struck by train; No; Raleigh, N.C.

1929 4791; Patton, James; 1929-Nov 13; 55 yr; M; Yes; 1/4; Heart failure; Yes

1929 4793; Patton, Lucy; 1929-Aug 14; 42 yr; F; Yes; 1/4; Tuberculosis; Yes

1929 4803; Pawnee Killer, Allen; 1930-Mar 2; 55 yr; M; Yes; FB; Pneumonia; Yes

1929 4866; Plenty Woman; 1930-Feb 28; 75 yr; F; Yes; FB; Angina pectoris; Yes

1929 3318; Pourier, Lizzie; 1929-Aug 16; 54 yr; F; Yes; 1/8; Intestinal obstruction; Yes

1929 5090; Pulliam, John Sr; 1930-Mar 22; 61 yr; M; Yes; 1/2; coronary sclerosis with occlusion; No; Leavenworth, Kans.

1929 5092; Pulliam, John Jr; 1929-Aug 7; 19 yr; M; Yes; 1/2; Tuberculosis; Yes

1929 5239; Red Bow, Christopher; 1930-Mar 21; 2 yr; M; Yes; FB; Pneumonia; Yes

---- ---- Red Bow, Lawrence; 1930-Mar 27; 6 da; M; Yes; FB; No data; Yes

---- ---- Red Cloud, Dawson; 1930-Jan 21; 1 da; M; Yes; FB; Cerebral hemorrhage; Yes

1929 5275; Red Deer; 1930-Feb 11; 80 yr; F; Yes; FB; La grippe; Yes

1929 5278; Red Dog, Fannie; 1930-Feb 2; 42 yr; F; Yes; 3/4; Tuberculosis; Yes

State **South Dakota**   Reservation   **Pine Ridge**   Agency or jurisdiction
    Pine Ridge   Office of Indian Affairs

Key: Year and Number On Last Census Roll; Surname, Given; Date of Death (Year-Month-Day); Age At Death; Sex; Tribe (Oglala Sioux unless given otherwise); Ward (Yes/No); Degree of Blood; Cause Of Death; At Jurisdiction Where Enrolled (Yes/No); (If no – Where)

Deaths Occurring Between July 1, 1929 and June 30, 1930 of Indians Enrolled at Jurisdiction

1929 5324;   Red Eyes, Richard; 1929-Oct 6; 9 yr; M; Yes; FB; Shot gun wound; Yes

1929 5364;   Red Kettle, Selina; 1929-Oct 23; 64 yr; F; Yes; 3/4; Cholilithineva[sic]; Yes

1929 5372;   Red Nest, Fred; 1929-July 6; 45 yr; M; Yes; FB; Tuberculosis; Yes

1929 5476;   Ree Woman; 1929-Dec 16; 98 yr; F; Yes; FB; Senility; Yes

1929 5508;   Richard, Peter; 1929-Dec 28; 81 yr; M; Yes; 1/4; No data; Yes

1929 5565;   Richard, Ramsey; 1929-Sept 29; 19 yr; M; Yes; 1/2; Tuberculosis; Yes

1929 5599;   Roan Eagle, Charles; 1930-Jan 19; 61 yr; M; Yes; FB; Tuberculosis; Yes

---- ----   Roland, Mollie B; 1929-Oct 19; 9 mo; F; Yes; 7/8; Cholera infantum; Yes

1929 5751;   Rulo, Jesse; 1930-Feb 1; 72 yr; M; Yes; 1/2; Heart disease; Yes

1929 5803;   Running Shield, Jacob; 1929-Oct 23; 6 mo; M; Yes; FB; Tuberculosis; Yes

1929 5837;   Ryan, James; 1929-Nov 4; 48 yr; M; Yes; 1/4; Pneumonia; Yes

---- -----   Shangreau, Vesta M; 1930-Mar 31; 1 yr; F; Yes; 11/16; Yes

1929 6007;   Shell Woman, Noah; 1930-Mar 1; 2 yr; M; Yes; 7/8; Pneumonia; Yes

1929 6043;   Short Bear, Alice; 1929-July 21; 16 yr; F; Yes; FB; Tuberculosis; Yes

---- ----   Sitting Hawk, Ethel; 1929-Oct 14; 3 mo; F; Yes; FB; No data; Yes

1929 6150;   Sitting Up, Gertrude; 1929-Oct 15; 3 yr; F; Yes; FB; Pneumonia; Yes

---- ----   Sitting Up, Richard; 1930-Jan 18; 3 da; M; Yes; FB; No data; Yes

---- ----   Sleeps, As C; 1930-Feb 24; 1 mo; M; Yes; FB; No data; Yes

1929 6241;   Soldier Hawk, Louisa; 1929-Aug 19; 17 yr; F; Yes; FB; No data; Yes

1929 6319;   Spotted Elk, Howell; 1929-Sept 18; 41 yr; M; Yes; FB; Dysentery; Yes

1929 6325;   Spotted Elk, Mildred; 1929-Aug 21; 1 yr; F; Yes; FB; Diarrhea; Yes

1929 6543;   Swallow, John L; 1930-Mar 2; 57 yr; M; Yes; 1/4; Peritonitis; Yes

---- ----   Tail, Lloyd Lein; 1929-Sept 8; 1 yr; M; Yes; FB; No data; Yes

---- ----   Ten Fingers, Katherine; 1930-Mar 9; 8 mo; F; Yes; 3/4; No data; Yes

1929 6695;   Three Stars, Guy; 1930-Jan 23; 26 yr; M; Yes; 5/8; Phthysis[sic] pulmonalis; Yes

1929 6737;   Thunder Horse, Dawson; 1929-Sept 22; 1 yr; M; Yes; FB; Diarrhea; Yes

1929 6918;   Two Crow, Ethel; 1930-Mar 28; 8 yr; F; Yes; 7/8; Tuberculosis; Yes

1929 6945;   Two Crow, James; 1929-Sept 16; 1 yr; M; Yes; FB; Neglect; Yes

1929 6959;   Two Elk, Nettie; 1930-Feb 18; 55 yr; F; Yes; FB; Tuberculosis; Yes

1929 6972;   Two Lance, Francis; 1930-Mar 26; 19 yr; M; Yes; FB; Peritonitis; Yes

1929 7113;   Walks Under Ground, Florence; 1929-July 22; 10 yr; F; Yes; FB; Diarrhea; Yes

---- ----   War Bonnet; 1929-Sept 30; 8 hr; F; Yes; FB; No data; Yes

---- ----   Weasel Bear, Albert; 1929-Sept 11; 9 mo; M; Yes; FB; No data; Yes

1929 7232;   Whirlwind; 1930-Jan 31; 56 yr; M; Yes; FB; Pneumonia; Yes

1929 7275;   White Bear, Peter; 1929-Nov 1; 21 yr; M; Yes; FB; Tuberculosis; Yes

1929 7731;   White Elk, Maggie; 1929-Sept 21, 67 yr; F; Yes; FB; Malignant tumor; Yes

State **South Dakota** Reservation **Pine Ridge** Agency or jurisdiction
Pine Ridge Office of Indian Affairs

Key: Year and Number On Last Census Roll; Surname, Given; Date of Death (Year-Month-Day); Age At Death; Sex; Tribe (Oglala Sioux unless given otherwise); Ward (Yes/No); Degree of Blood; Cause Of Death; At Jurisdiction Where Enrolled (Yes/No); (If no – Where)

Deaths Occurring Between July 1, 1929 and June 30, 1930 of Indians Enrolled at Jurisdiction

----	----	White Face, John J; 1930-Jan 1; 10 mo; M; Yes; FB; No data; Yes
1929	4804;	White Face Woman; 1919-Aug 5; 65 yr; F; Yes; FB; Ascities; Yes
1929	7379;	White Finger Nails; 1929-Nov 30; 73 yr; F; Yes; FB; Influenza; Yes
1929	7411;	White Horse, Joseph; 1929-July 23; 82 yr; M; Yes; FB; Senility; Yes
1929	7562;	Wood, John; 1930-Jan 30; 84 yr; M; Yes; FB; Chronic intestinal nephritis; Yes
1929	7663;	Yellow Boy, Chas; 1929-Aug 13; 4 mo; M; Yes; FB; Diarrhea; Yes
1929	7673;	Yellow Boy, Dora; 1930-Mar 25; 33 yr; F; Yes; FB; Embolism; Yes
1929	7708;	Yellow Hawk, Millie; 1929-Nov 23; 50 yr; F; Yes; FB; Mitral insufficiency; Yes
-----	----	Yellow Horse; 1929-Nov 26; 6 da; F; Yes; FB; Injury at birth; Yes
----	----	Yellow Bird, Josephine; 1930-Jan 22; 2 yr; F; Yes; 5/8; Pneumonia; Yes

143

DEATH ROLL

EXCLUSIVE OF STILLBIRTHS

1931
(April 1, 1930 - March 31, 1931)

PINE RIDGE RESERVATION
PINE RIDGE SOUTH DAKOTA

Key: Year and Number On Last Census Roll; Surname, Given; Date of Death (Year-Month-Day); Age At Death; Sex; Tribe (Oglala Sioux unless given otherwise); Ward (Yes/No); Degree of Blood; Cause Of Death; At Jurisdiction Where Enrolled (Yes/No); (If no – Where)

Deaths Occurring Between April 1, 1930 and March 31, 1931 of Indians Enrolled at Jurisdiction

1930   42;   Afraid Of Hawk, Albert; 1930-May 7; 11 yr; M; Yes; FB; No data; Yes

1930   36;   Afraid Of Hawk, Kenneth; 1930-May 14; 1 yr; M; Yes; FB; Pneumonia; Yes

1930   123;   American Horse, Sleep; 1930-Apr 8; 86 yr; F; Yes; FB; Heart trouble; Yes

1930   162;   Apple, (Patrick); 1931-Jan 18, 83 yr; M; Yes; 1/2; Pneumonia; Yes

1930   193;   Arapahoe, Daniel; 1930-Aug 13; 34 yr; M; Yes; FB; No data; No; Boston, Mass.

1930   220;   Babby, Agnes; 1930-Apr 23; 40 yr; F; Yes; 3/8; Influenza; No; Lead, S. Dakota

----   ---   Bad Cob, Ollie; 1930-Dec 14; 2 mo; F; Yes; FB; Acute gastritis; Yes

----   ---   Bad Wound, Noah Jr; 1930-May 6; 8 mo; M; Yes; 5/8; No data; Yes

1930   552;   Beard, Webster; 1931-Feb 22; 25 yr; F; Yes; 1/2; Tuberculosis; Yes

1930   430;   Bear Tail, Rhoda; 1930-Oct 20; 23 yr; F; Yes; 1/2; Typhoid fever; Yes

1930   390;   Bear Robe, Paul Jr; 1930-Sept 25; 21 yr; M; Yes; FB; Tuberculosis; Yes

1930   373;   Bear Nose, Orville; 1931-Mar 13; 2 yr; M; Yes; FB; Spinal meningitis; Yes

1930   452;   Belt, Gilbert; 1930-May 17; 19 yr; M; Yes; FB; Tuberculosis; Yes

1930   445;   Belt, Theda; 1930-May 21; 12 yr; F; Yes; FB; No data; Yes

----   ---   Bird, Edward; 1931-Feb 27; 1 mo; M; Yes; 7/8; Starvation; Yes

1930 7039;   Bird All Over; 1930-Dec 28; 83 yr; M; Yes; FB; No data; Yes

1930   587;   Bird Necklace, George; 1931-Feb 8; 82 yr; M; Yes; FB; Uremia; Yes

1930   623;   Bissonette, Bernard F; 1930-Apr 14; 8 mo; M; Yes; 3/4; Althropsie[sic]; Yes

1930 5732;   Bissonette, Lavina; 1930-Apr 5; 2 yr; F; Yes; 13/16; No data; Yes

----   ----   Bissonette, Lucille A; 1930-May 23; 10 mo; F; Yes; 3/4; No data; Yes

1930   654;   Black Bear, Madge; 1930-Sept 19; 13 yr; F; Yes; FB; Tuberculosis; Yes

1930   685;   Black Bird, Esther; 1931-Jan 1; 1 yr; F; Yes; FB; Tuberculosis; Yes

1930   807;   Black Bird, George; 1931-Jan 8; 28 yr; M; Yes; FB; Tuberculosis; Yes

1930   792;   Blind, Silas; 1930-Apr 27; 66 yr; M; Yes; FB; No data; Yes

1930   847;   Bone, Jasper; 1930-Oct 22; 19 yr; M; Yes; FB; No data; No; Gordon, Nebr.

1930 6928;   Black Owl; 1930-June 6; 57 yr; F; Yes; FB; Mitral insufficiency; Yes

1930   846;   Bone, Walter; 1930-July 31; 58 yr; M; Yes; FB; Heat stroke; Yes

1930   989;   Broken Nose, Christina; 1930-May 13; 4 yr; F; Yes; FB; No data; Yes

----   ---   Brown, Theodore E; 1931-Jan 7; 8 da; M; Yes; 5/89; No data; Yes

1930 1124;   Bullard, Frank; 1930-Dec 8; 53 yr; M; Yes; 1/4; Burns; Yes

----   ----   Bear Eagle, Cora; 1930-May 6; 8 mo; F; Yes; 5/8; No data; Yes

1930   822;   Calls Her; 1931-Feb 11; 70 yr; F; Yes; FB; Cerebral hemorrhage; Yes

1930 1260;   Charges Enemy, James Jr; 1930-May 25; 7 yr, M; Yes; FB; No data; Yes

----   ----   Chase In Winter, Madeline; 1930-May 3; 25 da; F; Yes; FB; No data; Yes

Key: Year and Number On Last Census Roll; Surname, Given; Date of Death (Year-Month-Day); Age At Death; Sex; Tribe (Oglala Sioux unless given otherwise); Ward (Yes/No); Degree of Blood; Cause Of Death; At Jurisdiction Where Enrolled (Yes/No); (If no – Where)

Deaths Occurring Between April 1, 1930 and March 31, 1931 of Indians Enrolled at Jurisdiction

---- ---- Chase In Winter, Mary; 1930-May 5; 27 da; F; Yes; FB; No data; Yes

1930 1260; Chasing Hawk, Rosa; 1930-Oct 14; 66 yr; F; Yes; FB; No data; Yes

---- ---- Chips, Inez Elaine; 1930-Sept 26; 1 mo; F; Yes; FB; Typhoid fever; Yes

1930 1239; Cazeaux, Mary; 1930-Aug 18; 66 yr; F; Yes; FB; Septic pneumonia; No; Hot Springs, S. Dak.

1930 1512; Comes From Among Them, Albert; 1931-Feb 5; 31 yr; M; Yes; FB; Tuberculosis; Yes

1930 1513; Comes From Among Them, Lillian; 1930-July 8; 26 yr; F; Yes; FB; Tuberculosis; Yes

---- ---- Comes From Among Them, Rose Marie; 1930-Oct 3; 3 mo; F; Yes; FB; No data; Yes

1930 1518; Comes Killing, Carrie; 1930-Aug 3; 50 yr; F; Yes; FB; Tuberculosis; Yes

---- ---- Comes Last, Loraine; 1930-Nov 30; 5 mo; F; Yes; FB; No data; Yes

1930 1612; Cottier, Louis A; 1930-July 29; 13 yr; M; Yes; 13/16; Infected tooth; Yes

1930 1658; Craven, Agnes; 1930-Dec 27; 23 yr; F; Yes; 1/2; Tuberculosis; Yes; No; Rapid City, S.D.

1930 1695; Crooked Eyes, Susie; 1930-Oct 23; 73 yr; F; Yes; FB; No data; Yes

---- ---- Cut Grass, Stella; 1931-Mar 17; 10 mo; F; Yr; FB; Pneumonia; Yes

1930 1469; Dirt Kettle, Grace; 1930-Oct 17; 8 mo; F; Yes; FB; No data; Yes

1930 1884; Distribution, Harriet; 1931-Feb 25; 72 yr; F; Yes; FB; Pneumonia; Yes

1930 1959; Dull Knife, Winnie; 1930-July 19; 14 yr; F; Yes; FB; Tuberculosis; Yes

---- ---- Eagle Elk, Guss; 1930-Apr 24; 1 hr; M; Yes; FB; No data; Yes

---- ---- Eagle Heart; 1930-June 28; 2 da; F; Yes; 5/16; No data; Yes

1930 2131; Feather, Moses; 1930-Oct 10; 2 yr; M; Yes; FB; No data; Yes

1930 1078; Fox Belly, Julia; 1930-Aug 25; 68 yr; F; Yes; FB; Acute indigestion; Yes

---- ---- Frazier, Harriet A; 1931-Mar 1; 2 mo; F; Yes; 7/8; No data; Yes

1930 2288; Frazier, Josephine; 1931-Feb 10; 27 yr; F; Yes; FB; Tuberculosis; Yes

1930 2318; Frog, Mary; 1931-Mar 9; 93 yr; F; Yes; FB; Old Age; Yes

1930 2358; Garnier, Florence; 1930-Nov 28; 21 yr; F; Yes; FB; Tuberculosis; Yes

1930 2412; Ghost Bear, Mathew; 1930-June 24; 19 yr; M; Yes; 7/8; Tuberculosis; Yes

---- ---- Good Shield, Moses; 1930-Apr 2; 5 da; M; Yes; FB; No data; Yes

1930 2583; Good Voice Elk, Abel; 1930-Apr 30; 5 mo; M; Yes; FB; No data; Yes

1930 2632; Grass, Carrie; 1930-May 10; 2 yr; F; Yes; FB; No data; Yes

1930 6734; Grass, Cecelia; 1930-July 19; 12 yr; F; Yes; 5/8; No data; Yes

1930 2637; Grass, Victoria E; 1930-Sept 25; 1 yr; F; Yes; FB; No data; Yes

1930 2655; Green, Harry; 1930-Dec 22; 48 yr; M; Yes; FB; 1/8; Gastric ulcer; No; Interior, S. Dak.

1930 2679; Guerier, Nellie; 1930-June 24; 49 yr; F; Yes; 3/4; Carcinoma of breast and arm; No; Geary, Oklahoma.

State **South Dakota** Reservation **Pine Ridge** Agency or jurisdiction
Pine Ridge Office of Indian Affairs

Key: Year and Number On Last Census Roll; Surname, Given; Date of Death (Year-Month-Day); Age At Death; Sex; Tribe (Oglala Sioux unless given otherwise); Ward (Yes/No); Degree of Blood; Cause Of Death; At Jurisdiction Where Enrolled (Yes/No); (If no – Where)

Deaths Occurring Between April 1, 1930 and March 31, 1931 of Indians Enrolled at Jurisdiction

1930 2869; High Eagle, Jennie; 1930-Dec 3; 64 yr; F; Yes; FB; No data; Yes

1930 2878; High Shield, William; 1931-Mar 3; 61 yr; M; Yes; FB; Heart block; Yes

1930 2948; Hollow Horn, Earl; 1930-May 27; 6 mo; M; Yes; FB; No data; Yes

1930 2949; Holy Bear; 1930-May 24; 68 yr; M; Yes; FB; Struck by train; No; Norristown, Penn.

1930 2960; Holy Day; 1930-July 11; 75 yr; F; Yes; FB; Heart failure; Yes

1930 3492; Iron Crow, Nellie; 1931-Mar 24; 32 yr; F; Yes; FB; Tuberculosis; Yes

1930 3154; Iron White Cow; 1931-Jan 29; 68 yr; F; Yes; FB; Tuberculosis; Yes

1931 3159; Iron White Man, Joseph 1930-Apr 14; 70 yr; M; Yes; FB; Pneumonia; Yes

---- ---- Janis, Daniel; 1930-May 31; 17 da; M; Yes; FB; Premature birth; Yes

1930 3239; Janis, Lawrence; 1930-May 7; 1 yr; M; Yes; 7/8; Pneumonia; Yes

1930 3262; Janis, Mable; 1930-Apr 12; 38 yr; F; Yes; 3/4; Puerperal infection; Yes

1930 3327; Jensen, Joseph L; 1930-Dec 13; 19 yr; M; Yes; 1/4; Tuberculosis; Yes

---- ---- Kicking Bear, Angeline L; 1930-Dec 6; 3 mo; F; Yes; FB; Pneumonia; Yes

1930 3408; Kicking Bear, Mabel; 1930-Dec 24; 35 yr; F; Yes; FB; Carcinoma of stomach and liver; No; Rapid City, S.D.

1930 3412; Kills Across, Madge; 1930-Dec 24; 18 yr; F; Yes; FB; Tuberculosis; Yes

1930 3411; Kills Across, Sophia; 1930-Apr 5; 45 yr; D; Yes; FB; Tuberculosis; Yes

1930 3420; Kills Alone, Martha; 1930-Dec 23; 60 yr; F; Yes; FB; Pneumonia; Yes

---- ---- Kills Back, Andrew V; 1930-July 8; 1 mo; M; Yes; FB; No data; Yes

1930 3455; Kills Enemy At Night, Henry; 1931-Mar 7; 51 yr; M; Yes; FB; Paresis; Yes

1930 3471; Kills In Water, George; 1930-Apr 28; 3 yr; M; Yes; FB; No data; Yes

1930 3491; Kills Small, James; 1930-Aug 13; 33 yr; M; Yes; FB; Tuberculosis; Yes

---- ---- Lakota, Walter J; 1930-Apr 19; 3 da; M; Yes; FB; No data; Yes

---- ---- Lays Hard, Everett; 1930-June 12; 2 da; M; Yes; FB; No data; Yes

1930 3849; Little Bird, Maude; 1930-July 9; 72 yr; F; Yes; FB; Tuberculosis; Yes

1930 3877; Little Cloud, Gloria; 1930-Aug 17; 2 yr; F; Yes; FB; Tuberculosis; Yes

1930 3918; Little Hawk, Luke; 1930-July 31; 50 yr; M; Yes; FB; Urinary retention; Yes

1930 4066; Living Outslde, Evangeline; 1930-May 27; 34 yr; F; Yes; Tuberculosis; Yes

1930 4104; Lone Elk, Angeline; 1930-Oct 15; 27 yr; F; Yes; FB; No data; Yes

---- ---- Locke, Fay Elwood; 1930-Sept 30; 5 mo; M; Yes; FB; Cholera infantum; Yes

1930 4154; Long Horn, Samuel; 1930-July 25; 19 yr; M; Yes; FB; Tuberculosis; Yes

1930 640; Long Skunk; Emily; 1930-Apr 3; 21 yr; D; Yes; FB; Tuberculosis; Yes

1930 4203; Looks Twice; 1930-Dec 29; 78 yr; M; Yes; FB; No data; Yes

1930 4218; Loves War, Laura; 1930-Oct 29; 69 yr; F; Yes; FB; Tuberculosis; Yes

149

State **South Dakota** Reservation **Pine Ridge** Agency or jurisdiction
Pine Ridge Office of Indian Affairs

Key: Year and Number On Last Census Roll; Surname, Given; Date of Death (Year-Month-Day); Age At Death; Sex; Tribe (Oglala Sioux unless given otherwise); Ward (Yes/No); Degree of Blood; Cause Of Death; At Jurisdiction Where Enrolled (Yes/No); (If no – Where)

Deaths Occurring Between April 1, 1930 and March 31, 1931 of Indians Enrolled at Jurisdiction

1930 4245; Makes Shine, David; 1930-May 1; 16 yr; M; Yes; FB; Tuberculosis; Yes
1930 4273; Marshall, Minnie; 1930-Apr 13; 62 yr; F; Yes; FB; No data; Yes
1930 4368; Menard, Emma; 1931-Mar 23; 56 yr; F; Yes; 1/2; No data; Yes
---- ---- Mexican, Ramona May; 1931-Jan 23; 6 mo; F; Yes; FB; No data; Yes
1930 4431; Mexican, Rose; 1930-Dec 4; 69 yr; F; Yes; FB; Pneumonia; Yes
1930 4485; Mills, Frederick; 1931-Mar 14; 1 yr; M; Yes; 1/2; Pneumonia; Yes
1930 4448; Milk, Samuel; 1930-June 19; 16 yr; M; Yes; FB; Struck by train; No; Chadron, Nebr.
1930 4553; Morrison, Henry; 1930-June 13; 12 yr; M; Yes; 7/8; Tuberculosis; Yes
1930 4591; Mousseau, Nellie; 1930-June 23; 62 yr; F; Yes; 3/4; Cardiac hypertrophy; Yes
1930 4667; Nelson, Margery; 1930-May 6; 21 yr; F; Yes; 1/2; Tuberculosis; Yes
---- --- No Belt; 1930-Apr 13; 2 da; M; Yes; FB; No data; Yes
1930 4702; No Belt, Ellen; 1931-Feb 1; 67 yr; F; Yes; FB; Septicemia; Yes
1930 4703; No Braid, Abel; 1930-Dec 4; 67 yr; M; Yes; FB; Tuberculosis; Yes
1930 4705; No Braid, Asa; 1930-May 7; 20 yr; M; Yes; FB; Tuberculosis; Yes
1930 4067; No Fat, Nellie; 1930-Oct 26; 2 yr; F; Yes; FB; No data; Yes
1930 4725; Not Help Him, Maggie; 1931-Jan 30; 22 yr; F; Yes; FB; Tuberculosis; Yes
1930 4733; No Water, Leo; 1930-June 22; 15 yr; M; Yes; FB; Tuberculosis; Yes
1930 4816; Packed, Susanna; 1930-May 8; 7 yr; D; Yes; FB; Tuberculosis; Yes
1930 4908; Pine Bird, St. Clair; 1930-Sept 5; 18 yr; M; Yes; FB; Tuberculosis; Yes
1930 4918; Plenty Arrow, Lena; 1930-May 24; 15 yr; F; Yes; FB; Tuberculosis; Yes
1930 4922; Plenty Birds, Luke; 1931-Jan 15; 61 yr; M; Yes; FB; Tuberculosis; Yes
1930 4932; Plenty Stars, Oliver; 1930-Sept 3; 54 yr; M; Yes; FB; No data; Yes
1930 5437; Plenty Wounds, Virginia Vey; 1930-Nov 22; 3 yr; F; Yes; FB; Diphtheria; Yes
---- ---- Poor Bear, Marie; 1930-Aug 6; 3 mo; F; Yes; FB; No data; Yes
---- ---- Poor Bear, Rosie; 1930-Aug 20; 3 mo; F; Yes; FB; No data; Yes
1930 5068; Pouting; 1920-Nov 24; 71 yr; F; Yes; FB; No data; Yes
1930 5190; Pumpkin Seed, Alice; 1930-Aug 17; 32 yr; F; Yes; FB; No data; Yes
1930 5195; Pumpkin Seed, Peter; 1930-June 2; 1 yr; M; Yes; FB; No data; Yes
1930 5297; Red Bear, Mary E; 1930-May 28; 15 yr; F; Yes; 3/4; Tuberculosis; Yes
---- ---- Red Bow, Clarence; 1930-Apr 1; 10 da; M; Yes; FB; No data; Yes
1930 5388; Red Elk, Catherine; 1930-Apr 21; 5 yr; F; Yes; FB; Meningitis; Yes
1930 5409; Red Feather, Esther; 1930-Apr 3; 8 yr; F; Yes; FB; Acute cold; Yes
1930 5412; Red Feather, John; 1931-Jan 5; 57 yr; M; Yes; FB; Empyema, right side; Yes
1930 5427; Red Hat; 1930-June 6; 57 yr; F; Yes; FB; No data; Yes
1930 5449; Red Nest, Stella; 1930-July 26; 41 yr; F; Yes; Carcinoma of breast; Yes
1930 5485; Red Plume; 1931-Mar 12; 74 yr; F; Yes; FB; Pneumonia; Yes
---- ---- Red Shirt, Ethel; 1931-Feb 13; 8 mo; F; Yes; 7/8; No data; Yes
1930 5496; Red Shirt, Eva; 1930-June 8; 87 yr; F; Yes; FB; Senility; Yes

Key: Year and Number On Last Census Roll; Surname, Given; Date of Death (Year-Month-Day); Age At Death; Sex; Tribe (Oglala Sioux unless given otherwise); Ward (Yes/No); Degree of Blood; Cause Of Death; At Jurisdiction Where Enrolled (Yes/No); (If no – Where)

Deaths Occurring Between April 1, 1930 and March 31, 1931 of Indians Enrolled at Jurisdiction

1930 5534; Red Willow, Martha; 1930-Nov 12; 38 yr; F; Yes; Postpartum hemorrhage; Yes

---- ---- Red Willow, Mary Fern; 1931-Jan 20; 2 mo; F; Yes; FB; Pneumonia; Yes

1930 5530; Red White Cow, Lucy; 1931-Mar 5; 74 yr; F; Yes; FB; Tuberculosis; Yes

1930 5594; Richard, John; 1930-July 28; 15 yr; M; Yes; 9/16; Typhoid fever; Yes

1930 5765; Rooks, Rosa; 1930-Sept 29; 62 yr; F; Yes; 1/2; Pneumonia; Yes

1930 5788; Ross, Myrtle Anna; 1930-Apr 28; 22 yr; F; Yes; 1/2; T.b. of bowels; No; Belcourt, N. Dak.

1930 1539; Runs Alogn[sic] The Edge, Chester; 1930-May 12; 16 yr; M; Yes; FB; Tuberculosis; Yes

1930 5930; Sage Brush; 1930-Oct 23; 88 yr; F; Yes; FB; old age; Yes

1930 5950; Salway, Charles; 1930-Apr 12; 50 yr; M; Yes; 5/8; Heart failure; Yes

1930 5951; Salway, Jessie; 1930-Sept 19; 35 yr; F; Yes; 5/8; Typhoid fever; Yes

1930 6098; Sharp Pointed 1930-Sept 8; 88 yr; M; Yes; FB; Old Age; Yes

1930 368; Shield Woman; 1930-Nov 17; 54 yr; F; Yes; FB; No data; Yes

1930 6178; Shot Close, Jennie; 1930-Apr 6; 72 yr; F; Yes; FB; Tuberculosis; Yes

1930 6559; Shout At, Julia; 1930-Apr 12; 64 yr; F; Yes; FB; Tuberculosis; Yes

1930 6257; Sitting Hawk, Rosie; 1930-May 20; 40 yr; F; Yes; FB; Tuberculosis; Yes

---- ---- Six Feathers, Phoebe May; 1930-Dec 14; 6 mo; F; Yes; 21/32; Pneumonia; Yes

1930 6308; Slow Bear, Leona; 1931-Mar 22; 8 yr; F; Yes; FB; No data; Yes

1930 6364; Southerland, Clara B; 1930-May 5; 55 yr; F; Yes; 3/8; Pneumonia; No; Cheyenne, Wyo.

1930 6377; Spider, Leo; 1930-May 30; 3 mo; M; Yes; FB; No data; Yes

1930 6403; Spotted Crow, Bessie; 1930-Oct 31; 35 yr; F; Yes; FB; Nephritis Erysipelas; Yes

1930 6427; Spotted Elk, Andrew; 1930-Nov 17; 8 yr; M; Yes; FB; Tuberculosis; Yes

1930 6442; Spotted Owl, Eva; 1931-Jan 22; 17 yr; F; Yes; FB; Tuberculosis; Yes

1930 6488; Standing Cloud, Robert; 1930-Oct 15; 65 yr; M; Yes; FB; No data; Yes

1930 6564; Star Comes Out, Elmore B; 1931-Feb 8; 10 mo; M; Yes; FB; Convulsions; Yes

1930 6748; Tail, Cleveland J; 1930-Oct 11; 1 yr; M; Yes; FB; No data; Yes

---- ---- Tail, Richard F; 1930-Sept 27; 1 mo; M; Yes; FB; No data; Yes

1930 6758; Tapio, Bertha A; 1931-Mar 14; 29 yr; F; Yes; 1/2; Tuberculosis; Yes

1930 6834; Thunder Bull, Annie; 1930-June 17; 78 yr; F; Yes; FB; Cardiac apoplexy; Yes

1930 6838; Thunder Bull, Julia; 1931-Jan 12; 9 yr; F; Yes; FB; Tuberculosis; Yes

1930 6849; Thunder Club, Adelia; 1931-Aug 27; 49 yr; F; Yes; 3/4; Cancer of uterus; Yes

State **South Dakota** Reservation **Pine Ridge** Agency or jurisdiction **Pine Ridge** Office of Indian Affairs

Key: Year and Number On Last Census Roll; Surname, Given; Date of Death (Year-Month-Day); Age At Death; Sex; Tribe (Oglala Sioux unless given otherwise); Ward (Yes/No); Degree of Blood; Cause Of Death; At Jurisdiction Where Enrolled (Yes/No); (If no – Where)

Deaths Occurring Between April 1, 1930 and March 31, 1931 of Indians Enrolled at Jurisdiction

1930 6934; Troublesome Hawk; 1931-Jan 19; 65 yr; M; Yes; FB; Fracture right femur; Yes

1930 6935; Troublesome Hawk, Maude; 1930-Oct 5; 60 yr; F; Yes; FB; Pyonophritis[sic]; Yes

1930 7031; Two Bulls, Dora; 1931-Jan 6; 32 yr; F; Yes; FB; Tuberculosis; Yes

1930 7035; Two Bulls, Fred; 1930-Oct 16; 60 yr; M; Yes; 3/4; No data; Yes

1930 7079; Two Crow, Idelia; 1930-Sept 21; 2 1/2 yr; F; Yes; 3/4; Acute enteritis; Yes

1930 7068; Two Crow, Jeanette; 1931-Feb 3; 2 yr; F; Yes; 5/8; Pneumonia; Yes

1930 1929; Two Elks, Charles; 1930-Nov 6; 17 yr; M; Yes; FB; Tuberculosis; Yes

1930 901; Two Sticks, Daisy; 1930-July 6; 20 yr; F; Yes; FB; Puerperal septicemia; Yes

1930 7146; Two Two, Emil; 1930-Oct 14; 22 yr; M; Yes; FB; Tuberculosis; Yes

1930 7139; Two Two, John B; 1930-Apr 27; 2 yr; M; Yes; 7/8; No data; Yes

1930 7182; Under The Baggage, William; 1931-Feb 15; 1 yr; M; Yes; FB; Pneumonia; Yes

1930 7198; Vlandry, Susie; 1931-Jan 1; 60 yr; F; Yes; 1/2; No data; Yes

1930 7380; Whirlwind Bear; 1930-June 10; 70 yr; M; Yes; FB; Cardiovascular insufficiency; Yes

1930 7382; Whirlwind Horse; 1930-Sept 24; 68 yr; M; Yes; FB; Typhoid fever; Yes

1930 7442; White Bull, Emma; 1931-Jan 21; 66 yr; F; Yes; FB; Septic infection; Yes

1930 7458; White Butterfly, Chas; 1931-Mar 19; 65 yr; F; Yes; FB; Pneumonia; Yes

1930 7460; White Butterfly, Jessie; 1931-Mar 24; 17 yr; F; Yes; FB; Tuberculosis; Yes

---- ----; White Calf, Margaret; 1931-Jan 8; 3 mo; F; Yes; FB; No data; Yes

1930 7487; White Cow Tribe; 1930-May 9; 74 yr; F; Yes; FB; Stomach trouble; Yes

1930 7537; White Face, Clara E; 1930-Nov 21; 2 yr; F; Yes; FB; No data; Yes

---- ----; White Face, Victoria; 1930-Dec 21; 5 mo; F; Yes; FB; No data; Yes

1930 7562; White Horse, Jessie; 1930-Aug 23; 43 yr; F; Yes; FB; Carcinoma of uterus; Yes

---- ----; White Wash, Ramona; 1931-Feb 22; 1 da; F; Yes; FB; No data; Yes

1930 7621; White Whirlwind, Fannie; 1930-June 12; 57 yr; F; Yes; FB; Carcinoma; Yes

1930 7623; White Whirlwind, Peter; 1930-Oct 29; 47 yr; M; Yes; FB; Drowned; Yes

1930 7844; Yellow Boy, Lucy; 1930-June 28; 7 yr; F; Yes; FB; No data; Yes

1930 7827; Yellow Boy, Antoine; 1930-Oct 6; 6 mo; M; Yes; FB; Pneumonia; Yes

1930 7852; Yellow Bull, Betsy; 1930-Apr 6; 2 mo; F; Yes; FB; No data; Yes

1930 7855; Yellow Hair, Louis; 1930-July 9; 40 yr; M; Yes; FB; Heart trouble; Yes

DEATH ROLL

1932
(April 1, 1931 - March 31, 1932)

PINE RIDGE RESERVATION
PINE RIDGE SOUTH DAKOTA

State __South Dakota__ Reservation __Pine Ridge__ Agency or jurisdiction
__Pine Ridge__ Office of Indian Affairs

Key: Year and Number On Last Census Roll; Surname, Given; Date of Death (Year-Month-Day); Age At
Death; Sex; Tribe (Oglala Sioux unless given otherwise); Ward (Yes/No); Degree of Blood; Cause Of Death;
At Jurisdiction Where Enrolled (Yes/No); (If no – Where)

Deaths Occurring Between April 1, 1931 and March 31, 1932 of Indians Enrolled at Jurisdiction

1931   27; Afraid of Bear, Mamie; 1931-9-30; 1; F; Yes; F; Cholera Infantum; Yes
      7718; All Good; 1931-7-25; 77; F; Yes; F; Pulmonary Tuberculosis; Yes

1931 305; Baggage, Frank; 1931-4-24; 59; M; Yes; 3/4; Paralysis of Respiratory
            Center; Yes
      356; Beard, Eliza J; 1931-12-14; 9/12; F; Yes; F; Pneumonia Lobular; Yes
      420; Bear Shield, Hazel; 1931-6-29; 9/12; F; Yes; F; Cholera Infantum; Yes
      ---   Bear Tail, (unnamed); 1931-12-10; 9 days; F; Yes; F; No data; Yes
      507; Bettelyoun, Jane; 1931-8-26; 75; F; Yes; 3/4; Cardiac Failure; Yes
      582; Bird Necklace, Claude; 1932-3-27; 23; M; Yes; 5/8; No data; Yes
      598; Bissonette, Royal; 1931-7-1; 18; M; Yes; 3/8; Self-inflicted Revolver
            wound in head; Yes
      673; Black Bird, Rosa; 1931-7-2; 34; F; Yes; F; Pulmonary Tuberculosis;
            Yes
      680; Black Bird, Nora Lillie; 1931-7-10; 21; F; Yes; 3/4; Acute Cardiac
            Dilation; Yes
      744; Black Feather, Jessie V; 1932-3-29; 1; F; Yes; 13/16; No data; Yes
      774; Black Tail Deer; 1931-7-8; 73; M; Yes; F; Acute Enteritis; Yes
      785; Black Tail Deer, Philip; 1931-9-1; 12; M; Yes; F; [not given]; Yes
      784; Black Tail Deer, Sadie; 1931-5-20; 1; F; Yes; F; Pulmonary
            Tuberculosis; Yes
      776; Black Tail Deer, William; 1931-6-9; 17; M; Yes; F; Pulmonary
            Tuberculosis; Yes
      787; Black Track; 1932-1-9; 79; F; Yes; F; Pneumonia Lobular; Yes
      834; Bluffing Bear, John; 1931-6-23; 75; M; Yes; F; Advanced Pulmonary
            Tuberculosis; Yes
      914; Brave Heart, Ellis; 1931-5-16; 13; M; Yes; F; Pulmonary Tuberculosis;
            Yes
      ---- Brings Yellow, Levi; 1931-8-22; 1/12; M; Yes; F; No data; Yes
      ---   Brings Yellow, Orva; 1931-8-21; 1/12; F; Yes; F; No data; Yes
     1009; Brooks, John; 1931-8-4; 54; M; Yes; 1/2; Cirrhosis of Liver; Yes
     1075; Brown Cloud, Charles; 1931-4-6; 61; M; Yes; F; No data; Yes
     1080; Brown Ear Horse, Theresa; 1931-10-4; 6/12; F; Yes; F; No data; Yes
     1191; Bush, Leona Agnes; 1931-7-25; 1; F; Yes; F; Cholera Infantum; Yes
      972; Beings Three White Horses, Josephine; 1931-11-12; 27; F; Yes; F; Pul.
            Tuberculosis; Yes

1931 1302; Charging Wolf, Rachel A; 1931-5-7; 69; F; Yes; F; Pneu. Lobar; Yes
      ---- Chase In Morning, Winifred; 1932-1-29; 1/12; F; Yes; F; No data; Yes
     1371; Chips, Caroline; 1931-12-3; 29; F; Yes; F; Peyote Poisoning; Yes
     1381; Clear, Ellen; 1931-7-25; 74; F; Yes; F; Acute Enteritis; Yes
     1561; Conquering Bear, Amelia; 1931-8-2; 59; F; Yes; F; Chronic
            Myocarditis; Yes;

State **South Dakota** Reservation **Pine Ridge** Agency or jurisdiction
Pine Ridge Office of Indian Affairs

Key: Year and Number On Last Census Roll; Surname, Given; Date of Death (Year-Month-Day); Age At Death; Sex; Tribe (Oglala Sioux unless given otherwise); Ward (Yes/No); Degree of Blood; Cause Of Death; At Jurisdiction Where Enrolled (Yes/No); (If no – Where)

Deaths Occurring Between April 1, 1931 and March 31, 1932 of Indians Enrolled at Jurisdiction

1931 1671; Crazy Cat, Last Woman; 1931-11-25; 69; F; Yes; F; No data; Yes
1675 Crazy Ghost, Bertha; 1932-3-16; 50; F; Yes; F; Adv. Pul. Tubercul.; Yes
1699; Crier, Sophia; 1931-4-6; 71; F; Yes; F; Chronic Myrunditis[sic]; Yes
1710; Crooked Eyes, Jacob; 1931-6-28; 1; M; Yes; F; No data; Yes
5622; Chief Eagle, Mildred; 1931-7-27; 17; F; Yes; F; Pul. Tuberculosis; Yes

1931 ---- Dillon, John; 1931-6-16; 2 da; M; Yes; 1/2; No data; Yes

1931 1995; Eagle Bear, Cornelius; 1931-9-11; 1; M; Yes; F; Bronch. Pneumonia; Yes
2007; Eagle Bull, Sarah E; 1932-1-12; 3; F; Yes; F; Aspiration of Mucus and blood; Yes
2021; Eagle Elk, Guy; 1931-8-25; 1; M; Yes; F; Acute Nephritis; Yes
2046; Eagle Hawk, Forest; 1932-1-27; 7; M; Yes; F; Pulmon. Tuberculosis; Yes
---- Eagle Heart, John; 1931-4-5; 2 hrs; M; Yes; 16/16; No data; Yes;
---- Eagle Heart, Joseph; 1931-4-5; 6 hrs; M; Yes; 15/16; No data; Yes
2060; Eagle Shield; 1931-7-10; 76; M; Yes; F; Sun Stroke; Yes
2069; Ecoffey, Mary; 1931-5-5; 46; F; Yes; 1/4; Carcinoma Scirrhus uterus; Yes

1931 2165; Featherman, Edith; 1931-4-1; 1; F; Yes; F; No data; Yes
2198; Fights Bear, Jonas; 1931-10-9; 1; M; Yes; F; No data; Yes
2273; Flying Hawk; 1931-12-24; 75; M; Yes; F; No data; Yes
---- Frog, Buster; 1931-10-20; 18 da; M; Yes; F; No data; Yes

1931 2454; Ghost Bear, Louisa; 1931-1-14; 58; F; Yes; F; Mitral Stenosis; Yes
2485; Gillispie, Alvin; 1932-2-17; 14; M; Yes; 3/8; Spinal Meninghitis[sic]; Yes
2529; Goes In Center, Ethel A; 1931-12-13; 1; F; Yes; 3/4; Laryngeal Diphth; Yes
2551; Goings, Whitney Frank; 1932-2-20; 2; M; Yes; 9/16; Pneumonia Lobar; Yes
2569; Good Buffalo, Grace; 1932-3-9; 7; F; Yes; F; No data; Yes
2594; Good Plume, Louisa; 1932-1-2; 40; F; Yes; F; No data; Yes
2677; Grass, Elsa V; 1931-4-21; 3; F; Yes; F; Tubero. Peritonitis; Yes

1931 2739; Hand, Yvonne; 1931-4-17; 1; F; Yes; F; No data; Yes
2740; Hand Soldier, Moses; 1931-11-20; 75; M; Yes; F; Senility; Yes
2873; Helper, Mary; 1931-7-8; 53; F; Yes; F; Pul. Tuberculosis; Yes
2917; High Horse #2, Sam; 1932-1-12; 69; M; Yes; F; No data; Yes
2154; High Pine, Mary; 1932-3-10; 27; F; Yes; F; Advanced Pul. Tuberculosis; Yes
---- High Pine, Delbert; 1931-8-5; 3 da; M; Yes; F; Bron. Pneumonia; Yes

State **South Dakota** Reservation **Pine Ridge** Agency or jurisdiction
Pine Ridge Office of Indian Affairs

Key: Year and Number On Last Census Roll; Surname, Given; Date of Death (Year-Month-Day); Age At Death; Sex; Tribe (Oglala Sioux unless given otherwise); Ward (Yes/No); Degree of Blood; Cause Of Death; At Jurisdiction Where Enrolled (Yes/No); (If no – Where)

Deaths Occurring Between April 1, 1931 and March 31, 1932 of Indians Enrolled at Jurisdiction

1931 ---- Holy Cloud, Denver; 1931-12-19; 1/12; M; Yes; 7/8; Pneumonia Lobar; Yes
2999; Holy Cloud, Matilda; 1932-2-17; 55; F; Yes; 3/4; Tuberculosis; Yes
3077; Hudspeth, Paul; 1931-9-19; 23; M; Yes; 1/2; Pul. Tuberculosis; Yes
1353; Her Good Road; 1932-2-4; 57; F; Yes; F; No data; Yes

1931 3111; In Sight; 1931-4-19; 75; F; Yes; F; No data; Yes
3126; Iron Bull, Minnie; 1931-11-2; 67; F; Yes; F; No data; Yes
3146; Iron Cloud, Robert; 1931-9-29; 41; M; Yes; F; No data; Yes
3182; Iron Horse; 1932-3-31; 81; M; Yes; F; No data; Yes

1931 3231; Jack, Helen; 1931-4-5; 9; F; Yes; F; No data; Yes
3355; Janis, William; 1932-1-24; 60; M; Yes; 3/4; Mycarditis[sic] Hypertension Arteriosclerosis; Yes
3368; Jealous Of Him, Christinia[sic]; 1932-1-13; 18 da; F; Yes; F; Bron. Pneumonia; Yes

1931 3474; Kills A Hundred, Elijah; 1931-7-25; 47; M; Yes; F; Dysentery Bacillary; Yes
7498; Kills Bad, Ransom; 1931-7-9; 7/12; M; Yes; F; Cholera Infantum; Yes
3486; Kills Brave, Lucy; 1931-4-17; 65; F; Yes; F; Chr. Parenslymatus[sic] Nephritis; Yes
3497; Kills Crow Indian, Lottie; 1931-12-19; 21; F; Yes; F; No data; Yes
1682; Kills Her Own; 1931-8-30; 77; F; Yes; F; Cirrhosis of Liver; Yes

1931 3644; Ladeaux, Orlando; 1931-4-12; 4; M; Yes; 7/8; Acute Meninghitis[sic]; Yes
4681; Last Horse, Stewart; 1931-4-16; 20; M; Yes; F; No data; Yes
695; Licks Enemy; 1931-12-1; 75; F; Yes; F; Lob. Pneumonia; Yes
3925; Little Cloud; 1931-9-27; 70; M; Yes; F; Chronic Uremia; Yes
3931; Little Cloud, Ambrose; 1931-12-13; 1; M; Yes; F; T.B. Meninges; Yes
3982; Little Horse; 1932-2-15; 57; M; Yes; Old Age; Yes
4063; Little White Man, Samuel; 1931-7-27; 24; M; Yes; F; Pul. Tuberculosis; Yes
4134; Loafer, Alvina; 1932-2-24; 8; F; Yes; F; No data; Yes
4137; Loafer, Ida; 1931-10-17; 2; F; Yes; F; Lob. Pneumonia; Yes
4195; Lone Wolf, Laura; 1931-7-30; 3; F; Yes; F; Pul. Tuberculosis; Yes
4242; Long Wolf, Minnie; 1932-1-11;53; F; Yes; F; Pul. Tuberculosis; Yes
1140; Long Soldier, Arnold; 1931-4-6; 7; M; Yes; F; No data; Yes
8019; Looks At Her; 1932-2-17; 64; F; Yes; F; Carcinoma of uterus; Yes
4262; Looks Twice, Amelia; 1932-3-22; 29; F; Yes; F; Chr. Pul. Physis[sic] & Tub. Osteomyelitis; Yes
4013; Little Soldier; 1932-2-15; 66; F; Yes; F; No data; Yes

State **South Dakota** Reservation **Pine Ridge** Agency or jurisdiction
Pine Ridge Office of Indian Affairs

Key: Year and Number On Last Census Roll; Surname, Given; Date of Death (Year-Month-Day); Age At Death; Sex; Tribe (Oglala Sioux unless given otherwise); Ward (Yes/No); Degree of Blood; Cause Of Death; At Jurisdiction Where Enrolled (Yes/No); (If no – Where)

Deaths Occurring Between April 1, 1931 and March 31, 1932 of Indians Enrolled at Jurisdiction

1931 4297; Makes Life; 1931-10-11; 84; F; Yes; F; Dropsy & Rheumatism; Yes
4303; Make Shine, Raymond; 1932-1-29; 10; M; Yes; F; No data; Yes
4329; Marshall, Elizabeth; 1932-1-17; 79; F; Yes; 1/2; Cholecystitis acute senility; Yes
4346; Martin, Berry; 1931-4; 13; 50; M; Yes; 1/2; No data; Yes
4366; Martinez, Sophia; 1931-8-26; 8; F; Yes; 5/8; No data; Yes
4421; Medicine, Josephine; 1932-3-26; 12; F; Yes; F; No data; Yes
4488; Mesteth, Alonzo; 1931-10-29; 1; M; Yes; 13/16; Bron. Pneumonia; Yes
4487; Mesteth, Dorothy; 1931-10-26; 2; F; Yes; 13/16; Bron. Pneumonia; Yes
---- Morrissette, Lawrence; 1931-12-1; 23 hrs; M; Yes; 7/8; Asthema[sic]; Yes
4606; Morrissette, Oliver; 1931-12-31; 56; M; Yes; 1/2; Acute Cardiac dilation; Yes
4622; Morrison, Henry; 1931-12-2; 53; M; Yes; 3/4; Pul. Tuberculosis; Yes
---- Mousseau, Mary; 1931-7-21; 4 da; F; Yes; 7/8; unknown; Yes
---- Mousseau, Rosa A; 1931-11-24; 4/12; F; Yes; 7/8; unknown; Yes

1931 4748 New Holy; 1931-10-12; 74; M; Yes; F; Pneumonia Lob; Yes
---- New Holy, Virginia; 1931-9-8; 4 da; F; Yes; F; Bron. Pneumonia; Yes
4773; Noisy Walk, Stephen; 1931-4-22; 24; M; Yes; F; Ludwigs[sic] Angina; Yes
4782; No Neck, Ellen; 1932-2-12; 1; F; Yes; 7/8; No data; Yes
4778; No Neck, Guy; 1931-12-24; 32; M; Yes; F; Adv. Pul. Tuberculosis--cohexia[sic]; Yes

1931 4825; One Feather, Rosa; 1931-4-30; 52; F; Yes; F; Pul. Tuberculosis; Yes

1931 4870; Pablo, Ramona; 1931-5-9; 1; F; Yes; 17/32; Pneumonia Lobar; Yes
---- Pacer, Leo C; 1931-10-21; 27 da; M; Yes; F; No data; Yes;
---- Parts His Hair, Owen; 1931-9-16; 1 da; M; Yes; F; Fail. closure of foreman ovale; Yes
5031; Plume, Emma; 1931-7-7; 21; F; Yes; F; Pul. Tuberculosis; Yes
5033; Plume, Susie; 1932-1-4; 53; F; Yes; F; Cerebral Hemorrhage; Yes
5097; Pourier, Irene; 1932-1-14; 29; F; Yes; 1/4; Endocarditis Septic Ruptured Compensation; Yes
5142; Powder Woman, Bernice; 1931-5-10; 1; F; Yes; F; Pul. Tuberculosis; Yes
---- Pretty Bird, Bernice; 1932-3-24; 1 da; F; Yes; F; No data; Yes
5169; Pretty Bird, Lizzie; 1931-8-27; 35; F; Yes; F; Pul. Tuberculosis; Yes
5266; Pumpkin Seed, Bertha; 1931-8-26; 5/12; F; Yes; F; No data; Yes
5255; Pumpkin Seed, Victoria; 1931-7-30; 21; F; Yes; F; Pul. Tuberculosis; Yes

Key: Year and Number On Last Census Roll; Surname, Given; Date of Death (Year-Month-Day); Age At Death; Sex; Tribe (Oglala Sioux unless given otherwise); Ward (Yes/No); Degree of Blood; Cause Of Death; At Jurisdiction Where Enrolled (Yes/No); (If no – Where)

Deaths Occurring Between April 1, 1931 and March 31, 1932 of Indians Enrolled at Jurisdiction

5290;　Quiver; 1931-8-13; 77; F; Yes; F; Mitral Regurgitation; Yes

1931 5337;　Randall, Rebecca; 1931-12-19; 3; F; Yes; F; Pul. Tuberculosis; Yes
5358;　Rattling Chase, Eva; 1932-2-6; 15; F; Yes; F; Pul. Tuberculosis; Yes
5384;　Red Blanket, Anna; 1932-2-25; 47; F; Yes; F; No data; Yes
3910;　Red Breath Bear, Cecelia; 1931-5-19; 13; F; Yes; F; Pul. Tuberculosis; Yes
5484;　Red Feather, Alonzo; 1932-3-20; 38; M; Yes; F; No data; Yes
----　Red Paint, Grace; 1931-7-11; 4/12; F; Yes; F; Intero Colitis; Yes
5569;　Red Shirt, Fred; 1931-5-22; 60[?]; M; Yes; F; Pul. Tuberculosis; Yes
5570;　Red Shirt, Gertie; 1931-8-21; 56; F; Yes; F; No data; Yes
5571;　Red Shirt, Levi; 1931-6-17; 21; M; Yes; F; Advanced Pul. Tuberculosis; Yes
----　Richard, Ramsay W; 1932-3-7; 9/12; M; Yes; 3/4; No data; Yes
5799;　Rocky Bear, Lucy; 1931-7-28; 63; F; Yes; F; Carcinoma of stomach & liver; Yes
5837;　Rooks, Rhoda; 1931-10-7; 45; F; Yes; 1/2; Malta Fever; Yes
5877;　Rouillard, Nora; 1932-3-3; 18; D; Yes; 1/4; Pul. Tuberculosis; Yes
5950;　Running Hawk, Charles; 1932-1-7; 48; M; Yes; F; Carcinoma Hand; Yes
5979;　Running Shield, Martha; 1931-7-11; 14; F; Yes; F; Pul. Tuberculosis; Yes
5998;　Runs Close To Lodge, John; 1931-6-13; 30; M; Yes; F; Adv. Pul. Tuberculosis; Yes
6012;　Russell, Joseph A; 1932-2-19; 31; M; Yes; 5/16; Angina Pectoris; Yes

6083;　Scabby Face, Margaret; 1931-5-21; 22; F; Yes; F; Pul. Tuberculosis; Yes
6103;　Scout Woman; 1931-10-12; 56; F; Yes; F; Carc. of uterus; Yes
6245;　Short Step, Ada; 1931-9-29; 50; F; Yes; F; Carc. of liver; Yes
6316;　Sits Poor; 1931-6-3; 80; M; Yes; F; Pul. Tuberculosis; Yes
6336;　Sitting Hawk; 1932-3-26; 80; M; Yes; F; No data; Yes
6360;　Six Feathers, Harvey; 1931-11-20; 11; M; Yes; F; Chronic Pul. Tuberculosis; Yes
6380;　Sleeps, Mary; 1931-9-26; 1; F; Yes; F; Pul. Tuberculosis; Yes
7013;　Spotted Elk, Richard; 1932-2-18; 18; M; Yes; F; Adv. Pul. Tuberculosis; Yes
6517;　Spotted Horse, John; 1931-4-1; 62; M; Yes; F; No data; Yes
6523;　Spotted Horse Woman; 1932-3-15; 80; F; Yes; F; Influenza; Yes
6550;　Standing Bear, Charles F; 1931-6-29; 22; M; Yes; 3/8; No data; Yes
6585;　Standing Soldier, Elizabeth; 1931-10-13; 16; F; Yes; F; Lob. Pneumonia; Yes

State **South Dakota** Reservation **Pine Ridge** Agency or jurisdiction
Pine Ridge Office of Indian Affairs

Key: Year and Number On Last Census Roll; Surname, Given; Date of Death (Year-Month-Day); Age At
Death; Sex; Tribe (Oglala Sioux unless given otherwise); Ward (Yes/No); Degree of Blood; Cause Of Death;
At Jurisdiction Where Enrolled (Yes/No); (If no – Where)

Deaths Occurring Between April 1, 1931 and March 31, 1932 of Indians Enrolled at Jurisdiction

6857; Tells Her Name; 1931-7-8; 78; F; Yes; F; Pul. Tuberculosis; Yes

5892; Thompson, Dolly; 1931-11-13; 29; F; Yes; F; No data; Yes

6904; Three Stars, Clarence; 1931-8-28; 67; M; Yes; M; Toxemia; Yes

7118; Two Bulls, Eudora; 1931-9-23; 23; F; Yes; F; Pul. Tuberculosis; Yes

7164; Two Crow, Asay; 1931-9-24; 1; M; Yes; F; Entero Colitis; Yes

7151; Two Lance, Jr; 1931-5-8; 77; M; Yes; F; No data; Yes

----; Tyon, Elizabeth; 1932-3-25; 8/12; F; Yes; 5/8; No data; Yes

7287; Vegar, Fernando; 1931-4-3; 20; M; Yes; 3/4; No data; Yes

7342; Walks Under Ground, Esther V; 1931-7-2; 21; F; Yes; F; Pul. Tuberculosis; Yes

7403; Weasel, Orla; 1931-4-16; 2/12; F; Yes; F; Bronch. Pneumonia; Yes

7466; Whetstone, Jennie; 1931-6-27; 48; F; Yes; F; Brights Disease; Yes

7489; Whirlwind Horse, Eugene; 1931-4-16; 1; M; Yes; 9/16; Injury Hernia; Yes

1931 7527; White Bear Claws, Lucy; 1931-8-19; 14; F; Yes; F; Pul. Tuberculosis; Yes

7562; White Calf, Abner; 1931-5-9; 75; M; Yes; F; Acute Enteritis; Yes

7651; White Hawk, (Luke); 1931-7-16; 72; M; Yes; F; Lobar Pneumonia; Yes

----; White Magpie, Frankie; 1931-7-14; 15 min; M; Yes; F; No data; Yes

7705; White Shield, (Cain); 1932-1-28; 65; M; Yes; F; No data; Yes

7829; Wooden Gun, Victoria; 1931-6-13; 84; F; Yes; F; Old Age; Yes

7846; Wounded, Amy; 1931-9-12; 10/12; F; Yes; F; Diarrhea; Yes Fermentative; Yes

7833; Wounded, Levi; 1931-7-2; 22; M; Yes; F; Pul. Tuberculosis; Yes

7832; Wounded, Maggie; 1931-10-30; 74; F; Yes; F; Mitral Regurgitation; Yes

8022; Yellow Wolf, Flora; 1931-12-1; 53; F; Yes; F; No data; Yes

8024; Yellow Wolf, Thomas; 1931-5-18; 24; M; Yes; F; Pul. Tuberculosis; Yes

4209; Yellow Woman; 1931-9-11; 60; F; Yes; F; Chronic Pul. Tuberculosis; Yes

MISCELLANEOUS DELINQUENT DEATHS

PINE RIDGE RESERVATION
PINE RIDGE SOUTH DAKOTA

State __South Dakota__ Reservation __Pine Ridge__ Agency or jurisdiction
__Pine Ridge__ Office of Indian Affairs

Key: Year and Number On Last Census Roll; Surname, Given; Date of Death (Year-Month-Day); Age At Death; Sex; Tribe (Oglala Sioux unless given otherwise); Ward (Yes/No); Degree of Blood; Cause Of Death; At Jurisdiction Where Enrolled (Yes/No); (If no – Where)

Deaths Occurring Between April 1, 1931 and March 31, 1932 of Indians Enrolled at Jurisdiction

1931 ---- Blue Legs, Rebecca; 1927-2-20; 12 da; F; Yes; F; Unknown; Yes

360; Bear Eagle, Josephine; 1930-10-14; 6; F; Yes; F; No data; Yes

1450; Clifford, Lawrence; 1926-5-1; 8; M; Yes; 5/16; No data; Yes

---- Fire Thunder, Irene; 1925-5-14; 2 da; F; Yes; 5/8; Pul. Tuberculosis; Yes

2963; Hodge, Bleamus L; 1919-3-2; 2/12; M; Yes; 1/16; Bold Hives; Yes

7151; Two Crow, Mary; 1931-2-15; 44; F; Yes; 3/4; Pul. Tuberculosis; Yes

7664; White Horse, Frank; 1930-10-17; 49; M; Yes; F; No data; Yes

7922; Yellow Bird, Josephine; 1930-1-22; 2; F; Yes; 5/8; Bronc. Pneumonia; Yes

163